# THERE'S NOT AN APP FOR THAT

T0131152

# THERE'S NOT AN APP FOR THAT

## MOBILE USER EXPERIENCE DESIGN FOR LIFE

SIMON ROBINSON

GARY MARSDEN

MATT JONES

AMSTERDAM • BOSTON • HEIDELBERG • LONDON • NEW YORK • OXFORD
PARIS • SAN DIEGO • SAN FRANCISCO • SINGAPORE • SYDNEY • TOKYO

Morgan Kaufmann is an imprint of Elsevier

**Acquiring Editor:** Meg Dunkerley
**Editorial Project Manager:** Lindsay Lawrence
**Project Manager:** Punithavathy Govindaradjane
**Designer:** Russell Purdy

*Morgan Kaufmann* is an imprint of Elsevier
225 Wyman Street, Waltham, MA, 02451, USA

**Library of Congress Cataloging-in-Publication Data**
Robinson, Simon, 1984-
    There's not an app for that : mobile user experience design for life / Simon Robinson, Gary Marsden, Matt Jones.
      pages cm
    ISBN 978-0-12-416691-2
1.   Mobile computing. 2.   Application software. 3.   Human-computer interaction. I. Marsden, Gary. II. Jones, Matt.
III. Title.
    QA76.59.R63 2014
    004.01'9–dc23
                                                  2014019476
**British Library Cataloguing-in-Publication Data**
A catalogue record for this book is available from the British Library.

ISBN: 978-0-12-416691-2

For information on all MK publications
visit our website at www.mkp.com

Printed and bound in China

# Dedication

*In memory of Gary: thank you for everything*

# Contents

PREFACE                                      xv
ABOUT THE AUTHORS                            xvii
ACKNOWLEDGMENTS                              xix
PHOTO CREDITS                                xxi

**1.  INTRODUCTION**                         **1**

ECSTASY                                      1
ANGST                                        6
LOSING OURSELVES                             9
REBELLION NOT RETREAT                        13
LIFE UNDER A LID                             16
FUTURE, NOW                                  26
RESOURCES                                    27

## 2. FROM TOUCH TO FEELING    30

INTRODUCTION    32

BUILT AS BODIES, BUILT FOR MATERIALS    34

BREAKING THE GLASS: VISIONS OF WHAT MIGHT BE POSSIBLE    39

RISING TO THE CHALLENGE    44

RESOURCES    45

## 3. INSPIRED BY FOOD    48

INTRODUCTION    50

MULTISENSORY INTERACTION    51

MATERIAL PROPERTIES IMPACT INTERACTION    59

GOING BEYOND "GOOD FOR US"    63

TAKEAWAYS    65

RESOURCES    66

## 4. INSPIRED BY FASHION    70

INTRODUCTION    72

TOUCHING FABRIC AND TOUCHING THE SCREEN    74

WEARABLES THAT RESPOND TO WEAR    81

INTIMATE INTERFACES    84

PRET-A-PORTER    85

RESOURCES    86

## 5. INSPIRED BY FITNESS    90

INTRODUCTION    92

DESIGNING FOR HOW OUR BODIES MOVE    95

EFFORTFUL DESIGN    99

ARE YOU DESIGNING FOR CYBORGS OR CENTAURS?    103

MOVING ON                                                           107

RESOURCES                                                           108

**6.  INSPIRED BY MATERIALS**                                       **112**

INTRODUCTION                                                        114

MODALITIES AND MULTIMODALITY                                        114

TANGIBLES: GETTING PHYSICAL                                         117

EMERGING INTERFACE MATERIALS                                        121

RESOURCES                                                           127

**7.  FROM HEADS DOWN TO FACE ON**                                  **130**

INTRODUCTION                                                        132

WHAT IS "HEADS DOWN"?                                               132

HOW DID THIS HAPPEN?                                                134

FACE ON                                                             136

SO WHAT'S TO BE DONE?                                               140

RESOURCES                                                           141

**8.  IN YOUR FACE TECHNOLOGY**                                     **144**

INTRODUCTION                                                        146

SURELY HEADS-UP DISPLAYS ARE THE ANSWER?                            147

IS SPEECH THE ANSWER?                                               150

WHY DO WE NEED TO THINK OF ALTERNATIVES TO
THESE EXCITING TECHNOLOGIES?                                        156

RESOURCES                                                           157

**9.  IN THE WORLD APPROACHES**                                     **158**

INTRODUCTION                                                        160

WEANING OFF HEADS DOWN: GLANCEABLE DISPLAYS                         160

APPS THAT BITE BACK                                          167

BEYOND THE INSTANT                                           168

DIRECT MANIPULATION AND THE POWER OF
THE WAND METAPHOR                                            169

WHEN HEADS DOWN WORKS                                        172

FACING UP TO REALITY                                         173

RESOURCES                                                    174

**10.  FROM CLINICAL TO CLUTTER**                            **176**

INTRODUCTION                                                 178

ORDERED CHAOS                                                182

SO WHAT'S TO BE DONE?                                        189

RESOURCES                                                    189

**11.  INSPIRED BY MESS**                                    **192**

INTRODUCTION                                                 194

DESIGNING FOR MESSY ORGANIZATION                             194

DESIGNING FOR MESSY INTERACTION                              198

DESIGNING FOR MESS MEDIA                                     203

MESS AND CREATIVITY                                          206

USING CLUTTER IN THE WORLD                                   207

TIDYING UP                                                   215

RESOURCES                                                    216

**12.  INSPIRED BY UNCERTAINTY**                             **218**

THE THRILL OF NOT BEING SURE                                 220

ILLUSTRATING THE VALUE OF UNCERTAINTY: NAVIGATION
WITHOUT NAVIGATING                                           224

FINDING YOUR OWN WAY                                         228

RESOURCES                                                    229

**13. FROM PRIVATE AND PERSONAL TO PUBLIC AND PERFORMANCE**     **232**

INTRODUCTION     234

TOGETHER MOMENTS     236

PERFORMANCE AT THE PERIPHERY     243

LEANING IN     246

OUT OF THE SHADOWS AND ONTO THE STAGE     252

RESOURCES     252

**14. MOBILES AS PROPS**     **254**

INTRODUCTION     256

DESIGNING TO ENCOURAGE PEOPLE TO USE THEIR MOBILES TOGETHER     261

DESIGNING AS IF MOBILES WERE PUBLIC RATHER THAN PRIVATE DEVICES     264

SUPPORTING ROLE TO LEADING ACTOR     271

RESOURCES     271

**15. EXTRAVAGANT COMPUTING**     **274**

INTRODUCTION     276

SMALL SCREEN, LARGE SCREEN     278

SELF-EXPRESSION AND EMBARRASSMENT     283

WRITING YOUR OWN SCRIPT     294

RESOURCES     295

**16. FROM DISTANCED TO MINDFUL INTERACTION**     **298**

INTRODUCTION     300

DISTANCING US     301

BECOMING MINDFUL     307

RESOURCES     308

## 17.  DESIGNING MINDFUL COMMUNICATION APPS          310

INTRODUCTION                                          312

MODES OF INTERACTION                                  313

SPACE                                                316

IDENTITY: WHO WE ARE                                 320

AN APP FOR THAT                                      321

SOLVING THE PROBLEM WITHOUT APPS                     335

RESOURCES                                            336

## 18.  MINDFULNESS WITHOUT APPS                     340

INTRODUCTION                                          342

GETTING RID OF APPS 1: BUILDING A JUST-IN-TIME SCHEME    342

GETTING RID OF APPS 2: BACK TO PEOPLE AGAIN          345

RESOURCES                                            347

## 19.  FROM SOME TO ALL                             348

INTRODUCTION                                          350

CHALLENGES                                           352

OPPORTUNITIES                                        360

DESIGNING FOR SHARING                                361

DESIGNING TO ACCOMMODATE LITERACY LEVELS             365

DESIGNING PLATFORMS THAT EMPOWER                     369

DESIGNING TO MAKE A BIG DIFFERENCE                   370

THE ROAD AHEAD                                       377

RESOURCES                                            378

## 20. BRINGING THINGS TOGETHER     **383**

THE WAY FORWARD     383

NO TIME LIKE THE PRESENT     387

BEYOND PHONES AND APPS     405

PATHWAYS TO THE FUTURE     409

RESOURCES     410

INDEX     413

# Preface

Apps are changing the world. If you work for a bank, an airline, an art gallery, or even a local coffee shop, you'll probably have helped create an app to connect and transact with your customers and visitors. As users, we consume these bite-sized chunks of digital goodness voraciously, with some estimates putting total app downloads to date at over 100 billion.

People find apps effective, satisfying, and enjoyable. Meeting their needs, filling dead time, solving their problems. So, why are we writing a book that argues for some new thinking?

We celebrate the success that is apps, services, and the ecology of mobile devices; but, we want to ask the question: what do the current approaches to mobile interaction overlook? Is there more to user experience than can be expressed through today's heads-down, glass-blunted, and private me-centered reality?

All three of us have had the great fortune to work and collaborate with research labs, practitioners, and industry. The job this book attempts to do is to connect the great app innovation out there with the sorts of alternative thinking that have been brewing in university and industry labs for several years.

What does this additional set of perspectives get you?

- If you are an **app developer**—either an individual with great ideas (or wanting them) or working at scale in a bigger team—we hope you will gain three types of insight. First, there will be inspiration on new types of services that can help users see and interact with their worlds in exciting ways.

- Second, if you already have an idea, the book may provoke you to think of interesting, effective ways to provide interactions with your service.

- Third, and finally, by surveying emerging interface styles and materials, we'll prepare you for the ever more rich opportunities to provide user experiences that really match the lives we all lead: the best is yet to come!

- You might have picked up this book, though, because you are **researcher** or **student** who is new to the field and wants a fast way into some of the hot research topics in user experience. We have reviewed a great number of articles from leading conferences and journals, trying to make this work of world-leading researchers accessible. We've provided full details of all the labs, projects, and papers we've followed so you can take your reading further.

- Perhaps, though, you are neither an app developer nor a researcher. Perhaps you simply are **intrigued** by what the present approaches to technology you use everyday do to your experience of life, and how the future might be different. Perhaps you are a worried parent or grandparent, anxious about your digital native children and grandchildren. We hope we've written the book in a way that connects with your interests too. After all, the changes we are trying to provoke are meant to make your life better and less worrisome!

This is a book and not a bible. We've surely made some errors in thinking through the complexities as we outline what might be effective evolutions of what is currently called "mobile." You may agree with what we've written, or can think of much better ways of looking at the problems. We hope so, as this is hopefully just the start of a conversation you can continue with your colleagues, students, or even children.

**Simon Robinson**

**Gary Marsden**

**Matt Jones**

Swansea, UK & Cape Town, South Africa

October 2014

# About the Authors

Simon Robinson is a researcher in the Future Interaction Technology Lab at Swansea University. His work so far has focused on mobile technologies that allow people to immerse themselves in the places, people, and events around them, rather than just in their mobile devices. His research—much of which has been part of the thinking behind this book—has been featured by New Scientist, Gizmodo, CBC Radio, and other international media venues, and has also been published in many international academic conferences and journals. In the past few years his emphasis has turned toward developing similarly face-on user experiences for resource-constrained communities in regions such as South Africa and India. Simon is an avid rock climber, and loves the fact that climbing doesn't need a touch screen to make you feel full of life.

More at simon.robinson.ac.

Gary Marsden was a professor of computer science at the University of Cape Town, pioneer and passionate advocate of HCI for development, and community builder. He became internationally known for his work in mobile interface design and ICT for development (ICT4D)—for which he was a recipient of the ACM SIGCHI's Social Impact Award in 2007. He went to great lengths to show how mobile technologies were revolutionizing how developing countries were advancing apace. In doing so, he raised the profile of what developing world actually meant. Gary died suddenly of a heart attack on December 27, 2013, and is survived by his wife Gil and his two children, Holly and Jake.

Matt Jones is a professor and Head of Department of Computer Science, Swansea University. His research work focuses on human-centered computing with particular emphasis on mobile and ubiquitous computing and resource-constrained communities in regions such as India and South Africa. His work in these contexts has been recognized by an IBM Faculty Award and, in 2014, by a Royal Society Wolfson Research Merit Award. Matt has had many active collaborations and interactions with industry, NGO, and governmental stakeholders including Microsoft Research, Nokia Research, and IBM Research. In his spare time he tries to live life face on with his energetic family, and enjoys nothing more than an exhilarating early morning cycle ride to the glorious beaches of the Gower.

More at undofuture.com.

# Acknowledgments

So many people have helped us, it's hard to know where to begin. It's impossible to list everyone by name as we've been supported by an international community of scholars, practitioners, and friends. To all of you who have produced the ideas we have drawn on, debated issues with us, and dreamed about better futures: thank you.

Without the encouragement, critique, and guidance provided by Meg, Heather, Lindsay, and Punitha at Morgan Kaufmann, and the early reviewers of the text, the book would be far less useful and usable than we hope it is: thank you.

We've worked closely with a number of people in doing the research and development work reported in parts of the book. So, thank you Rod, John, Steve, Nic, Thomas, Bill, Edwin, Shikoh, Andrew, Pierre, Jen, Will, Harold, George, Yvonne, Scott, Liam, Emma, Patrick, Tom, David F., Kristen, Ian, David B., Amit, Nitendra, and Richard.

Then there are all the organizations and companies who have supported and funded our work over the years; thank you EPSRC, RCUK, NRF, Microsoft Research, IBM Research, Samsung, Nokia Research, Hasso Plattner Institute, Royal Society, and Orange. We are also grateful to our universities for the supportive and stimulating environments they provide.

We are so thankful to our family and close friends who've kept us motivated and allowed us the time to complete this project. Thank you, *thank you,* then: Jen, who was not only a major part of much of the work in the book, but was also a great support, too (Simon); Gil, Jake, and Holly (Gary); and Clare, Sam, Ben, and Rosie (Matt).

Finally, while joyful to see this book emerge, we (Simon and Matt) are profoundly sad that Gary died before the book was printed. Without Gary we would not have started the work; it was so hard to finish it without him by our side.

Thank you, Gary.

# Photo Credits

| Page 121, Figure 6.3 | Tokens of Search (Salu Ylirisku, Siân Lindley, Giulio Jacucci, Richard Banks, Craig Stewart, Abigail Sellen, Richard Harper and Tim Regan, 2013). Reproduced by permission of Salu Ylirisku. |
| --- | --- |
| Page 122, Figure 6.4 | UltraHaptics (Tom Carter, Sue Ann Seah, Benjamin Long, Bruce Drinkwater and Sriram Subramanian, 2013). Reproduced by permission of Tom Carter. |
| Page 124, Figure 6.6 | MimicTile (Yusuke Nakagawa, Akiya Kamimura and Yoichiro Kawaguchi, 2012). Reproduced by permission of Akiya Kamimura. |
| Page 125, Figure 6.7 | Tilt Display (Jason Alexander, Andrés Lucero and Sriram Subramanian, 2012). Reproduced by permission of Jason Alexander. |
| Page 126, *Putting it into practice: Futuristic to feasible emotional communication* box | Intimate Mobiles (Fabian Hemmert, Ulrike Gollner, Matthias Löwe, Anne Wohlauf and Gesche Joost, 2011). Reproduced by permission of Fabian Hemmert. |
| Page 137, Figure 7.1 | BodySpace (Steven Strachan, Roderick Murray-Smith and Sile O'Modhrain, 2007). Reproduced by permission of Steven Strachan. |
| Page 146, Figure 8.1 | Adapted from "Wearcompevolution" by Glogger (http://commons.wikimedia.org/wiki/File:Wearcompevolution.jpg). Licensed under CC BY-SA 3.0 (http://creativecommons.org/licenses/by-sa/3.0/). |
| Page 147, Figure 8.2 | Google Glass, worn by Thad Starner. Reproduced by permission of Clint Zeagler. |
| Page 149, Figure 8.3 | Ubi Displays (John Hardy, Carl Ellis, Jason Alexander and Nigel Davies, 2013). Reproduced by permission of John Hardy. |
| Page 149, Figure 8.4 | Babbage Cabbage (Owen Noel Newton Fernando, Adrian David Cheok, Tim Merritt, Roshan Lalintha Peiris, Charith Lasantha Fernando, Nimesha Ranasinghe, Inosha Wickrama and Kasun Karunanayaka, 2009). Reproduced by permission of Owen Noel Newton Fernando. |
| Page 163, Figure 9.2 | Adapted from "Pebble watch word clock" by JohnnyMrNinja (http://commons.wikimedia.org/wiki/File:Pebble_watch_word_clock_4.png). Licensed under CC BY-SA 1.0 (http://creativecommons.org/licenses/by-sa/1.0/). |
| Page 170, Figure 9.3 | Mobile spatial interaction (Peter Froehlich, Lynne Baillie and Rainer Simon, 2008). Reproduced by permission of Peter Froehlich. |
| Page 180, *The quest for cyborgs* box | Implanted User Interfaces (Christian Holz, Tovi Grossman, George Fitzmaurice and Anne Agur, 2012). Reproduced by permission of Christian Holz. |
| Page 187, Figure 10.2 (left) | Kitchen scene. Image reproduced by by permission of Alex S. Taylor. |
| Page 187, Figure 10.2 (right) | Digital fridge design. Reproduced by permission of Alexey Dmitriev. |
| Page 188, Figure 10.3 | The Whereabouts Clock (Abigail Sellen, Rachel Eardley, Shahram Izadi and Richard Harper, 2006). Reproduced by permission of Abigail Sellen. |

| Page 198, Figure 11.2 (left) | StoryBank public display. Image reproduced by by permission of David Frohlich |
| Page 200, Figure 11.3 | Pass-Them-Around (Andrés Lucero, Jussi Holopainen and Tero Jokela, 2011). Reproduced by permission of Andrés Lucero. |
| Page 205, Figure 11.7 | Augmented bowl (Alex S. Taylor, Shahram Izadi, Laurel Swan, Richard Harper and Bill Buxton, 2006). Reproduced by permission of Alex S. Taylor. |
| Page 207, Figure 11.8 | DIRTI – Dirty Tangible Interfaces (Matthieu Savary, Diemo Schwarz, Denis Pellerin, Florence Massin, Christian Jacquemin and Roland Cahen, 2013). Reproduced by permission of User Studio. |
| Page 211, Figure 11.12 | Aestheticodes (Rupert Meese, Shakir Ali, Emily-Clare Thorne, Steve Benford, Anthony Quinn, Richard Mortier, Boriana Koleva, Tony Pridmore and Sharon Baurley, 2013). Reproduced by permission of Rupert Meese. |
| Page 221, *Uncertainty at the heart of enjoyable experiences* box | Smart rock climbing (Johannes Schöning, Oliver Paczkowski, Ilija Panov, Carsten Keßler, Krzysztof Janowicz, Hans Jörg Müller, Martin Raubal and Antonio Krüger, 2007). Reproduced by permission of Johannes Schöning. |
| Page 235, Figure 13.1 | Jenga blocks falling. Reproduced by permission of Patrick Oladimeji. |
| Page 249, *Learning in to research discussions* box | Audio Gifts (Emma Thom and Matt Jones, 2013). Reproduced by permission of Emma James (née Thom). |
| Page 269, *From one precious personal device to multitudes of utensils* box | Pick Up and Play (Roy Martens, 2013). Reproduced by permission of Roy Martens. |
| Page 277, *The view from an artist: "Shouldn't you call it Baroque computing?"* box | "The rebel angels" by Anthony Majanlahti (https://www.flickr.com/photos/antmoose/34649325/). Licensed under CC BY 2.0 (https://creativecommons.org/licenses/by/2.0/). |
| Page 279, *Projected performance* box | SideBySide (Karl D.D. Willis, Ivan Poupyrev, Scott E. Hudson, and Moshe Mahler, 2011). Reproduced by permission of Karl D.D. Willis. |
| Page 282, Figure 15.1 | Performative pico projection (Liam Betsworth, Huw Bowen, Simon Robinson and Matt Jones, 2014). Reproduced by permission of Liam Betsworth. |
| Page 289, *Case study: Hafod world heritage site* box | Performative pico projection (Liam Betsworth, Huw Bowen, Simon Robinson and Matt Jones, 2014). Reproduced by permission of Liam Betsworth. |
| Page 292, *Case study: Hafod world heritage site* box | Surround You (Liam Betsworth, Huw Bowen, Simon Robinson and Matt Jones, 2014). Reproduced by permission of Liam Betsworth. |
| Page 317, Figure 17.3 | Adapted from Edward Hall's classification of personal space. Reproduced by permission of Jennifer Pearson |
| Page 319, Figure 17.4 | Huggy Pajama (James Keng Soon Teh, Adrian David Cheok, Roshan L. Peiris, Yongsoon Choi, Vuong Thuong and Sha Lai, 2008). Reproduced by permission of James Keng Soon Teh. |

| | |
|---|---|
| Page 322, *MobiSurf: Communicating mindfully together through an ecology of devices* box | MobiSurf (Julian Seifert, Adalberto L. Simeone, Dominik Schmidt, Christian Reinartz, Paul Holleis, Matthias Wagner, Hans Gellersen and Enrico Rukzio, 2012). Reproduced by permission of Julian Seifert. |
| Page 323, Figure 17.5 | Less-prescriptive photo sharing (Thomas Reitmaier, 2013). Reproduced by permission of Thomas Reitmaier. |
| Page 330, Figure 17.9 | Share Face2Face (Thomas Reitmaier, 2013). Reproduced by permission of Thomas Reitmaier. |
| Page 370, *The "open source" bicycle* box | Adapted from "cubabike" by havankevin (https://www.flickr.com/photos/marionenkevin/220157144). Licensed under CC BY 2.0 (https://creativecommons.org/licenses/by/2.0/). |
| Page 376, *Design pointers* box | Envisioning cards (Batya Friedman and David Hendry, 2012). Reproduced by permission of Batya Friedman. |

# CHAPTER 1

## Introduction

## Ecstasy

Once upon a time, building a compelling, usable, useful mobile service was hard.
Very hard.

The devices had small, fiddly keyboards, seemingly designed by evolved svelte beings, not the fat-thumbed, clumsy typical users. Displays were black and white, pixelated, and very small, with the classic "snake" line game being hailed as a major user-pleasing feature. The only onboard sensors, if you could call them that, were the one attached to the battery, to warn of an imminent end to talk time, and the phone's aerial, which could determine the strength of the nearest mobile network signal.

Researchers and designers like us stared down at the materials we had to work with and sighed. While desktop and laptop computers at the time were advancing with dazzling screens, subwoofer audio, and lovely web browsers, it felt like we had traveled back in time to join the ranks of developers who struggled with programming the small displays of early photocopiers and ATM machines (remember the submarine periscope-like single-line displays?).

The austerity conditions we faced did lead to innovation as we tried to overcome the limitations with clever workarounds. Figure 1.1 is an example of this: we wanted to provide access to hundreds of phone and network service functions but avoid the frustrating madness of multiple, nested menu hierarchies given the very small screen we had to work with. The solution involved allowing users to spell out what they wanted, with the software filtering the list of possibilities dynamically. So, pressing 9 (**w**xyz) - 3 (d**e**f) - 2 (**a**bc) would quickly lead to the "weather" service being accessed.

Figure 1.1 Back to the future: small screens and fiddly keyboards challenged designers like us to provide usable, let alone rich, user experiences.

Things are so different now, thanks to a combination of three factors:

- First, there's the relentless progress Moore's Law has brought, with processor speed doubling every 18 months while costs remain the same.

- Then, market forces brought fierce competition to pack devices with as many hardware and software innovations as possible, from eye trackers to brighter and bigger displays (Figure 1.2).

- And, of course, there was Steve Jobs. His genius was to inspire and provoke teams at Apple to see the richness that touch screens, app stores, and an ecology of devices and platforms could bring.

The fruits of this work were richly illustrated at an Apple tech conference in 2012, where visitors enjoyed an art installation consisting of over 100 iPads glued together (Figure 1.3).

Figure 1.2 Now things seem so much better. With services like this from Google, the device presents useful content with little or no effort on the part of the user.

Figure 1.3 iPad art installation. Visitors look on in delight watching app store downloads in real time.

This long, shiny strand was synchronized to show the apps that were being downloaded from iTunes in real time. Like a great dark pool, the display entranced viewers, surfacing as it did the world's appetite for apps—for everything from dieting to connecting with the Dalai Lama—as well as exposing the work of an army of developers who are daily providing new snacks.

Today's smartphones seem to provide an incredible user experience. While there are lots of research papers and books about what user experience is, take a look at the user in Figure 1.4 for perhaps the best definition we can find. This shopper has waited hours to get his hands on the latest, greatest device. He just can't hide his raw ecstasy at getting his hands on a shiningly seductive piece of the future.

Figure 1.4 Ecstasy.

# What is user experience?

This book is about enhancing mobile user experience, so let's say up front what we think user experience (UX) is about, and what makes for a good one.

Sometimes people use UX as an up-to-date way to refer to the well-established notion of usability. But UX is far more than usability. In the days of computers as workbenches or simple home appliances, the ideals of a system being efficient, effective and satisfying—key elements in conventional usability thinking—were enough. However, now that we carry and wear devices, encountering digital services at theme parks, during surgery, or 30,000 ft above the ground, innovative ways of guiding and evaluating effective design are needed.

UX thinking, then, attempts to reorientate designers towards considerations about how to impact a user's emotional response and develop artifacts that have real meaning or value for people as they go through their everyday lives.

One group of human-computer interaction (HCI) researchers wanted to understand what "user experience" really means, so they carried out a survey of 275 UX professionals and academics. After analyzing respondents' answers, they identified several common features in people's definitions of what contributes to a user experience:

- UX is seen as a person's response when using a device, product, service, or object through some sort of user interface.

- UX is dynamic, so it can change before, during, or after use; and, it is context-dependent, the experience being affected by where the artifact is being used.

- The UX response, of course, is also subjective, affected by the user's background, previous experiences, and many other factors.

But what is this "response"? A good three-pronged answer is provided by Don Norman in his book *Emotional Design*:

- Firstly, it's the response you get as soon as you encounter the object (the *visceral*).

- Secondly, its the reaction that emerges as you use it (the *behavioral*—akin to the usability of old).

- And, finally, it's about *reflection*, and how it makes you see yourself in relation to others, with good UX helping you feel good about your choices and values.

## Angst

So, perhaps this book should stop right here.

Clearly the future looks bright; the ingredients and recipes for highly effective mobiles are in place. Users can live a fulfilled, better, more successful life as long as they can find and install the app for the bit of their lives—at work, at home, for fun—that needs a boost; and surely there's an app for all of that.

We don't want to deride this marvelous and diverse work—and the sparks of genius—that have brought the mobile industry to this place. Collectively, the three of us have worked in mobile human-computer interaction and user experience for over 40 years, and we've been as excited as anyone else to see mobiles go from quirky, clunky, dumb devices to the magic wands billions of people carry with them everyday.

So what are we worried about?

Think back to that picture of all of those iPads arranged as a vast pool. This dark surface is a technological echo perhaps of another deep, disturbing body of water. Narcissus was a figure in Greek mythology who cared only for himself, thinking no one else was beautiful enough to be worthy of his love. (See the front cover for the way we've adapted the very famous image of Narcissus by Caravaggio.) To teach him a lesson, the Gods, as they tended to do at that time, came up with a hideously ingenuous and appropriate punishment. Narcissus was enticed to a dark pool and, looking down, thought he saw a wonderful water spirit. As he put his hand into the water to touch the beauty, the ripples obscured the image, and Narcissus lost sight of what he wanted to connect with. When the water calmed, the image returned, and he was scared to touch it again in case the spirit left. Not realizing it was his own reflection, Narcissus stayed at the pool, looking down into the water, dying slowly as those who really cared for him, the wood nymphs, mourned nearby.

While we might not all possess Narcissus' physical beauty, as we look into our smartphone and tablet screens, gently prodding and caressing the digital water, are we falling in love with our own reflection, never to leave, oblivious to the actual life around us? With a few prods and taps, heads down, we can command forth such amazing content from search engines, tweets, and status updates that mention us or others in our social network, or images that give our lives a story. All the while, do we diminish the chances to look our fellow commuters in the eye; to smirk at our partners' hopeless jokes while at the pub; to feel the adrenaline surge as we begin to feel lost in an unfamiliar city; to feel frustrated if we don't know the answer, or a little nervous having to approach a stranger for help?

*Life is what happens when we're busy downloading apps... (with apologies to John Lennon)*

# The Rime of the Ancient Mobile Interaction Designers

Maybe we are having a collective midlife crisis, though, as we question what the current dominant technologies and design approaches are doing to the real experiences of life. Indulge us then for a little while, like the wedding guest in the *Rime of the Ancient Mariner*.

Back in 1998, Gary and Matt were in Glasgow, UK to attend the very first annual International Symposium on Human Computer Interaction for Mobile Devices and Services (still a great conference to hear about some of the most innovative research in this field). We'd attended a session presented by key Wireless

*'Hold off! Unhand me, grey-beard loon!*

*...*

*He holds him with his glitter-ing eye—*
*The Wedding-Guest stood still,*
*And listens like a three years' child:*
*The Mariner hath his will"*

Application Protocol (WAP) developers. WAP was the first serious framework to provide online content and transactions over the mobile phone networks.

After the conference, we left Glasgow to visit friends. We wanted to go out to watch a movie and, being tech-aholics, inspired by our WAP encounter, decided to see if we could connect our *PalmPilot* (a cutting-edge handheld "personal digital assistant") to the Web to see out what was on offer in the local area. There were five of us in the living room of an upstairs flat, the sun in true Scottish fashion shining outside. First, we had to move the sofa out of the way to expose the landline phone socket and plug in the portable modem. Then, one of us had to burrow under a low coffee table to find a power socket, plug in the adaptor and stretch the cable over to the sofa to power the modem. Both the modem connector and the power cable clip did not firmly fit into the PDA's socket, and had to be held delicately in place with our hands; too much movement and we'd have to begin the involved process of connecting to the Web again.

So, at the heart of this spider's web tangle of wires we all sat around the device, watched, and took it in turns to prod the screen with the stylus, repeatedly trying different settings (data speeds, carrier types, control codes…) to connect to our gateway server back in London. We chatted and laughed, trying not to move too much as we didn't want to break the connection with a jiggle of the wires. After a long time, we *heard* the data squeak up and down the telephone line. We saw the Lycos search page—Google hadn't been invented yet—slowly appear, slightly faster than a fax page being printed.

Of course, there were no movie listings for the little town in Scotland, but it didn't matter: it felt like we were at the start of something incredible—the ability to draw content from anywhere in the world into our everyday lives. We weren't sitting in a high-end university lab; we were in a bedsit, full of slightly tatty, student-era furniture.

By now, like the wedding guest of the poem, you might be tiring and wanting to hurry on to the main event. But pause for a moment, at that scene frozen from years ago. To get what we hoped would be some location-relevant content from the Web we had to really interact with our location: shifting sofas, scuttling around on all fours to find sockets, gingerly holding wires together. We worked together around one device; it was a social experience, an enduring memory. We had to use our wits and physical deftness—there really is a skill in using your phone and forefinger to pinch a wire in place at just the right angle.

It wouldn't happen like this today. With a few flicks of a screen, a swish over a keypad, any one of us individually could call up the listings, book the seats, and have the tickets downloaded for scanning by a QR reader. Maybe several of us would use our personal devices to sit silently, pausing to utter, heads still down, *"What about Iron Man?"*

The future has taken us so far from that sitting room in Scotland. We've lost so much in the process.

**Search for:**
*Rime of the Ancient Mariner*

## Losing ourselves

Let's look more closely at what happened to Narcissus. At first, the pool caught his eye, the image he saw distracting him from his meanderings through the woods. He probably didn't pause to consider the dangers of taking a closer look—what harm could it do, after all?

As he reached into the water, distraction began to turn to obsession. The pool in short order became his focus—his everything.

Soon he stopped trying to interact, scared that the creature in front of him would vanish. He had become consumed by the pool, now passively fixated with what it provided: in anguish at his situation but unable to move away.

What are the equivalent steps to losing ourselves to the digital?

**Step 1:** First comes the distraction; a stage most mobile users are already at (and have been for some time). Sitting on a wonderful beach outside Athens in 2001, Matt was watching a game of beach volleyball. Both players were knocking the ball deftly back and forth with one hand; occasionally they shouted at each other, teasing or celebrating a point. Looking more closely, though, something odd was happening: each player was using their other hand to hold a mobile and chat; not to each other, of course, but to someone elsewhere. This happened some time before smartphones had arrived, but presaged what we now see everyday. People who are in extraordinary places, in the company of their friends, with the opportunity to really feel alive, the sand on their feet, warmth on their face, the joy of sensing their skeleton and muscles flex and react to a physical challenge; all of this, but they dip in and out of the experience, distracted by the digital.

**Step 2:** The more serious stage, though, is where the physical becomes a mere prop for or, even worse, a distraction to the digital. The world within the shiny box becomes more important than the one outside. If you need evidence of how this digital primacy is taking hold, go and sit in a bar, restaurant, or café terrace in any major city. You'll see people from all sorts of cultures, backgrounds, and countries, lost to the world, focusing on the digital. Consider a young tourist couple in Paris, sitting opposite each other, their table facing out towards a view of the Eiffel Tower. Matt did this recently and watched in slight sadness as, in the world's capital of romance, the two spent 20 minutes sipping cappuccinos, mostly in silence. They weren't staring, love-struck into each other's eyes, though. Instead, they were tending their social network profiles, every now and then interrupting each other with a remark that usually elicited no response from the other.

## Connecting is disconnecting

We're more connected than ever before. But, as a side effect, we're also perhaps more *disconnected* than ever before, too. A study by Andrew Przybylski and Netta Weinstein of the University of Essex, UK, found that simply having a mobile phone present could interfere with human relationships. Phones *"inhibited the development of interpersonal closeness and trust,"* even when not actively being used.

They also *"reduced the extent to which individuals felt empathy and understanding from their partners."*

Rather than our ultra-connectedness helping to support and extend our existing lives, it seems to be making us overextend ourselves and try to cover all possible strands of our networks at the same time. Connecting to people and places through our devices rather than our surroundings, then, might have big impacts on our relationships and social lives.

Digital primacy does not just mean that people become more focused on their devices and the services they offer, or the seemingly more interesting, useful, and dynamic worlds they provide. In this second phase of loss, the physical world becomes less real unless it can be augmented by the digital. The craving to check in, tweet what's happening, upload a picture, and broadcast and share every moment is becoming more and more common.

## Really there?

A popular and revealing image from late 2013 shows a large crowd of onlookers and well-wishers eagerly waiting for the papal election announcement. However, the photo, taken from behind the crowd, primarily shows most people's hands held up with phones or tablets in hand to capture a photo for themselves.

**Search for:**
*2013 papal conclave phones photo*

Think about occasions where you've seen a similar scene. In the photo, people have made a conscious pilgrimage to see the election of a new pope, but the main view is a blanket of screens—a familiar picture at any recent festival or concert, too. While everyone in the crowd can say, "I was there," how many could, in all honesty, claim "I saw it"? Bizarrely, then, screen focus happens even when the goal of being in a place is to socialize with other people, or to share in experiencing an event.

**Step 3:** Eventually the pool consumed Narcissus. After distraction, it became his focus, then it took him. Maybe we're really pushing the connection now, but it is worth pausing to think about what might happen as we stare more deeply into the digital.

In the early days of human-computer interaction and usability practice, the designer's job was to make the machine easier for the human to use. To help people to be more efficient, effective, and satisfied. Are we now beginning to see a reversal, with the focus on making the human easier to use and be used by the machine? Are designers—people like you and us—forging systems that simply provide more and more ways to gather content and data from users, using these later to make money through advertising and other sales opportunities? Some neuroscientists are even beginning to worry that an increasing reliance on digital memories and other human augmentation might reduce our capacity to think for ourselves.

A world of smarter phones but dumber humans might seem an unlikely outcome of mobile technology progress, but the voices of dissent and caution resonate with many people's everyday worries about what our devices are turning us into. Talk to parents of any child born after around 2005, and listen to their concerns about how their children are becoming more and more "plugged in"—part of, not apart from, the digital.

# Two manifestos

We are not the first or only people to ask whether the new landscape of mobile devices, with cloud services floating all around, should concern or provoke us to try alternative ways of using the technological creativity and innovation that is effervescing all around the world from California to Korea, Mumbai to London. In particular, if after reading the last few pages you are either beginning to be drawn to the cause or, conversely, feel cross at our provocation, take a look at Jaron Lanier's *You are Not a Gadget* and Sherry Turkle's *Alone Together*.

*"I want to say: You have to be somebody before you can share yourself"*

**Jaron Lanier**

*"We have invented inspiring and enhancing technologies, and yet we have allowed them to diminish us. The prospect of loving, or being loved by, a machine changes what love can be. We know that the young are tempted. They have been brought up to be. Those who have known lifetimes of love can surely offer them more"*

**Sherry Turkle**

# Rebellion not retreat

One response to our angst and the calls of the likes of Lanier and Turkle (see the *Two manifestos* box) is to unplug and disconnect; that is, to retreat.

Like any addiction, the first step would be to recognize the control and deadening effect the substance was having on our lives and then—one day at a time—reduce the influence it has over us. Perhaps we could just tweet twice a day, or only check others' social network updates at lunchtime. Perhaps at the weekends and evenings we would declare a "digital fast."

We might even advocate that our users go on "digital detox" retreats to reconnect with the "real" world. Someone who did just this is Susan Maushart. Writing in *The Winter of our*

*Disconnect*, Maushart tells how she and three teenagers survived six months completely off-grid. Describing the experience as a return to the *"Old Country,"* she argues that she and her children not only spent more time reconnecting with each other but discovered the joy in doing things—from reading to playing instruments—more intensely, more deeply.

While we have a lot of sympathy with these sorts of strategies, the purpose of this book is not to argue for a return to a mobile-free existence. We are not part of a Technology Abstinence Movement, with attractive alternatives like conversation clubs to tempt addicts away from hunched-over tweeting.

We are also not lifestyle coaches or therapy gurus. The three of us are designers, computer scientists, researchers, and unashamed gadget lovers. So, our response is to design and think our way out of this mess: we want to rebel and look for a revolution in design thinking.

*Our response is to design and think our way out of this mess: we want to rebel and look for a revo-lution in design thinking.*

Jaron Lanier warns us that ways of living using digital devices and services are on the cusp of being "locked in." The way we see ourselves, express who we are, connect with others, and experience the world around us is being framed by the dominant digital design decisions. From the form factors and input-output mechanisms of mobile devices to the structure of blog sites and social network profiles, we are being handed scripts that constrain and codify in a narrow way what being a person is. But there is hope, as Lanier notes:

> *"There are aspects to all these software designs that could be retained more humanistically. A design that shares Twitter's feature of providing ambient continu-ous contact between people could perhaps drop Twitter's adoration of fragments. We don't really know because it is an unexplored design space."*
>
> **Jaron Lanier**

There's Not an App for That | Introduction

*We don't really know because it is an unexplored design space.* This book is an adventure to try and better chart the design space that meanders off the conventional technology roadmap. We want to explore alternative ways of incorporating mobiles into our lives.

Turkle speaks of her book as a letter, long and thought through, not a passing status update, seeking a response from both her daughter and the wider readership. This is our letter back. Three technologists who pick up her request, *"...to look again towards the virtue of solitude, deliberateness and living fully in the moment."*

## Rebelling against the machine

It was a hot summer's afternoon and one of us was getting to know Houston, visiting there for research discussions. The smart car we were in had a sophisticated built-in sat nav.

*"Turn left at the next intersection"*

We ignored its instruction.

*"In one mile turn left at the next intersection"*

We glided past the second exit, enjoying the skyscraper skyline ahead.

*"Exit at the next possible opportunity and rejoin the highway"*

The automated voice was starting to sound exasperated. We ignored it again.

*"Goodbye. You are now on your own"*

And with that, the machine's screen dimmed and then darkened to "off."

While this behavior was slightly disconcerting, it was exhilarating to have been given back control, allowed to take risks and make mistakes rather than blindly following directions (see Figure 1.5). We'd beaten the machine.

Figure 1.5 This "Ignore Sat Nav" road sign in Wales, UK, warns drivers of roads that are unsuitable for certain vehicles. A simple reminder that we shouldn't always blindly take instructions from our gadgets.

## Life under a lid

*Butterflies in a display case or butterflies flitting from flower to flower on a sunny early summer's day? The lifeless forms are so much easier to inspect in detail than the awkwardly animated reality, aren't they?*

In the 19th century a common pastime amongst educated, refined folk in the UK involved capturing butterflies with a dainty net and sticking a sharp, thin pin through the thorax. British fair play at its best.

After the creature had stopped fluttering its wings, it would be added to a collection like the one in Figure 1.6. Quite a horrifying hobby for sure—why would people do this to something so free and beautiful? Trying to trap the creatures' vibrant vitality under glass.

Today's mobiles are a bit like those Victorian butterfly boxes. They desperately attempt to present and capture the wonder of life. What they actually do, we suggest, is blunt the experience.

This book is about providing you with inspiration to bring more of real life to the mobile apps and services you create: to look at how people experience and enjoy the

Figure 1.6 Butterflies under glass.

physical world around them, and then to design to accommodate and exploit those insights.

We've identified six entrenched current design features leading to user experiences that are less real than people deserve:

- Touch screen dominance

- Heads-down thinking

- Clinical helpfulness

- Calm, understated interactions

- Stuck in the cloud(s)

- Design for the few

In each of the sections of this book we'll explore why these are problems, and then go on to look at opportunities for design that can be seized by taking different perspectives. Before we do that though, here's a hint of our thinking so you can see what's ahead.

## Touch screen dominance

When you think about presenting content and interactions on a mobile device, screens that you can tap, pinch, and swipe seem a wonderful resource. There's so much you can communicate on a display, and finger gestures, even with one hand, can be expressive. These touch screens have been hailed as a highly successful "natural user interface" (or NUI in the acronym tech-world soup). But selecting something on the interface and manipulating it doesn't really feel natural.

In a marvelous, and now famous blog "rant," former Apple designer Bret Victor provokes us to think about what real touch is, by pointing to the richness of physical interactions and our incredible abilities to perceive, for instance, textures, weights, and volumes.

So, if you are reading this book on a tablet right now, swipe your hand to turn back a page, and then return to this one. Now find a paper book and do the same thing. There's a clear difference in the sensation. Many people love their Kindles, Nooks, and other e-readers because they can travel on holiday without having to carry around a set of heavy books. While these devices are a clear benefit, without the physical weight in your backpack or bag, how do you know you've got the books you want with you?

Touch screen dominance has blinded us from thinking more about what real touching, feeling, and physical manipulation can offer. How could we use a more human view of "touch" to enhance the materials we build our mobiles from, the sensations they could stimulate, and the interactions they might afford?

## Provoking new thinking

Throughout this book we'll be trying to get you to think of alternative ways of presenting content and interacting with your users.

One technique that can help generate interesting deviations from the norm, whatever the platforms you are building on, involves imagining a world where certain characteristics commonly taken for granted are removed.

So, what about the world where you can't see anything any more, or your sight is partial? What would your mobile device feel like then? A research team in the UK came up with the *Haptic Lotus*, shown below, through just such an experiment.

The *Haptic Lotus* is designed to be held in both hands, its petals opening and closing as it gets nearer or further away from a target location. The team deployed the device as part of an "immersive haptic theatre experience," where audience members explored a pitch-black room carrying the device. While there were many fascinating insights from the work, let's pick out just two of the comments from people who took part:

*"The device was like a purring cat, or a pet."*

*"It was interesting to have something 'alive' in your hands. It was companionable."*

Using Bret Victor's inspirational piece as a starting point, beginning at Chapter 2 we'll be looking at how to break the dullness of glass screen prods to develop designs that are more "'alive' in your hands."

## Heads-down thinking

Several years ago there was an amusing marketing stunt that saw a telephone company put padded covers onto lampposts. The joke was that as people were always looking down, texting, tweeting, and status updating while walking, they needed protection for when they bumped into street furniture.

While funny, the problem with heads-down life isn't that people will have daily collisions. Try this short experiment when you are next in a crowded street. Attempt to walk into someone who is looking down at his or her phone. Usually they'll react amazingly deftly, weaving out of your way. On the rare occasion when you meet, apologize!

# Not always lucky

While we often can integrate heads-down interaction with walking and navigating a busy street, there are of course dangers. A real video that quickly became popular on YouTube a few years after the marketing stunt mentioned earlier shows a visitor to a shopping mall concentrating so hard on her mobile that she falls into a fountain.

HCI researchers Joanna Lumsden and Patrick Drost have investigated the risk of mobile screen focus through a study in their lab. A group of people was recruited to use a screen to verify text entry while at the same time walking around a circuit and avoiding virtual "hazards." Lumsden summarized the results for a news article as *"one in five bollards, lamp posts, raised kerbs or even moving vehicles is likely to go unnoticed by people texting,"* and *"the safest thing is for people not to text as they walk along."*

No, most of the time the problem is not that people will hit something, but rather that they are missing things. Here's another field experiment you can try. Take your mobile back to that busy street and start recording a video. Hold the phone up at roughly

Figure 1.7 Heads up walking down the street (left); the same street, texting heads down (right).

shoulder level and walk along the pavement for a few minutes. Next, repeat this process, but this time hold the phone down and look at the screen as if you were composing a text while walking. Reviewing the clips, perhaps you'll notice differences like the ones in Figure 1.7

Starting in Chapter 7, we explore ways of staying connected with the world around us while using mobiles. Recently, of course, there's been much excitement about "heads-up" displays, especially in the form of Google's *Glass* wearable. Surely that kind of approach solves our problem? In fact, it makes things worse. The digital world is now permanently in view or in ear, tempting users to foreground the digital and let the life around them blur into the background.

## Clinical helpfulness

There are plenty of mobile services that try to tidy up the messiness of our lives, to reduce the complexity, confusion, and frustration. Today's mobile search and mapping tools (for instance) aspire to tell us all we need to know, perhaps even before we realize we have a need.

Beginning at Chapter 10, we will challenge this tendency to design out the roughness of living. User experience design does not need to be about just creating joyful, happy

Comedian Dean Obeidallah tried living without a phone for a single day: "Instead of texting or checking my e-mail, I began to actually look at the people I was sharing the streets with. It truly resembled a movie set filled with extras from all walks of life."

Dean Obeidallah

users. We will look at the value of being lost, of not being certain, and of making our own way. Good UX often delights, but let's consider how to engender that surge of fright as adrenaline injects into our veins.

## Blunt reality or mirror world tidiness?

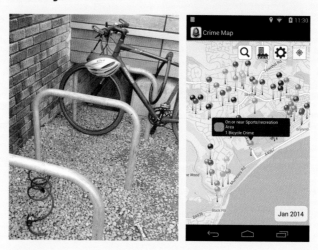

Parking my bike at the gym, I couldn't miss the severed lock next to the stand: a blunt reminder about the need for a strong protection for my bike! After my workout, I searched one of the app stores and found a lot of "crime mapping" offerings. Commonly, they show a variety of police statistics each as a neat and tidy pin on a map. Useful, I suppose, but lacking the impact of the clear crime signal of the forlorn lock next to the bike stand. Maybe a future bike lock like mine would respond to this sort of data by refusing to lock (or resisting me, at least) in areas where there have been recent thefts. Less futuristically, the mobile I was listening to music on as I cycled in could disrupt the music with the snarl of a lock cutter to warn me of potential dangers.

My gym visit, incidentally, was preceded by an energetic ride along the beautiful Swansea coast and up steep hills to the grazing moors behind the city, dodging wild ponies that had decided to try tarmac instead of turf. Safely inside the gym, in contrast, I experienced mechanical, digitized exercise on a running machine that simulated uphill slopes until I had had enough (see Figure 1.8). Reflecting now on the two experiences, I see again how much is lost when we design out the friction from an experience.

**MJ**

In the attempts to over-help users, have we built an infrastructure that tidies up the world too much? How can we design so that the digital spills out into the physical world, forcing it to deal with the constraints and affordances humans have evolved to cope with?

## Calm, understated interactions

There's a very famous concept video made by Apple in 1987 called "The Knowledge Navigator." It features two characters, the first being a professor surrounded by the props of scholarship: wood paneling on the walls, high shelves of books and a library

Figure 1.8 Heads down in the gym; and, the running machine has apps.

**Search for:**
*Knowledge
Navigator
video*

ladder, a globe. Amidst this environment familiar to academics down the ages is something from the future. The professor is working with what we would now call a tablet computer. He touches and gestures the surface to interact with information, but for much of the video is also in conversation with a personal assistant. This assistant isn't human but digital, appearing as a talking head at the top of the screen.

Watching the film now, what's remarkable is not just the accuracy of the prediction of how technology might turn out several decades later. More striking is the vision of technology as a personal, discreet support.

Most of the time mobiles aren't used by professors in quiet studies; they are in the hurly-burly of less rarefied environments: a late night metro train rattling home; or a long line waiting for the barista to finish making the latte. But even in these diverse, lively places, you can see the same sort of quiet turns to the technology: glances at the screen, taps on the glass, and casual swipes along the screen. Mobiles are an ever-present support that can gently reassure and provide.

Jump to another world altogether. This time we are in Bangalore, India, at a school for disadvantaged Grade 6 and 7 children. There's a "personal" computer, but it is surrounded by a group of children. Maybe they are waiting their turn to take control of the keyboard and mouse? Getting closer to them we can see they are not spectating but all performing together. Each of them has a mouse and they are energetically and excitedly working together on a number of learning tasks. Subdued, discreet interaction this is certainly not.

For several years now there has been much enthusiasm for digital "crowds" in the cloud, the aggregation of individuals over the net, their wisdom and their collective power a resource. Unlike any real crowds—or even the smaller groups of Indian school children using the multiple mice—these crowds are quiet.

Starting in Chapter 13, we explore what we can do to move away from always seeing our mobiles as personal, private devices. We'll look at ideas that promote a more public and extravagant use of our gadgets.

## Stuck in the cloud(s)

*Tweet of the Day* was a fascinating BBC Radio 4 series aired in 2013. Broadcast every day for a year with each program lasting just 90 seconds, listeners first heard a clip of a song, followed by a very brief story about the bird that produced it. Cunningly, the program daily reminded listeners that birds in all their physical glory, amongst trees, hedgerows, and on the wing, tweeted long before the digital cuckoo of Twitter arrived.

Mindfulness is a practice and philosophy—stemming originally from Buddhism—that has become popular in the mainstream over the past several years. Instead of being overwhelmed in one's thoughts and feelings, people are trained to become aware of how their physical and mental selves are intertwined. Exercises help them focus on the moment they are living in, rather than trying to unmuddle the complexities of the often racing thoughts of the past, present, and future. Practitioners of the method may well have been less surprised to find that *Tweet of the Day* was about actual birds, not status updates, than many of us app developers!

Starting in Chapter 16, we'll consider what might be called "mindful" interaction. Instead of creating apps that keep our users' heads "in the cloud" we look at ways to design so they can really be aware of who and what they are interacting with. We'll also consider how this viewpoint disrupts current app frameworks, pointing to interfaces based on data generated by physical surroundings and the people around us. Current designs, in contrast, distance these aspects, giving users the tunnel vision of task focus.

## Design for the few

Billboard displays and magazine ads for mobiles usually show smart, fit people living the good life: laughing with friends on shopping outings, or smiling as a business deal is closed. The kids in the Bangalore school remind us that the world—thankfully—is bigger than these pictures.

Hundreds of millions of users—in regions like India, China, and South America—are getting their first taste of computing and information interaction via mobile devices. Meanwhile, most mobiles are designed with a "first world" perspective.

All three of us have been really fortunate in having opportunities to look at future mobile services for these communities who are on the other side of the "digital divide." Mobiles can make a transformative difference to these communities. In Chapter 19, we'll consider the approaches proposed and the challenges that still need to be addressed.

## Alternative trajectories for mobile user experience design

In the rest of the book we'll be looking at a number of orthodox design approaches and directly challenging them. We explore the following design journeys:

- From Touch to Feeling

- From Heads Down to Face On

- From Clinical to Clutter

- From Private and Personal to Public and Performance

- From Distanced to Mindful Interaction

- From Some to All

## Future, now

If you are an app developer, creating new services under a tight deadline, you may be wondering how you can use this book. Let's be clear from the start—there are plenty of others on how to improve the basic usability and design of smartphones and touchscreen devices. This isn't one of them. Instead, our aim is to lay out new design spaces and thinking that has been bubbling in research labs and our heads for some time.

It seems obvious how things should develop in the mobile market—more apps, better screens, longer battery life, faster and faster networks, drawing us more and more towards the tempting pool that leads us to digital worlds that offer so much.

We want to help undermine this certainty by providing alternative perspectives; changing the future but starting now.

In each chapter there are examples of existing approaches, apps, and services that are critiqued to illustrate how things might be done differently. As well as provoking and inspiring, then, each chapter has sections that connect the far-out thinking with today's design concerns.

We'll also be surveying a wide range of interactive technologies that are not yet available commercially; as well as preparing you for the possibilities these materials will bring over the next 5 to 10 years, we consider how their properties and the design viewpoints they instantiate can be brought to enrich today's designs.

Each chapter begins with a summary to help you see the key issues. Throughout the book there are also a series of *Design Challenges* and *Design Pointers* that are there to help you understand the material and think about your own responses.

We don't want you to think this book is about telling you what to do. We know that there are many other ways of considering the issues we raise: we've highlighted some of these in breakout boxes called *Another Perspective*, and throughout the text we'll be posing questions to ask you what you think.

At the end of each chapter we've given a list of resources referred to in the text that you can use for further reading and study. In addition, to help you quickly jump to key sources you'll see *Search for* boxes dotted through the book: type these terms into a search engine and you should find content directly related to the topics they appear near to.

## Resources

Sherry Turkle's [1] and Jaron Lanier's [2] books have been a great inspiration as we prepared and wrote this book. More detail on the user experience survey we discussed can be found in [3]; and, a great starting book about the role of emotion in UX is [4]. Our small-screen menu research can be found in [5]. Bret Victor's "brief rant" is where we started from in thinking about going beyond "touch screens"; the post and follow-up comments can be found at [6].

Andrew Przybylski and Netta Weinstein's exploration of how mobile phones interfere with human relationships is in [7]. Susan Maushart's book [8], and "detox" websites such as [9] show one possible response to our mobile obsession.

The *Haptic Lotus* with its unique exploration of navigation and perception is described in [10]. Joanna Lumsden and Patrick Drost's research on accidents and mobiles is reported in [11] and [12]. Dean Obeidallah's day without a phone is covered in [13], and the YouTube real-life video of an unfortunate texting incident can be seen in [14]. Apple's *Knowledge Navigator* can be found at [15]. The full story on the Bangalore school children's collaborative interactions is told in [16].

[1] Turkle S. Alone Together: Why We Expect More from Technology and Less from Each Other. New York: Basic Books; 2011.

[2] Lanier J. You Are Not a Gadget: A Manifesto. New York: Alfred A. Knopf; 2010.

[3] Law EL-C, Roto V, Hassenzahl M, Vermeeren AP, Kort J. Understanding, scoping and defining user experience: A survey approach. In: Proceedings of the SIGCHI Conference on Human Factors in Computing Systems; ACM; 2009. pp. 719–28. http://dx.doi.org/10.1145/1518701.1518813.

[4] Norman D. Emotional Design: Why We Love (or Hate) Everyday Things. New York: Basic Books; 2005.

[5] Marsden G, Jones M. Ubiquitous computing and cellular handset interfaces – Are menus the best way forward? In: Proceedings of The South African Institute for Computer Scientists and Information Technologists Annual Conference; 2001. pp. 111–9.

[6] Victor B. A brief rant on the future of interaction design. 2011. Retrieved from http://worrydream.com/ABriefRantOnTheFutureOfInteractionDesign/.

[7] Przybylski AK, Weinstein N. Can you connect with me now? How the presence of mobile communication technology influences face-to-face conversation quality. J Soc Pers Relationships 2013;30(3):237–46. http://dx.doi.org/10.1177/0265407512453827.

[8] Maushart S. The Winter of Our Disconnect. London: Profile Books; 2011.

[9] Digital Detox. 2011. Retrieved from http://thedigitaldetox.org/.

[10] Linden J, van der, Rogers Y, Oshodi M, Spiers A, McGoran D, Cronin R, O'Dowd P. Haptic reassurance in the pitch black for an immersive theatre experience. In: Proceedings of the 13th International Conference on Ubiquitous Computing; ACM; 2011. pp. 143–52. http://dx.doi.org/10.1145/2030112.2030133.

[11] Lumsden J, Drost P. A comparison of the impact of avoidance cues in hazard avoidance during evaluation of text entry. In: Proceedings of the 22nd British HCI Group Annual Conference on People and Computers: Culture, Creativity, Interaction - Volume 2; British Computer Society; 2008. pp. 57–60.

[12] Derbyshire D. Millions 'putting lives at risk by texting while they walk.' 2010. Retrieved from http://www.dailymail.co.uk/sciencetech/article-1312656/.

[13] Obeidallah, D. A Day Without a Cell Phone. 2012. Retrieved from http://edition.cnn.com/2012/09/26/opinion/obeidallah-cell-phone/.

[14] Girl Falls In Mall Fountain While Texting. 2011. Retrieved from https://www.youtube.com/watch?v=mg11glsBW4Y.

[15] Apple's Future Computer: The Knowledge Navigator. 1987. Retrieved from https://www.youtube.com/watch?v=9b jve67p33E.

[16] Pawar US, Pal J, Gupta R, Toyama K. Multiple mice for retention tasks in disadvantaged schools. In: Proceedings of the SIGCHI Conference on Human Factors in Computing Systems; ACM; 2007. pp. 1581–90. http://dx.doi.org/10.1145/1240624.1240864.

# CHAPTER 2

## Problem 1
## FROM TOUCH TO FEELING

## WHAT'S THE PROBLEM?

Digital interactions through mobiles are an increasingly prominent part of day-to-day lived experience. But what are they doing to the richness of this everyday life?

Our starting point, in this first *Problem*, is to pause for a moment and think about the extent to which the smooth glass of our phones, which separates us from the digital world inside, numbs or dulls, rather than enlivens.

As you'll see as you read on, this book is a celebration of what it is to be truly alive—to revel in the complexity, ambiguity, messiness, and stimulation the world provides.

## WHY SHOULD YOU TACKLE IT?

If we look away from our interactions with gadgets, we see inspirations for what mobile experiences might be both now and in the future. We see a world of multisensory beings that taste, smell, see, and feel the world. Sometimes we are hit with a double espresso jolt of life—think of the pain of falling off a bike; other times we feel it much more subtly—as a gentle breeze brushes the hairs on the back of your neck. We live in a world where emotion is as important as efficiency.

We also experience a world that we can shape and manipulate through an equally broad spectrum of actions: from demolishing a wall with a sledgehammer to creating beautiful origami with deft finger folds.

Our challenge to you here, then, is to consider how these human skills can be put to better use, and inform the interaction designs we make both today and on the devices to come.

# KEY POINTS

■ "Touch," as in "touch screen," is a limited design resource compared to what humans are capable of in terms of the ways we can sense, respond, and manipulate.

■ We have been built for physical materials; digital materials currently lack many qualities to enable us to fully engage with them.

■ When we think about the physical world, we are reminded that not every interaction is pleasant, calming, and joyful. Facing up to a spectrum of emotional responses can introduce new thinking to interaction design.

■ Research labs and visionary designers have been exploring how to break through the glass to create digital experiences that engage better with these multisensory, emotional, and multimanipulator abilities.

# Introduction

Have you ever walked into a glass door? It's a shocking, dazing experience. The shock comes from the sudden, unexpected impact—one moment you are striding, unhindered, the world seemingly visible to you; the next you are stopped suddenly by the unseen barrier. You reel, perhaps curse, and after a while continue onwards.

Contrast the numbness from the glass door collision to having your senses fully stimulated. Think back to the last time you sunbathed on a beach. Lying there, you felt the warmth of the sun on your skin, noticing when comfortable heat began to turn to painful burn. Perhaps you dug your hands into the sand, rubbing the grains between your fingers, sensing the gritty texture. Despite your eyes being closed, you felt fully aware of the scene around you, listening to children splash close by, the gossipy chatter of neighbors anchored to beach chairs, the cawing of seagulls. You were alive in and alive to the place.

Or, if you are a more active sort, that feeling of vitality comes when you do sport or exercise. If you are a runner you'll know that feeling, halfway through a long route, where your legs fill with lactic acid, your heart and lungs feel like they might rip from your chest, and your eyes water with the exertion. Painfully, exhilaratingly alive.

Touch screens on smartphones have transformed mobile user experiences. They are widely seen as providing for diverse, deft manipulations: selections, pinches, swipes, magnifications, and so on. Rather than congratulating each other on the wonders of this technology, though, we want to provoke you.

## Design Challenge

What is the danger of these glass lids? Are they actually blunting our senses?

**Search for:**
*Bret Victor brief rant*

Each time we prod the screen with our fingers, it is as if we are walking into a glass door. Every tap is a micro-moment that dazes us. Bret Victor, the well-known interaction designer and blogger, calls this interaction style *"pictures under glass,"* worrying, as we do, about how the paradigm denies us a richer, sense-ful interaction.

There's Not an App for That | From Touch to Feeling

Modern glass doors and barriers have markings at eye level to warn the walker of danger (see Figure 2.1). What we'll be doing in this chapter is to act as the warning dots. We will highlight how impoverishing simple touch interaction is in comparison to real life, and point to alternatives.

We pose this question: how might we build experiences that allow us to feel fully alive? To move, that is, from touch screens to technologies and designs that encourage us to use all our senses to feel and connect to the world.

Figure 2.1 Warning! Glass can blunt experience.

## Alternative perspective

You might be thinking about objections to our focus here: surely mobile devices and their apps and services don't have to provide such an immersive set of experiences? After all, do we expect other tools (say a pencil or a pad of paper, or a cooking pot and a stirring spoon) to make us feel so alive? Surely, mobiles are just another object, and richer, visceral living can be left to other activities, like sunbathing or biking?

## Built as bodies, built for materials

Ben is one of Matt's children. He's 12, and for a few years has been developing a wonderful talent in creating origami models (see Figure 2.2 for an example). Dexterously he turns small, simple pieces of paper into dragons, boxes, or frogs.

Figure 2.2 Ben's origami.

We are built to manipulate, shape, and rearrange the world physically. Of course we use our hands, but we also "head" soccer balls, rush through leaves, kicking them into a storm with our feet, and deform beanbags with our backsides as we drop lazily down onto them.

Human-computer interaction researchers and designers have recognized the drive to get physical for decades. Beginning with the shift away from command-line interfaces—the blinking cursor on a screen that tells you nothing of the computer world beneath—to graphical user interfaces (GUIs), suddenly computers were turned from the foreign to the more familiar: there were pictures of documents, trashcans, and filing cabinets that the user could "pick up" and "move" using a mouse and keyboard.

While lots of today's interactions are much like the early GUIs, the mouse being replaced by our fingers, we've also seen a move to more tangible and direct interfaces. For many of us, at the moment, we are most likely to encounter these in gaming consoles, where we might hold a controller and use it as a baseball bat or ski pole, or stand with our arm outstretched imagining we are holding a bowling ball. There are other specialized applications too, such as systems to train surgeons to perform intricate surgery, holding an instrument that provides realistic force feedback as the trainee probes a simulated abdomen.

Back to Ben and another activity he loves to help with: cooking. We were finishing a soup making session, heating and stirring the final product together. Our tools were a pan and wooden spoon, and as he ladled the spoon through the liquid, it bubbled, occasionally hissing and spitting small flecks as it swirled over the hottest sides of its container. The soup was a highly responsive material, and one that engaged all our senses. We could see it; smell it; feel its texture—even our eyes watered as the vapors of garlic and onion hit their membranes.

Then, suddenly, there was panic. The pan spilt, and searingly hot soup hit Ben's legs. Wearing short trousers he was immediately in pain, the soup triggering the reflex to pull away. His skin started to blister, one material responding with urgency to the scalding temperature of the other. Running cold water over the burn, the skin began to cool, the

*"With an entire body at your command, do you seriously think the Future Of Interaction should be a single finger?"*

Bret Victor

*We are built for materials like this.*

dangerous heat soothed. Though pain is a highly discomforting experience, it's the body's way of protecting us from danger. The way Ben's body responded to the scalding soup and the cooling water starkly illustrates how we've evolved to cope with physical materials: we've been built for them. The *Uncomfortable interactions* box below considers how our ability to feel discomfort might expand our notions of user experience.

## Design Challenge

- We've been built as bodies that can manipulate and sense physical materials in virtuoso ways.

- We've adapted to these materials, but we're also vulnerable to them. They really can impact on us in bad ways (like the burning pain Ben suffered) or uncontrollably joyful ways (as any kid who has been tickled by their parent knows).

- Like other physical materials, we can be damaged (and repaired), and are grounded by the laws of physics.

- Maybe, then, we should strive to break away from simply digital interactions, through the blunting screen, because these other materials are more like us.

## Uncomfortable interactions

When most of us think about user experience, we think about happy, pleased users, delighted with their interactions. If in doubt about what good design should aim for, take a look at the television commercials made for any mobile phone manufacturer.

Steve Benford and his team, though, wonder about making *uncomfortable* interactions. They point to the way that societies and cultures have developed rituals, performances, and places that use discomfort to entertain, enlighten, or bond their members socially. So, we have theme parks where we scream as we fall 20 stories vertically, strapped precariously to a chair; we go to see harrowing movies and are provoked to reflect on deep issues; and, anyone who has tried a physically demanding assault course in a work team outing will know how that can bring the group together.

To explore the notion, the research team developed a number of prototypes like *Breathless*. Here, each user took on three roles in turn; all the while they wore a gas mask that was fitted out with a respiration monitor.

The basic discomfort of having their face fully encased by the mask was compounded by the activities they were then asked to perform. Each participant was asked to watch another user swinging in a chair (as in the image below), this second person's movements being controlled by a third user pulling a rope.

They then took the place of the swinging user, to find that when the controller stopped moving the rope, they had to breathe in time with the swing itself to maintain a smooth ride.

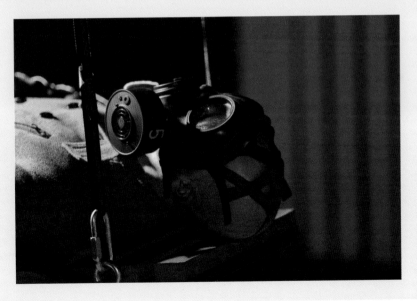

# Alternative perspective: Digital is natural

We're arguing in this chapter for a focus on natural, physical, body-based thinking and inspiration. However, there are lots of people who would reply that in the future, if not now, digital thinking will be the default. Take the interesting video created in 2013 to promote a major European Union conference on the future of ICT, for example. Called *"Digital is natural,"* during the clip several scenes unfold, and in each the actors are shown being confused or frustrated by nondigital interactions.

**Search for:**
*Digital is natural*

- In one scene, a diner is seen holding a paper menu, puzzled when his pinch-to-zoom gestures fail to have any effect. A couple across the room at another table looks over sympathetically.

- Later, at another restaurant, the most delicious looking, physically stimulating food arrives at a couple's table, and one of the two goes to take a picture of the plate. Her mobile battery is flat and her face shows such disappointment. "How can this meal be real without a socially shareable photo?" she thinks.

- Meanwhile, a middle-aged couple stop a young, skateboarding, modern-looking youth and ask him to take a picture of them with their nondigital camera. He holds the device at arm's length, and tries to touch the plastic back of the device to frame, focus, and shoot the picture. He doesn't "get" the viewfinder or big physical shutter button.

Our point of view is not that we need to resist the progress of the digital, pushing it away. Instead, we want to bring it closer to what we are as people in all our sensing, moving, material form. Our goal is to get you to think how the digital might *become* natural.

# Breaking the glass: Visions of what might be possible

We started this chapter by suggesting that the glass of our touch screens dulls our design thinking. Remember Narcissus at the pool back in Chapter 1? He stirred the waters with his hands but drew back quickly, frightened when the vision of beauty in front of him rippled away. If only he had forcefully thrust both hands in, cupped them and drenched his face with the water, perhaps he would have shaken himself from the trance, coming to his senses, waking to the world around him.

How can we get much more physical and touch the digital?

Groups of researchers have been looking at how the glass barriers of our modern day dark pools—the screens of smartphones, tablets, and the like—can be made permeable or broken down altogether, allowing users to reach in to the digital, or liberating the digital and taking it out into the physical world.

We've categorized these approaches into three types:

- **Illusions:** The glass is still there and solid but it *looks* like it is more permeable.

- **Hands-*in* interaction:** The glass screen is not the interface; you've reached into the digital and can grasp, gesture, and move with your hands instead of pinching, zooming, and swiping a flat surface.

- **Bits-*out* interaction:** The surface has been smashed and the digital world is flowing out: bits have become atoms.

Each of these approaches give us a glimpse of the future but can also inspire you to think how your current designs can go beyond the two-dimensionality of current screen approaches.

## Illusions

Jinha Lee and his collaborators at leading research labs, including MIT Media Lab and Microsoft Research, have built some fascinating examples of this first category. In a 2013 TED Talk, he describes how their ideas have evolved with a number of prototype interfaces.

**Search for:**
*Jinha Lee TED*

In one prototype, there is a stylus that can be pushed through the glass of a touch surface, allowing the user to create and manipulate objects apparently deep inside the display. The system is, of course, an illusion, with the pen collapsing in on itself as the user pushes. It is like the collapsible blade the magician pushes into the box containing the terrified assistant in the classic magic trick. Despite being an illusion, the way it opens up interaction possibilities by puncturing the human-digital barrier is compelling.

## Putting it into practice

The Sony PS Vita console includes a set of touch sensors on the back of the device. Many games have exploited this to provide extra controls. One, though, goes much further. *Tearaway* is a game that gives the player control over a paper character navigating a paper world to save it from the evil that wants to see everything ripped up. At various points in the game, the user can push and tap on the back of the device and see what looks like their own fingers reaching into the world to bounce the hero out of danger or flick the wicked crows away.

## Hands-*in* interaction

In his TED Talk, Lee then goes on to explain how they built a system that provides a way for the user to stick both hands into a digital world and more directly manipulate it. The prototype had two innovative elements that enabled this:

- **Under the lid interaction:** The prototype adapted a laptop screen, giving it a hinge that allowed it to be drawn up and towards the user, with the keyboard now behind the screen. A space was left for the user's hands to go under the screen to touch the keyboard and use the space behind it.

- **See-through screen:** The screen was unconventional too, as it was semi-transparent, showing the user digital content while allowing them to see through to the keyboard and their hands behind. With a depth camera—like those used

There's Not an App for That | From Touch to Feeling

on popular gaming consoles—to track hand movements, the user was then able to reach into the digital content, and, in Jinha's words, *"grab hold of the bits,"* picking out files from a 3D stack representation.

## Putting it into practice

There have been lots of apps that have used through-the-lens augmented reality techniques. That is, you hold up your phone at an object and some digital content is overlaid onto it or around it. Think of those apps that bring magazine adverts to life using clever image recognition.

One advance on these approaches would be to allow the user to get their hands on the augmentation, reaching in front of the screen they hold. So, when you look through the screen and see a car popping up out of the advert, you could reach in and flick it with your finger to see it speed off.

Again, it is worth looking at gaming consoles and games that have been experimenting in limited ways with such interactions for many years. While these devices have had to rely on clumsy visual markers or special objects, image recognition advances and future devices with depth-sensing capabilities will soon provide a richer palette of possibilities.

While behind-the-screen interactions of mobiles have fixated on such augmented reality scenarios, the hands-*in* style encourages us to think about manipulating the digital reality. So, if we propped up our mobiles or tablets on a stand and then put our hands behind the screen to work on digital content, what could we do? Perhaps we could sort through our photos in new and interesting ways? What about building a digital LEGO block building in three dimensions with both hands grabbing and snapping bricks together behind the screen, our hands visible using the rear camera?

## Bits-*out* interaction

While inspiring, these first two types of beyond-screen interactions still fail our Narcissus test—the digital materials remain under the surface, without a physical form of their own to break and awake us from the fixation.

An MIT team, though, led by a veteran of disruptive interface thinking, Hiroshi Ishii, are trying to change all this. In their visionary new world, physical materials and underlying computational models would be completely in sync, knitted together.

These "radical atoms" have three properties:

- They can transform their shape to reflect both the manipulations by the user and changes in the digital model.

- They have affordances—or cues to the user as to how to manipulate them—that dynamically adapt, keeping the user in the loop, as the materials shape-shift.

- They conform to physical laws and user considerations (such as not harming the person manipulating them!).

## Alternative perspective

Does giving physical objects digitally enhanced capabilities actually reduce the power users have to express themselves in rich ways? Perhaps what we are pointing to dulls rather than enhances someone's engagement with reality? Take the clay example on the following page: isn't there more joy and engagement with someone trying themselves to mold a perfect sphere, unaided?

We'd argue that computational enhancement of physical objects can be applied flexibly—in the *Perfect Red* case, shown in Figure 2.3, if you were a beginner, maybe the tool could help you develop your skill; if you are an expert then you'd use the digital power to create objects you just could not make on your own.

But what do you think?

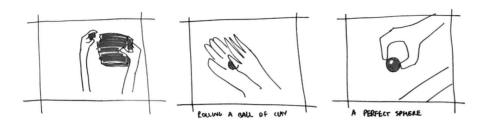

ROLLING A BALL OF CLAY    A PERFECT SPHERE

Figure 2.3 Digital-physical clay—*Perfect Red*. From left to right: Tear off a piece of *Perfect Red*; roll a ball and let it snap to a perfect sphere.

Think, then, about a computational clay (called *Perfect Red* by the researchers). It is like everyday modeling clay, but when you manipulate it, it responds in ways that objects in a computer-aided design world might. So, you start rolling it and it morphs into a perfect sphere (see Figure 2.3). Or, you split an object into two equal parts and any operation you do on one part—perhaps straightening it—will be automatically applied to another.

At the moment, *Perfect Red* is a fictional concept, but it and many other materials could be an everyday reality through advances in areas such as nanotechnology and mechatronics.

All of this seems a long way from today's smartphones, but it is a useful long-term vision that helps us question the richness of touch and manipulations possible on current devices and services. Right now, though, a shift to thinking more physically might improve the apps you are writing as the example in the following box illustrates.

## Putting it into practice: The mobile as a physical container

There are lots of apps that use shaking in an attempt to add a bit of fun or flair to the user interface—shake to activate a function; shake to see your photos collaged like a snow globe; you can even choose your baby's name by shaking to get a random suggestion. How, though, could we move on from these novelty uses of shaking to making a more physical-feeling connection between shaking the mobile and the effect it has on the contents "inside" the phone?

Imagine, then, your phone actually contained physical versions of the texts, emails, or status updates that have arrived: a box holding ball bearings, perhaps.

As you are walking down the street a message drops into the box, and then another, with a metallic sound and a vibration on the phone. As you continue to stride, the phone's accelerometer—measuring movements—is used to assess your gait, and the balls roll in the box, colliding into others and the walls of the device, all the time generating relevant vibrations and sounds. The feedback allows you to get a sense of what is going on without having to take the phone from your jacket.

As the researchers from Glasgow University who built the *Shoogle* system explain, it's like having keys and coins in your pockets that clink and clash as you move around. They've considered other ways of using the container-content notion, too: what if the mobile was filled with a liquid that would slosh around, again with richly realistic sounds and vibrations? Maybe, then, you could shake the mobile and hear and feel how empty or full the battery charge has become. Sure, you could look at the screen and access the power options to view detailed statistics, but perhaps the same information can be signaled in a way that uses human senses and abilities to assess situations in a more natural rather than machine-centered way.

## Rising to the challenge

So far we've tried to convince you that physically orientated thinking is an advantage and not a hindrance as you try to forge a future of exciting digital apps and services. We've also seen some inspiring starting points for beyond glass screen interactions.

At the start of this chapter, though, we said we wanted to draw on the user's experience outside the digital to inspire and inform the designs we build for our mobiles in the future.

To help you rise to the challenge of going from touch to feeling, in the next chapters we will turn to take inspiration from three elements of life that can make us feel fully alive: food, fashion, and fitness. Finally, as well as these human-centered areas, we'll present some inspiring new technology and materials that will enable interesting forms of touch, sensation, and manipulation.

## Resources

Bret Victor's "brief rant" on the future of interaction design is a succinct and persuasive argument for more expressive future touchables [1]. Jinha Lee's TED Talk illustrating how we might reach into the display can be watched at [2], and the paradigm shifting radical atoms vision is outlined in [3]. The *Tearaway* PS Vita game can be found at [4].

The physical to digital theme is continued in the attempt to make a mobile more of a physical container, as summarized in the box *The mobile as a physical container*, and detailed in [5].

While lots of user experience is about delight and joy, a good introduction to Steve Benford's uncomfortable interactions work is the magazine article at [6]. Finally, the "Digital is natural" video can be found at [7].

[1] Victor B. A brief rant on the future of interaction design. 2011. Retrieved from http://worrydream.com/ABriefRantOnTheFutureOfInteractionDesign/.

[2] Lee J. TED Talk: Reach into the computer and grab a pixel. 2013. Retrieved from http://www.ted.com/talks/jinha_lee_a_tool_that_lets_you_touch_pixels.

[3] Ishii H, Lakatos D, Bonanni L, Labrune J-B. Radical atoms: Beyond tangible bits, toward transformable materials. Interactions 2012;19(1):38–51. http://dx.doi.org/10.1145/2065327.2065337.

[4] Tearaway. 2013. Retrieved from http://www.playstation.com/en-us/games/tearaway-psvita.

[5] Williamson J, Murray-Smith R, Hughes S. Shoogle: Excitatory multimodal interaction on mobile devices. In: Proceedings of the SIGCHI Conference on Human Factors in Computing Systems; ACM; 2007. pp. 121–4. http://dx.doi.org/10.1145/1240624.1240642.

[6] Benford S, Greenhalgh C, Giannachi G, Walker B, Marshall J, Rodden T. Uncomfortable user experience. Commun ACM 2013;56(9):66–73. http://dx.doi.org/10.1145/2500889.

[7] Digital is natural. 2013. Retrieved from https://www.youtube.com/watch?v=aMTQBC ZIBTo.

# CHAPTER 3

## Opportunity 1.1
## INSPIRED BY FOOD

### WHAT'S THE OPPORTUNITY?

Food is a great starting point in our journey into thinking about how to make interactions enlivening. We'll be looking at its properties as a material; how we prepare, cook, and eat it; and the sensory and emotional reactions and responses it evokes.

### WHY IS IT ATTRACTIVE?

- Food is so much a part of most of our lives. We snack, munch, and drink throughout the day. It engages us directly in physical and emotional ways.

- Some early mobile phones were called "candy bars" because of their shape. Now, while most mobiles don't look like food, our relationship with them is similar—we snack and munch the content throughout the day.

- What we want you to think about in this chapter is how app design can recruit the way food engages us.

### KEY POINTS

- Preparing and eating food involves all our senses. Meanwhile, our apps often focus on the visual, and limited forms of audio.

- Our interactions with food are often *fluid*—we stir, mash, scoop, slurp, and chew. In contrast, the digital diets we serve up offer far more *discrete* styles—we bite through the features in chunks. Swipes and pinches are a good start in extending the interactive vocabulary, and games have good pointers to how we can do more.

- Food has diverse shapes, forms, and textures that change the way we can manipulate and experience it. Digital materials are in contrast flat and bland.

- Food affects people's emotions both positively and negatively. It can be a worry and a joy. We will see how thinking about the range of responses it evokes can help us create apps that shape behavior and go beyond providing something that is simply "good" for us.

## WHAT DO YOU THINK?

- One of the benefits of apps is that they are like snacks—they can provide quick gratification. Have you used any that are more engaging, like three-course dinners?

- How have you used audio or vibration to engage your users? Have you thought about how to effectively combine these outputs coherently with the screen display?

- Think of any apps you've come across that use fluid interactions like swipes, pinches, and zooms to complete a task. Forgetting about photos, maps, or games, what else can you think of?

# Introduction

Without food we die—within a few days of not eating, we'd begin to weaken and tire. Even the most resilient body would collapse in just over a month of being starved. Psychologist Abraham Maslow created a hierarchy of human needs to explain the needs that motivate people. Right at the bottom of that pyramid is food (along with other essentials like sleep and water): until these basic needs are sated, according to his theory, we are not driven by any higher-level concerns. Assuming we have enough to eat, though, everything connected with food, from the markets to the munching, can help make us feel fulfilled, helping us to meet the Maslow defined needs of socialization, esteem, and self-actualization.

**Search for:**
*Maslow hierarchy of needs*

Most of us live in cities, but despite our urban, human-built environments, many will look forward to their free time in gardens or communal allotments growing vegetables, fruits, and herbs to use in cooking. Perhaps, many of us can remember childhood lazy late-summer walks through fields, picking berries for pies made at our parents' sides. We connect to a distant past when, for most, the key daily activity was to forage, hunt, or tend, to provide for themselves and their community. Even those of us who fail to see the attraction in such earthy activities display these instinctive, long-developed food hunting skills as we prowl supermarket aisles, the hunting chariot or gatherer's sack replaced by the shopping trolley or wire basket.

When we have harvested or brought home the shopping and started to cook, we cut, beat, knead, tenderize, crush, and shape it. Then, we go a step further: we eat it. We allow ourselves to consume and be nourished and physically affected by the meals others and we provide. The effect on our bodies is both short term—the taste, smells, feeling of being full or, in the case of a problem, an upset digestive system—and long lasting—the nutrients and energy being incorporated into our vital systems.

Something that is so much a part of what we have always been and shapes what we become is a natural material to begin our exploration of what a really alive user experience might be. In the next several pages, we will look at some interesting investigations into food by digital researchers. Their work uncovers not just insights into how technology might fit into this big part of people's lives, but also provides inspirations about how we might break the glass to let life flow into and out of our digital devices and services to affect and influence us in more direct ways.

## Multisensory interaction

When you take a bite of something, what creates the taste? The obvious answer is the 10,000-plus taste buds laid out like mosaics over your tongue, throat, and roof of your mouth. However, our ability to distinguish classes of flavor—sweet, sour, salt, bitter, and umami—depends on the fusion of several senses. We can see the food we eat, smell it, get a sense of its texture, shape, and composition from movement and pressure receptors in our jaw and mouth, and hear it as we chew it.

Figure 3.1 Simulating taste using visual and smell stimulations.

Experimental work by Japanese researchers dramatically demonstrates the importance of multisensory experiences in human perception. Figure 3.1 shows the alien-like rig—called *MetaCookie+*—they developed as part of work into a new form of interfaces called gustatory—or taste—displays.

*MetaCookie+* fools the user into thinking a plain food is something richer in the following ways:

- When the user picks up the cookie, the system uses a camera to recognize it via the baked-in visual markers on its surface.

- These markers also allow the system to accurately overlay one of several coverings, such as almond or chocolate. The user sees the virtual covering through the head-mounted display they are wearing.

- As they take a bite, an air pump delivers a strong scent appropriate to the relevant cookie right under the user's nose.

So, while a user is actually chewing a simple, bland-flavored cookie, the system attempts to deliver a different experience to them through simulated visual and smell stimuli. Initial trials of the system suggest the technique can work, with over 70% of the cookies eaten being judged to taste like the food being simulated.

Another team from Japan has also been working on ways of amplifying or distorting the cooking and eating process through digital augmentation. Take, first, the *Chewing Jockey* system. This time, the user wears a headset that has:

- A microphone to pick up chewing noises;

- A jaw movement detector; and,

- A bone conductor speaker that sits behind the ear to provide output.

They've imagined a couple of ways the setup could be used to change someone's perception of eating:

- **Augmented food texture:** Potato chips can be made to sound even crisper; gummy sweets even more chewy and tender.

- **Gaming experience:** Pop a chewy sweet in the mouth, and as you chew you hear screaming sound effects, giving the impression that you are eating up living creatures. While, perhaps, a little distasteful, the researchers think this edible interface may have a role in some video games, with the gamer role-playing a creature hunting and eating.

Both of these two food-interaction systems require hardware for input and output that is currently not easily connected to mobile devices, but a third, the *Chop Chop* prototype, could be re-created on many smartphones.

The idea is neat and fun: a microphone (on the mobile, for instance) listens to the chopping noises as you prepare vegetables, and the system then responds with sound effects played through your headphones. Perhaps you hear the noise of a samurai sword slicing as you cut carrots with a simple knife; or a cartoon-like *"Kapow!"* or *"Zok!"* as a potato is finely prepared for a dauphinoise dish. This may be an intriguing way to connect the fun of popular mobile games like *Fruit Ninja* to physical activities.

## Putting it into practice

With these inspirations, how could you think about mobile design differently, today? Here are some starting points to help you think in new ways as you approach your next app:

- **Connect the physical to the digital:** Taking inspiration from the *Chop Chop* prototype, what other physical activities or sensations could be easily sensed and used to provide output to the user?

  - Perhaps your user is cycling fast down a hill, listening to an audiobook, the wind gusting over their face and head. Conventional thinking suggests a good thing to do for that rider is to sense the noise of turbulence and compensate for it, so the story playback isn't lost in the wind. Why not play with the biker, though? Amplify the sound of the air, use it to enhance the sense of speed and exhilaration that her other senses will be picking up. Of course, you may wish also to pause the playback while you do this, returning to the narrative as the bike slows at the bottom of the hill.

- Or, what about a children's guide to an ancient heritage site? Sensing when the user is walking, the system could generate a soldier's marching sound effect, or the noise of cracking and crumbling debris underfoot.

- **Think multisensory:** *MetaCookie+* emphasizes the role of using multiple forms of output, and *Chewing Jockey* uses several forms of input to control the system. Even on today's mobiles, then, why limit ourselves to predominantly touch input, and to visuals with relatively unsophisticated audio output? How could you use vibrations or clever sound effects to enhance how your user perceives your content? What can you sense from the microphone, and the accelerometer and compass, that could be used in combination with other inputs?

- **Don't blinker the user:** Why not allow your user to fully use their senses, encouraging them to look, smell, or touch the world around them while using your app? We'll be looking at ways of doing this when we consider how to move from *heads-down* to *face-on* interactions in Chapter 7.

## Design Challenge
### *What would being full look like?*

When we overeat, we feel bloated and full. When we exercise strenuously we feel tired, and if we sit too long in the sun we feel hot and bothered. Each of these sensations helps our bodies regulate activities—we decide to skip the dessert, we rest a while, or we move into the shade.

How could you design your app to give cues to users about the amount of time they've spent using it, or the number of interactions they've performed? Perhaps the visuals can become stretched or strained (for bloating), or make the user strain to read them (for tiredness); or, you could adjust the brightness and contrast to evoke an overpowering sunny day.

Physical responses encourage people to stop doing things they enjoy so that ill effects are reduced and they can return to these activities again and again. Maybe there is value in helping users to know when to stop using your app for the same reasons.

## Fluid dexterity

Watch a master chef wield a wok or frying pan. She knows instinctively when to shake or stir, to raise the pan out of the flames or let the heat lick the base. Steam and heat are sensed, and she'll also be keeping an eye on the flame itself, turning the gas up or down as necessary.

There are many thousands of cooking apps, of course, and phones and tablets are ideal form factors to lay on the kitchen surface or even prop up on purpose-designed kitchen stands. Like conventional recipe books, these provide step-by-step instructions along, sometimes, with videos or audio to illustrate the various tasks.

Novice computer programmers are often encouraged to think about programming like cooking, with their programs being the recipes. Recipe thinking fits machines well—it is what they do, following instruction by instruction in a discrete fashion. People, though, acquire many new skills through doing, moving and manipulating things around them. It's hard, then, to learn how to ride a pushbike, surf, or dance a tango simply by reading the step-by-step guide in a manual.

## Design Pointer

Think about designing in a way that keeps people in the flow of their activity, helping them develop competency in using your app to complete the task at hand. Avoid making them jump in and out of the primary task in a more stilted, robotic-like stop-start way as if they were consulting a cookbook.

In-the-flow thinking has influenced a number of research projects into augmented and "smart" kitchens. The *panavi* system is a good example, having several sophisticated input and output components to support interaction:

- An adapted wok-style pan contains accelerometers in its handle to sense the stirring and shaking.

- LED lights on the pan's handle show the current temperature of the food, and vibrations made by a motor embedded inside it reinforce this. The learner chef has to keep the lights and vibrations within the "safe" zone to perfect the food.

- A projector above the pan is used to display animations directly onto the food to indicate when to shake the dish.

- A conventional screen recipe display is also available at eye level.

Meanwhile, in the *Ambient Kitchen* project, based at Newcastle University in the UK, they've extended the range of kitchen tools augmented with sensors, with 27 different implements from whisks to vegetable scrapers having accelerometers inserted in their handles. Movements are inferred from readings coming from these tools individually, and fused together. For example, using information about which pan is being moved and which implement is in the cook's hands can help determine the specific action being performed.

Like *panavi*, the kitchen has been used to understand task-based learning, but also in many other explorations, including how to support people who are suffering from cognitive impairments such as dementia, with the hope that the technology can help them in staying at home and maintaining a degree of independence.

## Design Pointer
### *Think dynamic interaction*

- The *panavi* and *Ambient Kitchen* prototypes react dynamically to movement, temperatures, and other food triggers, helping the cook deal with the task rather than being elsewhere in the recipe.

- There is continuous interaction with the system, rather than the "touch-to-touch" or option-to-option style that characterizes mobile apps.

- They build on and develop creative, physical skills to really manipulate the materials at hand.

## Putting it into practice: Foraging

How can the sorts of fluid, in-the flow, dexterous manipulations of cooking stimulate you to think about making a difference to your app thinking? Let's take two example activities: mobile shopping and visiting a tourist archaeological site.

**Shopping:** In real-world shops, store owners carefully collect products they think will sell and "exhibit" them in a stimulating, highly browseable way. Shoppers in a clothes store, then, can push their hands into racks of clothes and quickly flick between options, pulling potential articles out and replacing them when they realize the color, style, or size just isn't "them." They can also move between sections and shelves, carrying items to compare with others in another part of the store.

In contrast, the predominant style in mobile shopping apps facilitates searching rather than foraging. More recently, some apps have introduced carousel-style presentations that hint at more dynamic, flexible browsing (see the image below). What could you do to take such ideas further?

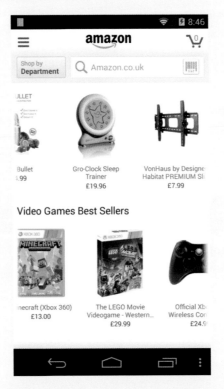

**Visiting:** The *Virtual Excavator* is an iOS app developed by a group of researchers in Helsinki and Glasgow. As well as the conventional touch-based interactions to find information, they have a simple trowel-like action to help visitors uncover finds.

Moving the device generates shaking sounds, and eventually the virtual object is displayed on the screen. Turning away from this specific domain, how could you use gestures or shakes to sift through virtual piles of potential "finds"—your email, documents, or photos, for instance?

# Material properties impact interaction

As we have seen already, food is highly interactive: we shape, break, cook, and consume it. Let's consider here three of its physical properties that help us to think further about the design of digital interactive materials.

## Function follows form

Conventionally in design we are told to ensure that form—the way something looks, feels, and affords interaction—follows function. That is, make it in a way that helps someone do what the object is intended to do.

But, sometimes, form affects functionality. Consider this extreme—and fun— example of how food's form can affect physical-digital functionality. The *Noisy Jelly* kit offers a new take on digital music. You make a series of jellies and place them on a thin piece of wood lined with tinfoil. The board is connected to a simple capacitive sensor attached to a computer. Different jellies have varying shapes and different levels of salt concentrations in them that affect how they conduct the current. The physical form also impacts on the sorts of manipulations— and hence musical sounds—the user is able to perform: larger, spherical ones affording conventional wobbling, and spiky pyramid forms more precise, targeted touches.

**Search for:**
*Noisy Jelly*

The eccentric *Noisy Jelly* reminds us that with food, the shape and physical properties affect the way we have to approach it for successful interactions. In the jelly system, if you use the same touch or swipe action for all of the shapes and mixtures, you won't produce the full range of music possible.

## Material that is consumed

The *FoodieFab* system connects two dinner parties over the Internet. One group can design a message with a short piece of text and a shape on their touch screen, then a 3D printer-like fabricator in the remote location etches out the design in "food media." The prototype can handle different food flavors and materials to create edible outputs that range from simple icing style patterns to complete objects such as muffins. Once the food has arrived, the diners pick it out of the fabricator and eat it.

In interaction research and design communities there are the beginnings of interest in what have been called "ephemeral interfaces": materials—like the fabricated food—that provide transient, short-lived displays or interaction opportunities. In today's app world, services like *Snapchat* are examples of how interfaces and media can be given similar properties.

## Not simply instant gratification

While food does seem to have a very short-term life—mere moments from our plate, to mouth, to gullet—stepping back a little lets us see that before this final act of eating, there's a much longer set of steps. We might sit down and plan a meal, creating a shopping list on our mobile. Then we go and shop for it, bring it home, and store it in the refrigerator or cupboard. Maybe several days elapse before opening the fridge reminds us that we have ingredients, and we begin to prepare the elements of our meal.

## Design Pointer
### *Think persistent interaction*

When you think about the interfaces you produce for your mobile apps, ask yourself what the user was doing before, and might do after, firing up the app. What did they last do when they used your system? Did they use your service on another platform, such as a tablet or smart television? Remembering these prior states and transactions can really be beneficial to users. Search providers have rapidly seen the value of such approaches, integrating, for example, the queries done on the desktop with content and search suggestions later available on the mobile app.

## Learning from how our feelings impact on food choices

When we sit down to eat, the food we put in our mouths elicits immediate sensations and feelings—of taste, heat, texture, and so on. Higher-level emotions are often invoked too—highly pleasurable feelings (think about a chocolate torte with double thick cream) and unpleasant guilty ones too (think, again, about that chocolate torte with double thick cream). These emotions impact on our future food intakes—building an addiction or making us resolute to try to cut back.

We are used to doctors, dentists and, now, devices giving us strongly worded advice to avoid overindulgence or certain food types, and to choose healthier, wiser options. These prescriptive, sometimes hard-to-hear, often detailed recommendations have their place, but since the publication of the book *Nudge* by Thaler and Sunstein in 2009, there's been an alternative set of strategies to deploy.

**Search for:**
*Nudge book*

Nudge approaches, as their name suggests, gently change behavior, trying to get the brain to autopilot to better habits rather than getting us to engage in a long, reflective, conscious deliberation. Often the nudge works by giving a person some context about themselves or others so they can quickly see the implications of their choices. Thaler and Sunstein report on a simple sign they placed near an elevator that said, "Most people take the stairs"; it had a dramatic effect on the number of people walking rather than using the lift.

A number of supermarkets are beginning to use handheld scanners, or downloaded apps on the shopper's own mobile, to record purchases while shopping rather than all at the end during checkout. These devices and services might of course also offer coupons or other information to prompt purchases.

In dreaming up new features for these platforms, the temptation for the developers of such innovations is to default to detailed recommendations, content, and interactions. The *lambent* cart handle points to an alternative nudge method. The design is called "lambent" because it uses simple, gently flickering lights, and is an ambient display—that is, it subtly displays information in the background, and in implicit rather than explicit ways:

- Each item placed into the cart is scanned by the shopper using a scanner built into the handle.

- Then, a row of LEDs illuminate from left to right to suggest the food miles for that item—an indication of the energy and resources that have been needed to get a product to the supermarket, local being seen as better than air freighted. The more lights, the more miles.

- The lights also glow green for organic food, and orange for a product that isn't.

- After each scan, the lights across the handle indicate the total food miles for the shopping trip so far.

In a trial of the system the researchers found that this simple display did have an effect on the way participants felt about their food choices. Quantitatively, 72% of things bought with the lambent cart had lower food miles than when an ordinary cart was used.

## Design Challenge

If you are developing apps or services that are designed to help users make choices, think about deploying nudge techniques.

Instead of simply drawing your user into a complex set of screens and content with the associated screen swipes and taps, think about simpler, social, meaningful visualizations and messages.

The techniques are not confined to lifestyle habits like eating and fitness. Think too how they might help to enhance work behaviors and productivity, or purchases a customer might make.

## Going beyond "good for us"

If you have a child or remember being one, lots of your interactions with food will revolve around developing good habits: "it's good for you"; "eat it all up"; "have you finished your peas?"

The nudge-type designs are also about helping users do the right thing. These approaches can fixate on defects in a user's behavior or skills, and prescribe suitable solutions. While more subtle than a child's nanny at teatime, nudging, the gentler nag, still sees us users as children that need to be coaxed to better behaviors.

Two researchers, Andrea Grimes and Richard Harper, have written persuasively about the problems of the "fixing" viewpoint, and posed an alternative design point of view.

There is another side to cooking and eating of course: indulgence, joy, excess, and fun.

They want to encourage designers to be more positive about human choice and everyday behaviors, pointing us to consider *celebratory* rather than *corrective* technologies.

Looking at cooking and food, Grimes and Harper illustrate four problems that technologists have tried to solve with digital support systems for cooking:

- We have already touched on two of them: **inexperience** and **poor diet choices**, with the augmented wok and shopping cart examples.

- They also describe the *Cook's Collage* that helps a person keep track of where they are in a recipe, letting them deal with the problems of **distraction** when in the flow making a meal.

- Then there are issues of **inefficiency**, with a number of systems being proposed to optimize the cook's time. For example, one shows what utensils are in a kitchen cabinet, with the aim of reducing the amount of time spent hunting for just the right implement.

Instead of trying to make up for deficiencies in a person's abilities or lack of knowledge, the alternatives proposed involve looking at the positives of the activity (see the following box). While Grimes and Harper's observations arise from looking at the domain of food, their insights can inform wider design choices, encouraging us to revel in the complexities, ambiguities, and mess of life rather than instinctively trying to sort it out. We will be exploring this in more depth in Chapter 10.

## Putting it into practice: Positive designs

In describing the celebratory technology perspective in the context of food, Grimes and Harper present dimensions that can inspire new devices and services, including:

**Creativity:** People like to experiment and adapt dishes rather then slavishly following instructions. How about a service that provides inspiration by giving them an awareness of what their friends are cooking that night?

**Pleasure and nostalgia:** Food can evoke strong memories and responses, as we've noted already. The *Memory Microwave* display they propose shows images associated with the food being heated up—perhaps photos of grandmother, who regularly made this sort of meal.

**Gifting:** Food often involves the giving and receiving of a gift: a simple gift of the time needed to make the meal, or a tangible take-home such as a home-baked cake. After a dinner party, guests could be given a tagged "jewel" that, when placed in a box back home, displays a photo of the meal. Over time, the jewels shared by friends would remind them of the long-term giving and receiving they had been blessed with.

**Relaxation:** Meals and parties often involve both food and a music track to set the scene. The music might fit the food theme—Mexican guitar for Mexican night—or style—refined dinner party versus pumping house party. Consider, then, a music app that uses the searches a user has made for shopping ingredients and recipes to suggest an appropriate playlist.

## Design Challenge

How can we take these ideas beyond food? For example, how could you apply the positive, celebratory design patterns suggested by Grimes and Harper in your next (non–food orientated) app?

# Takeaways

In these chapters about humans as sensing, engaged, and emotional beings, we are trying to encourage us all to break what we see as the dulling glass of touch screens. We want you to think about how people are stimulated as they interact with your app in an immediate, direct way, but also what these interactions make them feel about themselves. In Chapter 1, we saw that Don Norman helpfully characterized this range of emotional responses as going from the visceral to the reflective.

After this chapter you might want to think about experimenting with:

- More than visual output, more than finger poke input.

- Dynamic interactions that are fluid and flow-like, and less step-by-step, discrete and chunky.

- Matching your interaction style to the form of the materials you are manipulating.

- Thinking about ephemeral and—in contrast—persistent interactions.

- Using emotional responses to guide interaction choices.

- Thinking about apps that are celebratory in style rather than corrective or simple utilities.

## Resources

Maslow's hierarchy of needs can be found in [1]. Full details of our trio of interesting food-based interfaces can be found in [2,3,4]; the two augmented kitchen prototypes we drew on, meanwhile, can be explored further in [5,6] and an example of how all these explorations can inspire new thinking in conventional mobiles is described in [7], where a mobile is used like a trowel.

We also looked at how properties of the food itself rather than the tools can inform interaction design, thinking about jellies [8], food fabricators [9] and ephemeral—short-lived—interfaces [10].

In our exploration of eating, we encountered nudge approaches [11] and how they might be used in a supermarket context [12]. While many nudge systems try to make us better, Andrea Grimes and Richard Harper provoke us to think about how to be more joyful, using food and meals as a context for their broader interaction design arguments [13].

[1] Maslow AH. A theory of human motivation. Psychol Rev 1943;50:370–96. http://dx.doi.org/10.1037/h0054346.

[2] Narumi T, Nishizaka S, Kajinami T, Tanikawa T, Hirose M. Augmented reality flavors: Gustatory display based on edible marker and cross-modal interaction. In: Proceedings of the SIGCHI Conference on Human Factors in Computing Systems; ACM; 2011. pp. 93–102. http://dx.doi.org/10.1145/1978942.1978957.

[3] Koizumi N, Tanaka H, Uema Y, Inami M. Chewing jockey: Augmented food texture by using sound based on the cross-modal effect. In: Proceedings of the 8th International Conference on Advances in Computer Entertainment Technology; ACM; 2011. pp. 21:1–4. http://dx.doi.org/10.1145/ 2071423.2071449.

[4] Halupka V, Almahr A, Pan Y, Cheok AD. Chop chop: A sound augmented kitchen prototype. In: Proceedings of the 9th International Conference on Advances in Computer Entertainment; Springer-Verlag; 2012. pp. 494–7. http://dx.doi.org/10.1007/978-3-642-34292-9_43.

[5] Uriu D, Namai M, Tokuhisa S, Kashiwagi R, Inami M, Okude N. Panavi: Recipe medium with a sensors-embedded pan for domestic users to master professional culinary arts. In: Proceedings of the SIGCHI Conference on Human Factors in Computing Systems; ACM; 2012. pp. 129–38. http://dx.doi.org/10.1145/2207676.2207695.

[6] Hooper CJ, Preston A, Balaam M, Seedhouse P, Jackson D, Pham C, Ladha C, Ladha K, Plötz T, Olivier P. The French kitchen: Task-based learning in an instrumented kitchen. In: Proceedings of the 2012 ACM Conference on Ubiquitous Computing; ACM; 2012. pp. 193–202. http://dx.doi.org/10.1145/2370216.2370246.

[7] McGookin D, Vazquez-Alvarez Y, Brewster S, Bergstrom-Lehtovirta J. Shaking the dead: Multimodal location based experiences for un-stewarded archaeological sites. In: Proceedings of the 7th Nordic Conference on Human-Computer Interaction: Making Sense Through Design; ACM; 2012. pp. 199–208. http://dx.doi.org/10.1145/2399016.2399048.

[8] Noisy Jelly. 2012. Retrieved from http://noisyjelly.com/.

[9] Wei J, Peiris RL, Koh JTKV, Wang X, Choi Y, Martinez XR, Tache R, Halupka V, Cheok AD. Food media: Exploring interactive entertainment over telepresent dinner. In: Proceedings of the 8th International Conference on Advances in Computer Entertainment Technology; ACM; 2011. pp. 26:1–8. http://dx.doi.org/10.1145/2071423.2071455.

[10] Döring T, Sylvester A, Schmidt A. A design space for ephemeral user interfaces. In: Proceedings of the 7th International Conference on Tangible, Embedded and Embodied Interaction; ACM; 2013. pp. 75–82. http://dx.doi.org/10.1145/2460625.2460637.

[11] Thaler RH, Sunstein CR. Nudge: Improving Decisions about Health, Wealth and Happiness. London: Penguin; 2008 .

[12] Kalnikaite V, Rogers Y, Bird J, Villar N, Bachour K, Payne S, Todd PM, Schöning J, Krüger A, Kreitmayer S. How to nudge in situ: Designing lambent devices to deliver salient information in supermarkets. In: Proceedings of the 13th International Conference on Ubiquitous Computing; ACM; 2011. pp. 11–20. http://dx.doi.org/10.1145/2030112.2030115.

[13] Grimes A, Harper R. Celebratory technology: New directions for food research in HCI. In: Proceedings of the SIGCHI Conference on Human Factors in Computing Systems; ACM; 2008. pp. 467–76. http://dx.doi.org/10.1145/1357054.1357130.

# CHAPTER 4

## Opportunity 1.2
## INSPIRED BY FASHION

### WHAT'S THE OPPORTUNITY?

In this chapter we'll be looking at clothes—how they make us feel, how they respond to our bodies, and how we express ourselves through them.

Perhaps you've said it yourself: *"I feel naked without my mobile phone!"* It's a great way to emphasize how important these devices have become to our everyday lives. When people say this, they probably mean they don't feel ready to face the world without the mobile by their side. If you walked out of your house actually naked, you'd soon realize how clothes equip you for navigating modern-day living, from protecting you from the elements to allowing you to express who you are (an office worker, a surfer, a tourist…).

### WHY IS IT ATTRACTIVE?

Creators of fabrics think deeply about how their designs will feel and fit with the wearer. They have to think about how they will age with use and how to balance usability against fashionability.

All of these perspectives disrupt touch-screen thinking in two ways:

- They further push us to think about the limitations of what we feel when we touch the surfaces of our devices.

- They make us consider digital materials as something that can have a life, shape, and form that isn't trapped inside the boxes we carry, the glass lid closing off what we can do to it and how it can affect us.

## KEY POINTS

- Fabrics afford a variety of touch interactions. We can learn from these pats, taps, and scrunches, and apply them to current apps.

- Different fabrics can be perceived as warm, cooling, smooth, rugged, and so on. We'll look at how this rich vocabulary of feelings might make us see digital materials differently.

- Fabrics and clothes wear with use. Jeans become more comfortable as they are worn and washed several times. Shoes show how many miles we've pounded the pavement. What about digital materials?

- Skeumorphs are digital designs that look like something in the physical world. Some designers are moving away from them to emphasize the digital. We caution against blindly following this, and suggest benefits of informing app interactions with physical ones even when the surface design is more digital in look and feel.

- Clothes fit closely to our skin, and we can perceive their subtle effects on our bodies. We look at how more "intimate interfaces" thinking might be designed into our mobiles.

## WHAT DO YOU THINK?

- How are the clothes you are wearing now similar and different to the mobile and its apps in your pocket?

- What could you do to an app you are designing so that its design is informed by one of the fabrics you have on your body right now?

# Introduction

Anyone who has been in a clothes shop fitting room, tugging on too-tight tops or jeans, their image reflected back in the oversized mirrors, knows too well, perhaps, that clothing is material that has to fit the way we are made.

The clothes we wear remind us daily that we are physical bodies, born to inhabit and navigate a material world. We usually choose what we wear carefully to fit in with the weather, physical terrain, and activities we are likely to be engaged in. The fabrics we pull on, their cut, and the number of layers we wear will all be influenced.

When we choose unwisely, we can feel uncomfortable physically or emotionally. Matt painfully remembers turning up to a smart country house in the UK for a wedding: while he was wearing a conventional, tailored dinner jacket, he matched this with jeans and trainers. The subtle—and sometimes not so subtle—glances from fellow guests signaled the sartorial faux pas. Meanwhile, his daughter, Rosie, often goes out into the garden to feed her guinea pigs without wearing shoes, returning to the house with soggy socks and complaining of the cold!

Clothes, then, insulate us from the contexts we find ourselves in, or can be designed to amplify or resonate with them. Thick, waterproof jackets on a cold, wet day are an example of the first; swim costumes on a hot, sunny day or a gown in a glitzy ball of the other.

In terms of our bodies, depending on the materials and style chosen, they can either closely follow our own forms, like the compression tights of a runner, or, conversely, they

## Design Challenges

1. How do your apps "protect" the user from or "amplify" the contexts they find themselves in?

2. How can you design in a way that your services and apps snugly fit the user?

3. What about developing ones that allow users to change how they are perceived while still being identifiable?

can conceal, contort, or extend our physical shape and size (if you are old enough think back to the 1980s craze for shoulder pads; or, if you are younger, the more recent male youth preference for baggy jeans).

Let's look now, then, at the design and qualities of fabrics and clothes. We'll consider:

- Some of the properties of materials, how they feel and make us feel, along with how they respond and change with use; and,

- How this very physical set of materials, so close often to our skin, can inform how we design and manipulate the more distant digital materials, both today on current smartphones and apps and in the future as more organic devices emerge.

## The phone as an accessory

People have personalized their mobile devices in a number of ways for years. Stickers on the cases, beads hanging from the top or bottom, and, of course, personal lock screen images.

Researchers from the Mobile Life Centre in Stockholm, though, are extending this popular set of behaviors to allow people to fit their mobiles more directly to the outfits they are wearing. Their work centers on futuristic digital-physical materials that could be folded, bent, or even tied, as well as change colors to fit the wearer's outfit. However, they also point to approaches that can be implemented today.

First, then, there is an app concept—dreamt up by another researcher in Sweden—that allows the user to take a close-up of a detail on the clothes they are wearing and use it either as a screen saver image or as a sticker that could be placed on the back of the device.

Then, there's the *Mobile ActDresses* system. Here, some attachment to the mobile—a case or piece of jewelry hanging from the device, chosen to match the user's style and dress context—adapts the theme or apps available on the phone. The scenario they describe shows how the physical and digital worlds can be neatly woven together: "Jill rarely takes any step without her mobile phone…

*Just before entering her office, Jill attaches the company shell to her mobile phone handset, which makes the phone work both to let her into the building, as well as a company identity marker and label on her phone. Plus, it goes well with her outfit. The phone is now set into a mode that switches her contact list so that it automatically loads her work contacts as her primary address book in the phone…*

*…When leaving the office she immediately takes the shell off her phone, which then replaces her office applications with her favorite spare time applications on the front screen…."*

## Touching fabric and touching the screen

According to a report in the *Financial Times* in early 2013, Americans purchased over 10% of their clothes online, and Moody's, the credit rating agency, predicted that by the end of 2014 this market would be worth over $45 billion in the USA, alone. Increasingly, these purchases are being made on mobile devices.

These staggering figures are one of the motivations for many researchers and developers to provide a richer sense of the objects available to purchase online. Watch a clothes shopper and you will see how they feel, crunch, and stretch potential purchases to assess the items' qualities.

How can you communicate the richness of fabrics through the less lively touch screen display?

One team of researchers from London and Edinburgh have developed the *iShoogle* approach—"shoogle" being the Scottish word conveying a gentle, shaking action—to begin to answer this question. The system attempts to represent the "hand" of a textile, that is, the way the material feels.

Different textiles have distinct perceived sensations associated with them and garment designers have a well-established vocabulary to delineate the differences. So, a material could be described as smooth or rough; hard or soft; cool or warm; and so on.

The *iShoogle* researchers began by studying how people go about handling different materials both in a lab setting and in the real world of major clothes stores. In the retail context, shoppers used three common gestures to assess a material: rubbing or stroking the edge of a garment with their thumb and forefinger; or, grabbing the edge and scrunching it up in their whole hand.

However, there were lots of other less frequent gestures—ranging from pinching and flicking to patting the material. An interesting art installation called *soft(n)* further illustrates the extensive set of touches people can perform and perceive in interacting with objects (see the following box).

## Expressive touch in soft, interactive devices

Imagine a set of mobile devices that look much like large, comfortable pillows, soft to the touch and light enough to throw playfully into the air. Maybe you have an image like the one below in mind.

This *soft(n)* system is a group of wirelessly networked objects that contain sewn-in touch input sensors, motion detectors, and output devices allowing the devices to respond through lights, vibrations, and sound.

The researchers who developed the system are using it to better understand how people can express themselves and interact with others through touch interactions:

- Touch sensors respond to a wide variety of stimuli, pointing to opportunities that go way beyond the current limited vocabularies of touch in today's mobile devices.

- The surface responds to taps, pats, glides (what the developers define as a *"meandering touch"*), kneads, holds (*"a lingering, big touch"*), and many more.

## Design Challenge

How could your apps be enhanced if you thought in terms of the pats, glides, and kneads of *soft(n)*?

Watching how people work with these materials to assess them, there's a striking difference to the relatively limited touch gestures we currently see on mobile devices. The following box illustrates how even with today's capacitive displays, with the right software, much more expressive touches are possible.

## Putting it into practice: More than prod or pinch?

Research groups have demonstrated how conventional smartphone platforms can be used to provide touch interactions that take account of subtle variations in finger presses and pressures to extend the input vocabulary.

**Using touch screen inputs**: The *Fat Thumb* technique proposed by a team in Calgary University uses the inputs from the touch screen itself. The illustration below demonstrates how sensing how much of the user's thumb touches the screen can be used to provide one-handed screen gestures.

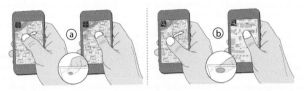

**Using additional sensors**: Other systems use additional sensors in the phone to recognize the touch variants. *Force Tap* can distinguish between soft and hard screen taps by using the device's accelerometer (or movement) sensor. The researchers who developed this approach suggest a range of applications including an enhancement to music-making apps, with notes being made by gentle or harder taps on an on-screen piano keyboard.

*TapSense,* meanwhile, developed at Carnegie Mellon University, can distinguish a touch from the user's knuckle, nail, fingertip, or pad by analyzing the sound generated on contact. Demonstrating their system on an iPhone, they've implemented a soft keyboard that allows input of both standard alphabet characters and alt characters (numbers and symbols) without the need to switch keyboard modes. Tapping on a key with your finger pad, as normal, generates the appropriate conventional character; a tip of finger tap, however, selects the alternative symbol.

In our own work, we've applied the idea of using the device's microphone to pick up and use touches the user makes. Our method, called *TapBack,* was deployed with "dumb" phones: phones without touch screens and no programmability. These phones have become less and less common in the developed world over the last 10 years or so, but they are still very widely used in developing regions such as rural India and Africa. The system allows users to control access to an interactive voice service over a standard telephone, as the following image illustrates.

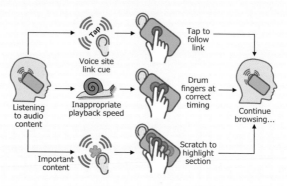

Moving from the physical to the digital, the *iShoogle* team wanted to explore the extent to which people could judge the texture of a garment simply by interacting with cleverly constructed interactive videos on an iPad.

Different types of cloth were filmed in high definition as they were manipulated by hand. Then, when the user touches the screen, the materials respond visually, with the system playing the most appropriate segment of video footage (see Figure 4.1).

Figure 4.1 Example interactive video responses in the *iShoogle* system.

In a controlled lab study the team showed that the approach can convey a range of properties effectively, simply through the screen interactions; as they conclude, *"a designer or a consumer [can] quickly create an interactive representation of a textile, requiring only the skill of taking good video footage."*

As with the *MetaCookie+* system we saw in the previous chapter, the way our perceptions can be influenced by clever manipulations of stimuli (in this case the visuals) is something we can use as designers to enrich the user experiences of interfaces. The following box illustrates how similar visual effects can provide more realistic interactions with book apps.

## Putting it into practice: Realistic paper interactions through touch?

The video techniques used for fabric interactions in *iShoogle* have also been used by the British Library in London to give scholars access to ancient and precious manuscripts displayed on a touch screen. Their system, *Turning the Pages*, allows a reader to grab hold of a page corner and bend it, and then to move it from one side of the book to the other to see the next page, just as with a physical manuscript. The interface uses lots of images of pages, manually photographed in various stages of being turned.

**Search for:**
*British Library turning the pages*

Work done by Matt and colleagues in New Zealand built on this idea so that it could be applied to any document, automatically providing page turning facilities. *Realistic Books* (see the image below) does this by using a mathematical model of how paper bends when it is picked up by thumb and finger and turned. The user can manipulate a single page at a time, or a chunk of them in one go.

In contrast with most current digital reading apps, the interface supports a number of useful document manipulations that can enhance a reader's understanding, efficient use, or pure enjoyment of a book:

- Instead of having to use a search term or go-to function, if the user roughly remembers where the content they want is located, they can grab hold of a chunk of pages and begin turning, seeing what's underneath immediately, and moving to another place if they've gone too far or not far enough.

- Think about the last time you picked up a book in a real book shop and quickly flipped through the full set of pages: with this system a reader can get a sense of the size and style of the book with fast, smooth, page animations.

Matt is a fan of e-paper mobile readers such as the Kindle or Nook. Every day, he reads his favorite newspaper on one of them. While the service is convenient—when he's traveling he can still get the op-eds he enjoys—and cheaper than buying the print edition, there's something less satisfying about the user experience.

For him, as with many people, reading something like a newspaper or magazine is as much about the distraction and relaxation it brings as the content it conveys. The lazy, casual, hopping from story to story and page to page is like a bird hopping between beds of earth, pecking for worms.

In contrast, the e-reader turns the experience into more of mechanistic, faster-paced one. This is partly due to pages being smaller than in physical versions, requiring more frequent page turns, but is also a function of the immediate page-to-page transitions as the next-page gesture is made.

The *Realistic Books* interface is an example of a skeuomorph. That is, we've retained features of the original design in the digital version. In mobile interface design there has been somewhat of a backlash against such a stance recently.

We've seen, then, the realistic looking notebook apps and calendars being replaced by some designers with flatter, computer-oriented visuals.

Even if you are flat-land convert, an escapee from skeuomorphs, try to consider how aspects of familiar, physical *interactions* can improve your designs. So, in the e-reader case, perhaps as the user holds their finger down onto a page, instead of jumping to the next page or looking up a dictionary entry, an ever-deeper portion of the book could be revealed in preview, like pushing through to later parts of the text. When the user releases their finger, the new portion of the book is displayed.

---

Clever animations can help bring your interface to life, but what the user actually feels is cold, solid glass under their fingertips, of course. Touch the folds, hems, or ridges on the clothes you are wearing right now, in contrast. What if a mobile device had such surfaces and materials that you could explore with your hands and fingers to control how it worked?

The research team that built *Stane* outer shells for mobile devices have done just this. Instead of the flat, highly polished cases we've become used to in mobile phones, their cases are textured with ridges that can be stroked or picked, and raised dots that can be tapped on or circled gently with the tip of a finger.

As the user caresses the case in these sorts of ways, a microphone in the case picks up the varying noises their interactions generate, and these are used to control applications. In one implementation the team shows how a music player could be operated with the textures, with different surfaces and gestures being used for volume control, track changes, and the like.

## Wearables that respond to wear

Clothes are meant for bodies. They come to life when they are slipped or pulled on. So close to the skin, they are directly affected by our living, breathing natures.

Joanna Berzowska's Extra Soft Labs in Canada has played with the notion of the changes that occur to clothes as we wear them, creating what they call memory rich

> "Clothing is able to witness some of our most intimate interactions; it is able to record our fear and excitement, our stress and our strain, through the collection of sweat, skin, cells, stains and tears. It becomes worn over time and carries the evidence of our identity and our history."
>
> Joanna Berzowska

**Search for:**
XS Labs

clothing. By stitching touch and movement sensors into fabrics along with lighting components, they've made a number of thought provoking garments.

There's the *Intimate Memory Shirt* that reacts to someone touching the wearer by lighting up a curved line of lights that fall from the neckline to the hem. The lights go out, bottom to top, in sequence after the touch so that the worn display also indicates how long ago the last touch happened. Breathing near the wearer's neck, perhaps a gentle whisper from a lover, also activates the lights, with different levels of breathing leading to more or fewer lights being lit.

In another garment, the *Spotty Dress*, there are thermo chromatic spots—patches of material that can be made visible or invisible by running an electric current through them. Before being touched, the dress displays a leopard print–like spotted pattern. With more and more interactions with others, though, the spots disappear. The researchers used these dresses with groups of dancers to see what movements and choreography they would provoke amongst wearers.

Such responsive digital-physical material is also used in the *Wo.Defy* dress developed by a team at Simon Fraser University. Intricate silk flowers sewn on the dress open and close depending on the breathing patterns of the wearer sensed by the garment.

In Chapter 13, we'll return to consider how these types of digital "devices" allow people to perform and display their interactions publicly in contrast to the more usual private, personal interfaces of today's mobiles. However, for now, let's focus on the way the designers of these garments capture and present the interaction history; that is, a record of how the garments have been touched by the wearer and people they've encountered.

If you look at your mobile's touch screen you'll probably see a patina of fingerprints on the surface, such as those in Figure 4.2. As with memory rich clothing, these are marks of use, a record of how you've been touching your mobile. If you've been snacking at the same time or perhaps just come off a hot beach after a day's sunbathing, the screen might be more smeared than normal. On a starkly cold day, maybe the screen is hardly marked.

Figure 4.2 Traces of past interactions.

## Design Challenge

These prints are physical traces of use. How might we record, analyze, and represent them digitally to give our users some further insights into the content or services they are interacting with?

One answer is suggested by the aptly entitled *Read Wear* scheme. While it was envisaged for mouse-and-keyboard computers, it can help us think creatively about repurposing the touches captured on-screen.

In the approach, the scroll bar of a document viewer is augmented with shaded marking to indicate which parts of the content have been viewed the most. Inspired by this, in the *Realistic Books* visualizer (see the box earlier), we used more sophisticated graphical processing to age pages of the document that had been most accessed. The aim in both of these examples was to give the reader quick clues as to perhaps the most significant or interesting sections of the book.

The visualizations are analogs of what we encounter in physical objects that help us make use of other people's choices: well-thumbed library books that fall open to often-read chapters; or a track across a woodland showing where many others have found a route previously.

**Search for:**
*Intimate interfaces MIT*

# Intimate interfaces

As well as responding to our bodies, clothes have a direct impact on the movement, pressure, and temperature sensors that we have on our skin surface. The *Communication-Wear* research team in the UK has built prototypes that attempt to exploit the close contact clothes have to our skin and the skin's ability to perceive subtle stimuli.

In one design, they've created a shape-shifting fabric inside a shirtsleeve. The pleated material runs from the cuff to the mid-forearm, and when a micro-motor is activated, a gentle, stroking sensation can be felt by the wearer. On the back of the shirt, towards the wearer's shoulders, there are textile patches that can be activated to induce a pleasant warming sensation on the skin's surface.

As the system's name suggests, the researchers' interest is in how to convey messages from someone to the wearer in a subtle, visceral way: imagine sending a "stroke" or "hug" message from your phone to someone with this shirt on and them feeling the pleats ripple or the pads warm in response.

While not as sophisticated as this shirt, it is possible for our nervous system to sense and react to vibrations in a phone carried in a pocket. The body's sensitivity and adaptation to these stimuli is illustrated by the slightly concerning phenomenon of the phantom phone vibration. If you generally carry your mobile stuffed into a trouser pocket, your thigh muscle might occasionally twitch in a way that makes you feel that your mobile is there and alerting you to a message. Your nervous system has learned a stimulus from lots of exposure to the phone's vibration output when it is close to the skin, and tricks you into checking your pocket only to find the device isn't there.

## Putting it into practice: Close to the skin in-pocket vibrations.

A team at Telefonica Labs in Barcelona has looked at using in-pocket vibration patterns to give a user awareness of a situation or content without having to take out the device and look at the screen, as this scenario from their work illustrates:

*"Matheo is a project manager with about 20 engineers reporting to him. Today he is taking the day off. Nevertheless, he usually checks his phone for urgent emails every 10 minutes to make sure everything is going well at work in his absence. This generates a lot of anxiety and prevents him from relaxing during his vacation. In order to address the problem, he has started to use a mobile device in his pocket that emits a soothing and mild vibration pattern every once in a while only when multiple emails flagged as urgent arrive in his inbox in a short period of time. Hence, Matheo doesn't have to constantly check his phone, while still peripherally perceiving information without being abruptly disturbed during vacation."*

This sort of design falls into the class of "apps that bite back," which we discuss in Chapter 9, the aim being to design in a way that promotes interaction only when there is something useful or interesting for the user to engage with.

# Pret-a-porter

Let's end this chapter with a small sensory experiment. Sit down; close your eyes. Reach down to your shoes and feel the material they are made of; move to your socks and up along your body to sense the clothes you are covered with. What are the ranges of sensations you perceive?

Now fire up your mobile and select your photo app. You can keep your eyes open and feel the surface of the device. Next, select the music app and repeat the experiment. What are the ranges of sensation you perceive?

Rise to the challenge: in your next app, without having to wait for futuristic new mobile hardware, what can you do to make digital materials more feel-able?

# Resources

We began in this chapter by considering how mobiles could be accessorized in innovative ways [1,2]. The importance of systems that can give users a more realistic experience while mobile shopping and the *iShoogle* attempt at doing just that are covered in [3,4]. This approach made us think about the types of touch that fabrics afford [5] and how we might build richer touches on conventional mobiles [6,7,8,9]. *iShoogle* deals with fabric; we saw too how similarly rich on-screen visualizations can improve digital book viewers [10].

The richness of touch given by fabric took us to the *Stane* physical and alluring device cases, patterned with physical elements that can provide additional touch inputs to mobiles [11]. Another feature of clothes—their closeness to our skins—was also investigated, drawing on [12,13]. Finally, we saw how the close proximity of our mobiles to our skins could be utilized via vibrotactile output [14].

[1] Juhlin O, Zhang Y, Sundbom C, Fernaeus Y. Fashionable shape switching: Explorations in outfit-centric design. In: Proceedings of the SIGCHI Conference on Human Factors in Computing Systems; ACM; 2013. pp. 1353–62. http://dx.doi.org/10.1145/2470654.2466178.

[2] Jacobsson M, Fernaeus Y, Nylander S. Mobile ActDresses: Programming mobile devices by accessorizing. In: CHI '12 Extended Abstracts on Human Factors in Computing Systems; ACM; 2012. pp. 1071–4. http://dx.doi.org/10.1145/2212776.2212388.

[3] Online clothes sales reach 'critical mass.' 2013. Retrieved from http://www.ft.com/cms/s/0/00904c94-7148-11e2-9b5c-00144feab49a.html.

[4] Atkinson D, Orzechowski P, Petreca B, Bianchi-Berthouze N, Watkins P, Baurley S, Padilla S, Chantler M. Tactile perceptions of digital textiles: A design research approach. In: Proceedings of the SIGCHI Conference on Human Factors in Computing Systems; ACM; 2013. pp. 1669–78. http://dx.doi.org/10.1145/2470654.2466221.

[5] Schiphorst T. Soft(n): Toward a somaesthetics of touch. In: CHI '09 Extended Abstracts on Human Factors in Computing Systems; ACM; 2009. pp. 2427–38. http://dx.doi.org/10.1145/1520340.1520345.

[6] Boring S, Ledo D, Chen X, Marquardt N, Tang A, Greenberg S. The fat thumb: Using the thumb's contact size for single-handed mobile interaction. In: Proceedings of the 14th International Conference on Human-Computer Interaction with Mobile Devices and Services; ACM; 2012. pp. 39–48. http://dx.doi.org/10.1145/2371574.2371582.

[7] Heo S, Lee G. Forcetap: Extending the input vocabulary of mobile touch screens by adding tap gestures. In: Proceedings of the 13th International Conference on Human-Computer Interaction with Mobile Devices and Services; ACM; 2011. pp. 113–22. http://dx.doi.org/10.1145/2037373.2037393.

[8] Harrison C, Schwarz J, Hudson SE. TapSense: Enhancing finger interaction on touch surfaces. In: Proceedings of the 24th Annual ACM Symposium on User Interface Software and Technology; ACM; 2011. pp. 627–36. http://dx.doi.org/10.1145/2047196.2047279.

[9] Robinson S, Rajput N, Jones M, Jain A, Sahay S, Nanavati A. TapBack: Towards richer mobile interfaces in impoverished contexts. In: Proceedings of the SIGCHI Conference on Human Factors in Computing Systems; ACM; 2011. pp. 2733–6. http://dx.doi.org/10.1145/1978942.1979345.

[10] Chu Y-C, Bainbridge D, Jones M, Witten IH. Realistic books: A bizarre homage to an obsolete medium? In: Proceedings of the 2004 Joint ACM/IEEE Conference on Digital Libraries. 2004. pp. 78–86. http://dx.doi.org/10.1109/JCDL.2004.1336103.

[11] Murray-Smith R, Williamson J, Hughes S, Quaade T. Stane: Synthesized surfaces for tactile input. In: Proceedings of the SIGCHI Conference on Human Factors in Computing Systems; ACM; 2008. pp. 1299–302. http://dx.doi.org/10.1145/1357054.1357257.

[12] Berzowska J. Memory rich clothing: Second skins that communicate physical memory. In: Proceedings of the 5th Conference on Creativity & Cognition; ACM; 2005. pp. 32–40. http://dx.doi.org/10.1145/1056224.1056231.

[13] Baurley S, Brock P, Geelhoed E, Moore A. Communication-Wear: User feedback as part of a co-design process. In: Proceedings of the 2nd International Conference on Haptic and Audio Interaction Design; Springer-Verlag; 2007. pp. 56–68. http://dx.doi.org/10.1007/978-3-540-76702-2_7.

[14] Pielot M, Oliveira Rd. Peripheral vibro-tactile displays. In: Proceedings of the 15th International Conference on Human-Computer Interaction with Mobile Devices and Services; ACM; 2013. pp. 1–10. http://dx.doi.org/10.1145/2493190.2493197.

There's Not an App for That | Inspired by Fashion

# CHAPTER 5

## Opportunity 1.3
## INSPIRED BY FITNESS

## WHAT'S THE OPPORTUNITY?

Many people get a great deal of joy from exercise and exertion. Be it a power walk at lunchtime or benching weights at the end of the day, people love to work out.

What is it about these activities that makes us feel good? Can we learn from these activities to enhance the user experiences our apps and services evoke?

Even when not explicitly exercising, people are often moving—we might be going somewhere, or simply demonstrating the impressive ways our bodies can stretch and balance in everyday movements, like scooping a puppy up from the floor into our arms. What can we learn from these abilities, and can we design to accommodate them?

## WHY IS IT ATTRACTIVE?

- The word "mobile" suggests "on the move," but our devices often immobilize us. Looking at fast-moving, effortful experiences challenges us to think about how to design for better mobility.

- There's also evidence that effort and exercise have many positive benefits on our engagement, mood, and social connection. These studies challenge us to think about the impacts of effortless mobile interactions on our well-being.

## KEY POINTS

- Designing for movement might require simple tweaks (like ensuring mobiles can be operated by our nondominant hand), or could use more sophisticated context awareness approaches to automatically adapt displays to fit our activity.

- Effort can impact how meaningful an experience is—we'll look at how to use exertion to question current designs, improving them by making them more *difficult.*

- Lots of future tech visions seem to point to a world where we are cyborgs— where our pockets, bags, and even the things we wear dress us in a new digital flesh that appears to make us more powerful beings. We look, in contrast, at how humans become as one in physical activities: the horse and rider; cycle and cyclist; dancer and partner. We'll see how these negotiations can point to a more graceful human-digital dance.

## WHAT DO YOU THINK?

- How many times have you had to stop to interact with your mobile today?

- Do you use any mobile devices while exercising? What do you notice about their designs, both good and bad points?

- Think of any app interactions that give you similar user experiences to those you have when you swim, cycle, walk, or vigorously climb the stairs.

# Introduction

Despite the universal worry—by health practitioners, governments, and parents—about our increasing levels of unhealthiness and inactivity, many people do in fact still spend significant amounts of time doing fitness activities or taking part in a sport. A recent Gallup poll showed that over 50% of Americans spend at least 30 minutes a day, three times a week getting physical. This survey polled adults, but younger age groups are more active, as any parent who has a second career as a taxi driver, shuttling their charges and friends to little league games, soccer matches, or swim meets can attest.

Digital purveyors have long capitalized on this huge physical market with devices (like wearable heart-rate monitors); services (such as apps to map your run); and, for those who don't want to leave their homes, the successful body-based games like Wii Sports and the similar ones for Microsoft's Kinect. There certainly is an app for any fitness or sports lover: hundreds of thousands of them, from ones that will improve your abdominal muscles to others that are aimed at lowering your golf handicap.

What is it about sport and fitness that makes these activities addictively satisfying? There are, of course, good sensible reasons to strive for fitness. It can make you live longer: the UK's National Health Service promotes it because evidence shows that regularly exercising can reduce serious illnesses like cancer and stroke by 50% and early death risks by a third. It can improve appearance and—if you skim through issues of magazines like *Men's Health* or *Cosmopolitan*—thereby increase your chances of finding a soul mate. Then there are the social benefits: it can give us something fun to do with friends on a rainy afternoon, sliding around in mud on a waterlogged rugby pitch.

As app developers, sensible, well-evidenced motivations are attractive—if we build an app for things that can *do* clearly useful things for people, then surely there's a chance our offering will catch the eye of browsers in the packed-to-the-rafters, candy-shop, colorful app stores. Perhaps, though, it is worth sometimes switching off our "logical" brain that focuses on helping people *do*.

Matt regularly gets up at 5:30 a.m., puts on his biking kit, and does an hour cycling along the seafront and up into the hills, and then heads back to the gym for a shorter

*We love to move, to sweat, to feel the blood pump and our chests constrict with effort, not always comfortable, but definitely alive.*

burst on the treadmills. Why does he do it when he could spend an extra hour and a half in bed every morning?

There are two types of *feelings* that have made the activity so compelling for Matt, that even on a cold, ice-forming morning, he still has to get up:

- **Body awareness:** Pushing hard up a hill or gliding along the flat, he has a wide awareness of what he is made of, and of his physical abilities, from the effortful extension of his calf muscles to the subtler sense of his finger joints deftly clicking through the gear changes. Then there is the impact on this full body experience of the weather—in the driving rain, he can feel the water stream down his face; opening his mouth, he can taste the salty spray that envelops him as the sea wind blows. The water seeps through his clothing as the journey progresses. It feels great.

- **Mindfulness:** But this feeling is often more than the immediate, from-the-skin-up type. Often, as the exercise intensifies, he experiences his body and mind ever closer bind together, his mind escaping the everyday and worldly, a sense of being beyond-alive—hyper-alive, perhaps. This is not a feeling of escaping or retreating from the physical, but of the physical and the mental being melded together.

Haruki Murakami, the famous author, wrote a book about how his running and writing practices intertwine, as this excerpt illustrates:

*"Sometimes I run fast when I feel like it, but if I increase the pace I shorten the amount of time I run, the point being to let the exhilaration I feel at the end of each run carry over to the next day. This is the same sort of tack I find necessary when writing a novel. I stop every day right at the point where I feel I can write more. Do that, and the next day's work goes surprisingly smoothly. I think Ernest Hemingway did something like that. To keep on going, you have to keep up the rhythm."*

**Haruki Murakami**

This chapter is not about designing apps for fitness (although you may well get some inspirations here). Instead, it is about considering how the feelings, rhythms, and effort of physical experiences might shape the designs we produce. Just as Haruki thinks about how running shapes his writing, let's think about how physicality can inspire our designs.

Kia Höök, a interaction design professor from Sweden, has long explored the importance of affect—or emotion—on successful design. She pointed out that what we currently call user experience and usability grew out of an earlier profession called *ergonomics* (the word first being coined in the mid-1800s). This discipline thought hard about the human body, encouraging designers of tools, furniture, and job practices to ensure their products made use of a person's capabilities and accommodated their limitations.

As our tools have become less physical—not many of us routinely have to pick up a hammer or chisel any more—and more digital, we have forgotten the importance of exploiting the physical in designing for effective experiences. As Höök puts it, *"…in some respects the ergonomists were more sensitive to the body than we are."*

In this chapter we will try to unpick some of the qualities of intense as well as gracefully subtle physical interactions common in fitness, sport, and other physically focused activities. In doing so we'll consider what this might mean to general mobile user experience design. In this way, we'll attempt to think about how we designers can become more sensitive to the body than we are now.

## Design Challenge

We often speak of doing things "in the cloud" or "being online." These are places that we can go to, away from the physical, and there's no doubt that sometimes the feelings we have there are exhilarating, immersive, and highly satisfying.

When we are highly engaged in digital interactions, the experience has some of the qualities of the almost transcendental state Matt feels when cycling. But there

There's Not an App for That | Inspired by Fitness

is a difference. The physical interactions related to the digital sensations are very limited in contrast to those in exercise: a prodding finger or a swiping movement in contrast to a pounding heart, stretched sinews, and a sweating brow.

What could you do now, using today's platforms, to your service to better align physical effort with the digital stimulation?

Looking a bit to the future, beyond current devices, what new forms of hardware could you imagine that might be necessary to more fully connect the physical and digital?

## Designing for how our bodies move

Walking, talking, tweeting on the move looks very natural. Our bodies seem to cope well. Every day we see people operating their devices on the move and in situations as diverse as the washroom to the grocery store. But what are these devices really doing to the way we physically engage with our world and propel ourselves through the spaces we live in? Because devices are now—to borrow the visionary ubiquitous computing researcher Mark Weiser's phrase—*"in the woodwork,"* engrained into our everyday experience, it can be hard to see the effects.

If we could look at places where mobiles aren't common, perhaps this would help. There are very few places left in the world where these everywhere devices are just being introduced, of course. Pedro Ferreira and colleague Kia Höök visited one of these to see how technology disrupts the rhythms of movement in that place as it takes hold. Their findings are a fascinating insight into the lives of the ni-Vans, inhabitants of Vanuatu, a remote grouping of islands in the South Pacific Ocean. But their work also raises questions about how we all have had to change the way we hold ourselves, altering our poise and balance, and the ways we move through our places and spaces to accommodate the changes that our smartphones demand.

Surrounded by water, the ni-Vans spend a great deal of time in it or on it. They skillfully pilot canoes to move between different parts of the land, to fish, and also just for fun.

Running into the water for a quick swim to refresh or clean is commonplace. Walking along the coastline also sometimes requires physical skill, focus, and presence to navigate the very sharp coral underfoot.

The scene is of a people physically connected to their land and the water that defines it. They readily exploit its resources using graceful, expert body moves to navigate its challenges. Into this paradise, as presented by the researchers, comes an interloper drawn in by the erection of GSM cell towers.

*"Farewell happy fields, Where joy forever dwells: Hail, horrors, hail,"* as the poet and author of *Paradise Lost*, John Milton might have observed. Not quite as bad as that though: the coming of the mobile brought benefits to the islanders, helping them to keep in touch over the geographically disparate communities. The less positive set of changes the researchers observed, though, concerned the way mobiles were affecting how they used and had control of their bodies:

- A spontaneous run into the sea is suddenly arrested as the islander remembers he has his new mobile hanging from a lanyard around his neck.

- Then, another ni-Van, with phone hanging from the neck, goes to retrieve an object bobbing on the water. His canoe glides gracefully as he uses one hand to hold onto the boat and with the other stretches out. Unaware that his phone is soon to touch the water as he continues to lithely lean out, his focus on the task is broken by a friend who calls out to warn him and *"…made him sit back in a very sudden move, causing the boat to rock slightly."*

In any teenager's home in the developed world, parents—people like the two of us who have children—worry and nag their children to unplug and put the gadgets down. The concern is about what the devices are doing to their *brains*: their attention, their social skills, the way it all might be nurturing an addictive set of traits.

What's interesting about the ni-Van stories is that they show we should also be thinking about what mobiles are doing to our physical interactions, how we might better design devices and software that fit with the ways we move as much as with the ways we think.

Ferreira and Höök from the ni-Van islander studies offer some starting points:

- Think about how to design services that a person can use with their non-dominant hand or no hands at all—freeing them to help with balance, to reach out, or to hold some more important object or tool.

- Think about where people will wear your technology. For those of you thinking about future wearable devices—be they watches, glasses, or the digitally enhanced fabrics we encountered earlier in Chapter 4—there's further pause for thought. The research points to the need to consider carefully what you get people to wear and where they might put or carry the device to avoid disrupting the natural ways they want to conduct themselves.

On Matt's cycle rides, he uses a sophisticated wearable—a watch with built-in GPS, altimeter, barometer, and compass, that connects to a heart-rate belt worn across his chest. It's a remarkable, robust (and stylish) piece of engineering. But the creators—strangely, given its use context—don't seem to have fully have thought about designing for body motion.

Simple things like changing the display to show different values—heart rate or distance traveled, for instance—involve a fiddly button push. Difficult at any time when traveling fast down a hill, even more so on a fresh, chilly morning with gloves on: to do it safely would involve a stop, a pulling of a glove, a press of the button, a putting back on of the glove, and starting up again. The joy and thrill of the ride punctured. Even looking at the display while riding, with its small, difficult-to-read digits, can interrupt the flow of the activity, particularly on a dark morning without the aid of a head-mounted torch.

## Putting it into practice: Using movement context to adapt interaction

With a little extra thought—and minimal extra cost—some of the road bumps in Matt's watch interaction could be smoothed. The watch has an accelerometer that could detect a shake of the wrist and switch displays (turning on the screen light momentarily too). It also knows how fast the rider is traveling, and could adapt the size of the digits, accordingly.

Can you think of any other improvements, and also some interaction and technical challenges that you would have to think about if you built a prototype of this design?

Joe Marshall and Paul Tennent from the Mixed Reality Lab in Nottingham, UK, have been giving further thought to designing for real mobile interaction. They make the good point that most services at the moment are not optimized for the highly mobile lives we lead; rather, current designs seem to have a built-in "stop-to-interact" ethos. In their work, they've identified a series of challenges we need to take account of if we want to break away from this stifling design stance and allow people to move freely while using our apps:

- **Cognitive overload:** There's only so much our brains can process while on the move—what does the user *need* to do or know at any given time? Furthermore, if we divert too much of our users' attention from the other things they are doing there could be some serious consequences (such as falling off a bike).

- **Physical constraints and terrain:** These are the sorts of issues faced when trying to operate a watch while riding. Giving another example activity, the researchers point out that running over rough ground can take a great deal of attention and quick, responsive physical actions to balance or steady oneself. Operating any mobile in such a context is unfeasible; you'd have to stop to interact.

- **Other people:** What designs are needed so that when you are on the move you don't impact on others in the space you are passing through, and that allow you to move smoothly through the crowd? In a more threatening environment, are there ways to operate your device without delaying until you get to a safer place where you can more obviously use your mobile?

We'll be returning to some of these issues and suggesting some additional solutions in Chapter 7 where we look to move from "heads down" to "face on" interactions.

# Effortful design

Effort and exertion are not the first things we think about when we picture people using apps on their smartphones. Indeed, for many of us who design these tools, the aim is to produce something that is *effortless*.

For over a decade, Florian "Floyd" Müller and his team at Exertion Games Lab in Melbourne have been demonstrating the benefits of combining innovative user interfaces with effortful, physical interactions. A number of years before the Wii and its gesture-based controls, Müller's team began exploring what they named "exertion interfaces." Summing up the motivation for their work, Müller and team quote the wisdom of Plato, who they claim said:

*"You can discover more about a person in an hour of play than in a year of conversation"*

If Plato were around today perhaps he'd have extended his analysis to say something like:

*"You can discover more about a person in an hour of play than in a screen full of tweets or a myriad of status updates"*

Physical games with others can be a powerful way of building up social bonds. Initially, this was the driver for Müller's team, with early prototypes focusing on how physical activities could be shared over a distance. In one example, two people were able to practice ball-shooting skills with each other while separated geographically. The system

*"...given the potential for fulfilling and rich experiences which support and enhance people's movement activities, it is imperative that we design for interaction in motion."*

Joe Marshall and Paul Tennent

used a large video projection in both locations, and sensors that could detect when one player kicked the ball at the wall that was acting as the screen showing their remote partner.

Building up connections between people is just one of the benefits or effects of shared physical games. More recently, Müller and collaborators looked at extreme effort in inter-action, what they term "brute force" interfaces, drawing inspiration from contact sports like rugby and American football where direct body-to-body collisions and struggles are all part of the game. In studying this form of activity, they've noted the theories that suggest such play-conflict can be useful to people as a way of venting aggression and emotions as a form of catharsis (but, as the researchers note, other theorists think aggressive physicality in games might have more negative effects, heightening such emotions).

While there are still debates about some of the positive benefits of physical interac-tion on the way players think and feel, there is a convincing amount of evidence that there are direct links between our movements and moods, memory, learning, and how engaged we feel.

Nadia Bianchi-Berthouze, from a leading human-computer interaction research group in London, has reviewed a series of studies that illustrate such links. In one, for example, when people were asked to sit in a slumped posture—think about the way you sit when you are fed up and tired—researchers found that psychologically they were more helpless and demotivated compared with people who were asked to stand upright and be open. This finding is a little startling in the light of the heads-down, hunched postures we can all observe on our daily commutes or in cafes and restau-rants. The way simple changes in physical interaction can affect our feelings was also demonstrated by experiments suggesting that nodding or shaking your head while thinking about a product can impact on your positive or negative assessment of the offer.

Knowing that the way we move or hold ourselves can change the way we process information or alter the way we feel has led a number of researchers to think about how to design their digital systems in new ways to exploit these links. Take for example the team at the University of Illinois that has built an educational game to help the player explore issues of climate change at a science museum. The player dons a polar bear hat, and for the duration of the game becomes a creature that has to deal with the difficulties of the changing ice environment. To swim they have to vigorously move their arms; to stomp across the ice they shuffle their weight from one foot to another.

This game—built around Wii body movement sensors—is motivated by work that has shown that people with heightened physical and emotional states can learn better, and their ability to remember things is improved. As the team at Illinois note, though, it is important to get the level of arousal just right—if someone is too stimulated and engaged, the intensity of the moment can overwhelm their ability to process the situation. A simple example of this is seen when crime victims—say, of a street robbery—have a very clear memory of one particular detail of the event (the shoes the robber was wearing, perhaps), but the bigger picture is lost.

As with this polar bear game, much of the work at the moment on exploiting exertion and effort to improve the user experience is being done in the context of play, and on systems that are used in a fixed environment, such as in someone's home. An interesting question for us mobile developers is to explore to what extent we can build in *effortful* gestures or movements to heighten the sense of engagement with the services our users interact with.

Imagine, then, that you want to post a comment about a restaurant or tourist attraction in front of you. For a negative review, perhaps you could clasp your hand tightly around the phone you've just written the review on, and forcibly throw the content towards the place. For a kinder comment, how would it feel to gently cradle the device and gesture in a way that is like releasing a dove into the sky?

Most of us living in countries that experience cold weather have sophisticated automated central heating systems in our homes. The work of heating our houses is hidden and simplified. All we have to do to warm up is to go to the thermostat and turn up the dial; within a short period the temperature rises. In contrast, think about what our ancestors used to have to do. They probably had a fire in the main living area that would be fueled by wood.

To make sure they had heating in the winter, they'd need to plan for the wood to be ready. This would have involved cutting down a tree, chopping it up with a heavy axe, and stacking it to season. They might even have had to think further ahead, tending a plantation in a wood to ensure a sustainable fuel supply. With logs in hand, each day would see them having to lay a fire, kindle it, and keep it alive throughout the evening, into the dark cold night.

The demands of central heating versus a wood fire at the heart of a home is one of the ways that Albert Borgmann, a philosopher, makes his compelling points about how technology can change perspectives on life. He distinguishes between two paradigms: the device paradigm and what he calls "focal things."

Devices can hide the world from us, disconnect us from some relationship or activity. So, central heating hides the effort and world needed to heat our homes. In a similar way, digital devices are potentially altering other activities, commodifying, say, social life or shopping.

In contrast, focal technologies require practice and commitment. Borgmann argues that these technologies are important as they help to bring meaning to people's lives, coordinating their view of their world.

Researcher Daniel Fallman has used Borgmann's philosophy to stimulate some interesting new ways to think about user experience, answering some important questions for us all:

- **"What is a good user experience?** ... experiences that require substantial effort; experiences that require a great deal of skill on the part of the user...

- **What user experiences are to be avoided?** ... where a user's wishes are effortlessly granted and nothing is demanded in return... Avoid designing for user experiences that might become substitutes for genuine, real-world experiences.

- **How does one determine the success or failure of a user experience?** User experiences are to be considered failures if they fail to motivate and engage the user either positively or negatively. User experiences are successful if they bring us closer to genuine places, people, and things."

**Daniel Fallman**

# Are you designing for cyborgs or centaurs?

Generations of children who have watched the phenomenally successful science fiction TV show *Doctor Who* have hidden behind sofas—or even left the living room—when the terrifying cyber-men appear. This monstrous race began benignly by replacing their human components bit by bit with the better technology. Ultimately, everything was mechanized, and they lost their humanity. Traveling the galaxy, whenever they encounter emotional beings they transform them into man-machines, in a process that is accompanied on screen by a chilling last expression of human emotion, a shocking scream.

Some futuristic visions for mobiles see us humans being upgraded with wearable or more permanently attached or embedded devices, our weaknesses mitigated by digital technology. Robert Scoble, an unashamed techno-utopian and widely followed blogger, has written about the dangers of people being left behind if they don't embrace these fixes. Forget about Web 2.0; it is all about Human 2.0.

Search for:
*Robert Scoble*

The fusion of new tools to ourselves can be framed in a much more romantic, helpful way, though. Kia Höök, who we met earlier in this chapter on her travels to Vanuatu, does just this when she tries to explain what it feels like when she is engaged in her passion for horse riding.

She speaks of the continuous negotiation between her horse and herself, a true partner-ship that is communicated through multiple channels, from the breath of the horse to her knees touching the beast's sides.

This sense of being at one with a "tool" is common in other sports too, such as cycling or rowing. When Matt is pelting fast along the road on his bike, he feels that his body and the bike merge and respond to each other in a way that leads to a highly pleasur-able "user experience." Turning into a corner by leaning his body, the front of the bike's carbon fiber frame resists the forces and prompts a quick change in how his weight is distributed on the turn, leading to an adrenaline-fueled moment of panic-excitement at the delight of avoiding a speedy tumble.

Over a number of years we, along with colleagues at Glasgow University, have been thinking about how to achieve this sort of satisfying and responsive form of interaction when using mobile devices. We called the approach "negotiated interaction" to empha-size the evolving, continuous "in the loop" form of back and forth between the user and the device or service we were building. In starting the work, we described what we felt is a more appealing symbiosis between machine and person:

> "We believe the appropriate comparison would be dancing, rather than the current command and control metaphor. When someone dances with a partner there is a soft ebb and flow of control; sometimes one person leads, sometimes the other, this chang-ing fluidly as they dance. We are proposing a similar interaction between a user and computer, where sometimes the user leads and at other times the computer according to the context of the interaction. This contrasts with most current approaches where one agent, be it the human or the computer, pre-empts the other and where most interac-tion is driven by events and proceeds to varying degrees in rigid, over-specified ways."

## Putting it into practice: Elegantly negotiated physical and digital interactions

### Exploring a digitally enriched environment

An example of how the approach could be used is that of location-aware information acquisition while walking in a town center:

- You might feel a "tick" on your phone's vibration motor, making you aware that there is information available about something in your environment.

- Your—not the device's—rich context understanding abilities would tell you how likely this "tick" was to be of interest; if you ignore the cue and walk on, the negotiation would end there and then.

- If you are curious, you might gesture with the phone at likely targets in your surroundings, and get a response from several of them.

- If you are further intrigued, you could continue to interact with these potential targets, possibly moving from the vibrotactile to an audio display, gaining information by an active exploration of the environment (something we have evolved to do naturally).

In this scenario, the user explores the possibilities in the situation by directly engaging (probing or playing) with it, being able to move at will through the space of possibilities, gaining more and more insight during the interaction. The multimodal feedback provided encodes both the system's current interpretation of the user's intention (e.g., that they are moving towards a target) and the probability of the target meeting the user's needs. After working through combinations of vibration and audio, if the joint dynamics of the information source and the user continue to intertwine, the display of the mobile device might be used for full details.

**Photo browsing application**

People really enjoy looking at their photos on their mobiles, but many of the standard browsing tools don't make it easy to explore the potentially very large sets of images their devices hold. Conventional approaches embody the sort of stop-start interactions we've seen before, where the flow of the activity is interrupted in a less than satisfying way. So, the user may have to drill down a hierarchy of photo folders, backtracking when they don't see what they're looking for, or swipe through a fixed stream of photos that does not respond to their interest by, for instance, taking account of how long they spend looking at a particular photo.

Search for:
EPSRC negotiated interaction

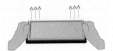  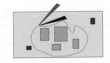 

The *Flutter* prototype, in contrast, uses the negotiated, responsive approach (see image above, from left to right):

- The user begins by shaking the mobile to introduce new photos onto the display. If a photo isn't touched it soon fades from view.

- If the user interacts with a photo then the system uses this to learn what piques the user's interest, and provides related images in a dynamic way.

- Photo groupings that make sense to the user are easily made by drawing a boundary around collections of images. This connects them and any metadata already associated with each image. These interactions then allow the user to express in gestures their view of "interesting," a notion that is much harder to articulate in search keywords or multiple traversals through a rigid menu structure.

- Flipping the device clears the display.

# Moving on

With all of the *Opportunities* we present in this book, our intention is to give you starting points to impact on your approach to app and service design. While some of the ideas are abstract and conceptual, others directly practical, and others framed in respect to future hardware advances, we want you to try and apply everything to your current practices.

So, open up your phone again and pick one of your favorite apps—maybe even one you have had a hand in designing. Play around with it for a while and then answer these questions:

- To what extent can you use it while walking, running for a bus, or carrying a baby or luggage? Could you adapt it to better fit these contexts?

- How could the notion of putting in effort on the user's part improve the user experience?

- Is the basic interaction style machine-dominant, or one of graceful togetherness?

## Resources

In this *Opportunity*, our inspirations were fitness, activity, and movement. We began by looking at exercise habits—the Gallup poll mentioned can be found at [1]. We heard from Haruki Murakami [2] how physical experiences exhilarate, and from Mark Wiser how computing is now *"in the woodwork"* [3]. We encountered the last people on Earth to get a mobile phone service, seeing how mobiles impacted their graceful movements in [4], and thought too about how devices and services have to be carefully designed for physical communities found in many less-remote locations [5]. Our section on how exertion, activity, and engagement are linked and how we might exploit these relationships in designing systems drew on several research articles [6,7,8,9,10,11,12].

When we exercise we are often "at one" with our activity, be it running, cycling, or horse riding. By thinking more about this feeling [13] we considered how it might affect the way we design our apps [14,15].

[1]  Americans Exercising Less in 2013. 2013. Retrieved from http://www.gallup.com/poll/163718/americans-exercising-less-2013.aspx.

[2]  Murakami H, Gabriel P. What I Talk About When I Talk About Running. London: Random House; 2011.

[3] Weiser M. Ubiquitous computing. 1996. Retrieved from http://www.ubiq.com/hypert ext/weiser/UbiHome.html.

[4] Ferreira P, Höök K. Bodily orientations around mobiles: Lessons learnt in Vanuatu. In: Proceedings of the SIGCHI Conference on Human Factors in Computing Systems; ACM; 2011. pp. 277–86. http://dx.doi.org/10.1145/1978942.1978981.

[5] Marshall J, Tennent P. Mobile interaction does not exist. In: CHI '13 Extended Abstracts on Human Factors in Computing Systems; ACM; 2013. pp. 2069–78. http://dx.doi.org/10.1145/2468356.2468725.

[6] Müller F, Agamanolis S, Picard R. Exertion interfaces: Sports over a distance for social bonding and fun. In: Proceedings of the SIGCHI Conference on Human Factors in Computing Systems; ACM; 2003. pp. 561–8. http://dx.doi.org/10.1145/642611.642709.

[7] Müller F, Agamanolis S, Vetere F, Gibbs M. Brute force interactions: Leveraging intense physical actions in gaming. In: Proceedings of the 21st Annual Conference of the Australian Computer-Human Interaction Special Interest Group: Design: Open 24/7; ACM; 2009. pp. 57–64. http://dx.doi.org/10.1145/1738826.1738836.

[8] Bianchi-Berthouze N. Understanding the role of body movement in player engagement. Hum Comput Interact 2013;28(1):40–75. http://dx.doi.org/10.1080/07370024.2012.688468.

[9] Lyons L, Slattery B, Jimenez P, Lopez B, Moher T. Don't forget about the sweat: Effortful embodied interaction in support of learning. In: Proceedings of the Sixth International Conference on Tangible, Embedded and Embodied Interaction; ACM; 2012. pp. 77–84. http://dx.doi.org/10.1145/2148131.2148149.

[10] Borgmann A. Technology and the Character of Contemporary Life: A Philosophical Inquiry. Chicago, IL: University of Chicago Press; 1987.

[11] Fallman D. The new good: Exploring the potential of philosophy of technology to contribute to human-computer interaction. In: Proceedings of the SIGCHI

Conference on Human Factors in Computing Systems; ACM; 2011. pp. 1051–60. http://dx.doi.org/10.1145/1978942.1979099.

[12] Fallman D. A different way of seeing: Albert Borgmann's philosophy of technology and human-computer interaction. AI Soc. 2010;25(1):53–60. http://dx.doi.org/10.1007/s00146-009-0234-1.

[13] Höök K. Transferring qualities from horseback riding to design. In: Proceedings of the 6th Nordic Conference on Human-Computer Interaction: Extending Boundaries. 2010. pp. 226–35. http://dx.doi.org/10.1145/ 1868914.1868943. NordiCHI '10. ACM.

[14] Multimodal Negotiated Interaction in Mobile Scenarios. 2007. Retrieved from http://gow.epsrc.ac.uk/NGBOViewGrant.aspx?GrantRef=EP/E042171/1.

[15] Williamson J, Brown LM. Flutter: Directed random browsing of photo collections with a tangible interface. In: Proceedings of the 7th ACM Conference on Designing Interactive Systems; ACM; 2008. pp. 147–55. http://dx.doi.org/10.1145/1394445.1394461.

# CHAPTER 6

## Opportunity 1.4
## INSPIRED BY MATERIALS

## WHAT'S THE OPPORTUNITY?

In this last chapter on *From Touch to Feeling* we've let our inner technophile and gadget geekiness come to the fore. We look at new forms of interaction material—hardware and devices—that have the potential to dramatically break the glass between your users and the apps you create in the future.

## WHY IS IT ATTRACTIVE?

Being aware of what is coming down the line in terms of hardware can help you prepare for the exciting future possibilities. It also forces you to think about what these enable relative to the "impoverished" touch and feeling interfaces possible today.

## KEY POINTS

- Today's style guides for popular platforms have little to say in terms of going beyond visual displays. What about other modalities, such as audio, haptic, and gestural options?

- Linking the mobile to the physical world using tangible interface concepts could provide compelling new services and interaction styles.

- Research labs are developing exciting input and output materials, from ultrahaptics to displays that can mutate into a range of shapes.

- Although some of the proposals are very futuristic, it is feasible to turn the thinking into mobile interfaces, today.

# WHAT DO YOU THINK?

- Make a list of the nonvisual inputs or outputs you regularly make use of on your mobile.

- Have you thought how nonvisual elements could improve your own apps?

- Have you ever used an app that includes near-field communication (or RFID tags)? What was good about the interaction? What were the problems?

# Introduction

So far, we've encountered a number of example prototypes that go far beyond the simple glass-blunted touch interactions commonly deployed by apps and devices. In this chapter, we step back a little and think about the classes of approach that you can consider both now, in trying to stimulate interesting methods to engage your users, and in the future as technologies develop. The three groups of interaction innovation we'll look at are:

- Modalities and multimodality

- Tangible interfaces

- Emerging interface materials

# Modalities and multimodality

If you've looked at the UI guidelines for the two major mobile platforms, Android and iOS, you'll have noticed that—unsurprisingly—a lot of the emphasis is on the way the visuals look and respond, and the sorts of screen touches that work, as the excerpts below illustrate.

**From the Android guidelines:**

- *"**Keep it brief.** Use short phrases with simple words. People are likely to skip sentences if they're long."*

- *"**Pictures are faster than words.** Consider using pictures to explain ideas. They get people's attention and can be much more efficient than words."*

- *"**Give me tricks that work everywhere.** People feel great when they figure things out for themselves. Make your app easier to learn by leveraging visual patterns and muscle memory from other Android apps. For example, the swipe gesture may be a good navigational shortcut."*

**Search for:**
*Android design guidelines*

**From the iOS guidelines:**

- *"**Users know the standard gestures.** People use gestures—such as tap, drag, and pinch—to interact with apps and their iOS devices. Using gestures gives people a close personal connection to their devices and enhances their sense of direct manipulation of onscreen objects. People generally expect gestures to work the same in all the apps they use."*

Search for:
iOS design
guidelines

There is, however, very little guidance or indeed basic encouragement to consider alternative ways of communicating input, feedback, or output to a user. The only two we could find in the entire official guidelines for both Android and iOS are:

- **Android:** *"Delight me in surprising ways. A beautiful surface, a carefully-placed animation, or a well-timed sound effect is a joy to experience."*

- **iOS:** *"Shake to initiate an undo or redo action."*

As we've seen earlier, there are opportunities even with the relatively limited sensors and actuators built into mobiles to make the interface more alive, breaking through the glass:

**Let the user feel the interaction:** Some apps use simple confirmatory buzzes when a function is activated or a task is achieved. In the last few chapters we've seen more sophisticated examples of how we might be guided by and give guidance to an app through additional touch interaction. We saw, for example, how in-pocket pulsing vibrations could communicate ambient awareness of events, and how tapping or scratching on the back of a device might provide another form of input.

**Let the user hear the interaction:** Sounds are a powerful, quick way to provide alerts: they can be used to enhance the dynamics of a touch gesture (think about the "whoosh" you could add to a swipe movement), and, like vibrations, are a useful way to confirm an action has been initiated. Of course, you need to allow users to disable all of these noises at will—people are uncomfortable with them when others are around—but there's currently an underuse of subtle sound design, so experiment with it. Many people spend a great deal of time listening to audio through headphones plugged into their mobiles. More ambitiously, then, can you think of distorting or amplifying a physical activity through sound interfaces, such as the ones we saw in the discussion around food interactions? What about augmenting or modifying the quality of the audio in the phone call or music playback to communicate some device, service, or content aspect?

**Let the user do bigger gestures:** Think of the phone as a tool that can be used to manipulate material, or in a way that sees it as material itself. Think of it as a pan or a trowel, a ball that could be thrown, a piece of clothing that could be put on. What sorts of new interactions does this bring?

If combined carefully to provide multimodality, our palette of visuals, sound, vibrations, shakes, and gestures can enhance user experience in three ways:

- Reinforcing inputs or outputs provided in another form;

- Supporting redundancy—a swoosh noise accompanying a message being sent, for example, can reassure a user who looks away just as the visual animation is displayed on screen; and,

- A greater sense that the user is directly manipulating an object rather than dealing with a remote abstraction (think back to the *Flutter* prototype in the previous chapter, and the photos sliding off the surface when the display was tilted).

Having said all this, though, it is extremely important to avoid simply adding new sounds, touch interactions, vibrations, dramatic gestures, and the like just for the sake of novelty or gimmick. User experience has to be crafted, and the things you add that go beyond the basic visual display and conventional set of on-screen gestures have to be meaningful and of value. A number of guidelines have been written to help guide effective combinations; an early set encourages two overarching goals that you should keep in mind (see the *Guidelines for multimodal design* box on the following page).

## Putting it into practice: Guidelines for multimodal design

There are many collections of modality design guidelines for mobile devices. At a core level, however, there are a number of key pointers, such as researcher Leah Reeves and colleagues' guidelines for multimodal user interface design:

1. *"Maximize human cognitive and physical abilities. Designers need to determine how to support intuitive, streamlined interactions based on users' human information processing abilities ...."*

So, giving information in a way that requires the user to pay attention to two different modalities (say speech and text) to understand the message can increase the cognitive load and make it harder for the user to learn.

2. *"Integrate modalities in a manner compatible with user preferences, context and system functionality. Additional modalities should be added to the system only if they improve satisfaction, efficiency, or other aspects of performance for a given user and context."*

So, avoid adding modalities for novelty or whim—modality creep could be as seducing as feature creep in software design, and similarly dissatisfying.

# Tangibles: Getting physical

Tangible user interfaces—TUIs—connect a physical set of objects that can be manipulated, moved, passed around, or even kicked to some form of digital processing. When you manipulate the objects, an action is activated or input created that the system can then process. The tangible elements sometimes also contain output elements, allowing them to display feedback or content or to be manipulated or even moved by the computational components.

A good way of understanding TUIs is to think about the *iCon* system that's been developed by a group of researchers in Taiwan, illustrated in Figure 6.1. It's a useful example as the tangibles it recruits are the sorts of everyday objects you might have on the desk cluttered around your computer—coffee cups, drinks bottles, marker pens, and so on. Its use is also easy to grasp, as these objects are connected cleverly to commonly used apps on the computer that lives on the desk such as a music player, photo gallery, or web browser.

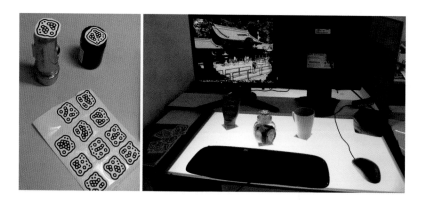

Figure 6.1 The *iCon* system: Tangible objects are tracked around the desk.

With the system, you pick up any of the objects on your desk, stick a simple marker on it—like a barcode or QR code—and use an application on the computer to associate the object with an action. So, you might connect your coffee cup to the volume control of the music player such that when you turn the cup one way, the volume is increased, and decreased in the other direction. Markers on top of the objects are detected by a webcam above the desk and, in the research prototype, stickers on the bottom of an object were recognized by one under the desk through the surface's transparent material.

While widely discussed in research labs, tangible thinking is only currently applied to mobiles in the most modest of ways—shaking to undo an action, perhaps; and using the turning of the physical screen to reorient the display from landscape to portrait. Some of the examples in Chapter 2 give a flavor of what could be done with the sensors

There's Not an App for That | Inspired by Materials

and outputs in most phones at the moment—go back and read the box *Putting it into practice: The mobile as a physical container* if you missed that earlier, for instance.

One technology that might encourage more tangible thinking in designs is near field communication (NFC). Built into increasing numbers of mobiles, this short-range wireless transmitter and reader technology can be used to pass content from and to a user's mobile by placing the device next to another object containing an NFC chip.

Advertising boards equipped with *"touch for more information"* points are now common in many UK cities (see Figure 6.2), and more sophisticated posters are possible with multiple tags.

Figure 6.2 Touch to interact.

Several research prototypes have placed a grid of chips under a map, allowing a visitor to touch various points to be shown tourist highlights. Alternatively, touching the *"You are here"* icon on the map and then another location could be a fast way of activating a route calculation on the visitor's mobile, the mapping service showing the directions on the phone's screen.

NFC interaction—and other near field approaches such as Apple's *iBeacon* protocol—should provoke us to think imaginatively about how to push the digital world out into our physical environments, moving interactions that are currently in our head and under the glass to those that are in our hands and all around our homes, offices, and places we encounter.

An interesting example of this digital to tangible transformation is the *Tokens of Search* prototype illustrated in Figure 6.3. It consists of:

- A beautifully crafted box made of Finnish birch (two of the researchers in the project are from Helsinki);

- A tablet display; and,

- Three different types of NFC-containing objects: knots and tags (seen in the figure) and standard NFC stickers that can be stuck on anything (like a postcard or mug).

Designed to be placed in a communal area at home—hence its high-end, attractive design—family members can associate a web link or set of links to any of the knots, tags, or stickers from any device they have (like their computer or mobile). They then attach the now tangible search token to something in the home, or simply leave it around for others to find. Scanning the token with an NFC-ready device takes them directly to the content found earlier by their housemate.

Figure 6.3 The *Tokens of Search* prototype.

# Emerging interface materials

In the previous two sections, we've pointed to ways you might think about producing more sense-ful interactions by adding to the repertoire of input and output forms you use in your app, or recruiting other objects to add tangibility to your designs. The new interfaces you create equipped with these perspectives can be implemented with today's technologies.

In research labs, though, there are some very exciting new materials that are being developed that will further enable you to break through the glass of touch-based interfaces. To give a feel of what is to come within the next five years or so, let's look at two classes of material—ultrahaptics and deformables.

## Touching the air: Ultrahaptics

Imagine holding your hand above your mobile's display and feeling an in-air vibration that gives you the sense of an object under your fingers: "pressing" the object might, for instance, pause music playing on the device. This would be particularly useful if your mobile was in a cradle in your car where you cannot take your eyes off the road but can reach over and feel for a number of controls projected out of the display in this way. Or, consider looking at a map and then using your finger to feel the population densities found in different regions, sensing this additional layer of content that is displayed above the screen using ultrasound (see Figure 6.4).

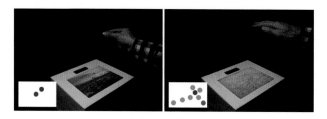

Figure 6.4 The *UltraHaptics* display. Left: A pinch-zoom gesture, with tactile feedback felt above the surface. Right: A population density map is explored with the aid of several different tactile properties.

These and other applications are envisaged by the research team at Bristol University exploring the feasibility and value of what they call *UltraHaptics*. To create the in-air feedback, they use a grid of ultrasonic output devices that sit underneath a surface.

The ultrasound—which operates at 40 kHz—can penetrate the material to reach a user's fingers. The prototype does not use the sort of display found on tablets and mobiles, though, as currently there are not glass surfaces that ultrasound can travel through. To demonstrate their concepts, then, they project the display onto the surface using an overhead projector, and the user's hand position is tracked by the sort of depth camera using in Microsoft's Kinect gaming device. In time, though, the ultrahaptics approach could be realized in commercial products with surfaces that do allow ultrasound to pass through and an integrated finger tracker built into the device.

There's Not an App for That | Inspired by Materials

# Reshaping the display for input and output: Deformables

Turning to interactions *on* rather than *over* the screen, let's see what might be possible when the current fixed, rigid glass screens begin to have the ability to mutate and deform.

Tactus Technology's display technology could already be incorporated into commercial devices. In the example, shown in Figure 6.5, one portion of the screen is layered with a material that can bubble out of the display to provide fixed, hard buttons, in this case providing a full keyboard on a tablet. When the user dismisses the keyboard, the surface flattens quickly to return to a conventional looking, entirely flat surface.

Figure 6.5 Tactus Technology: Buttons that morph out of the screen.

The next example, the *MimicTile* (Figure 6.6), also shows an approach that might become popular as it could, with adaption, be used with a range of existing fixed screen devices. A deformable—that is, bendable, flexible, graspable—material is attached with a cable to the phone and can be operated using one hand, as the illustration shows. In the image, the user is bending the tile down towards the back of the device, but it can also be bent upward. But the tile does not just simply provide an interesting new controller; it also can provide touch feedback by becoming more or less rigid using the shape memory alloy wires it contains. The more rigid it is, the harder it becomes to bend. One of the demo videos the researchers provide shows how the tile is used in a photo browsing app. Bending the tile back zooms the image in; when the maximum zoom is reached the material becomes stiffer and more difficult to bend.

Figure 6.6 *MimicTile:* Deformables with shape memory.

In near time, we can imagine other forms of interesting additional surfaces and materials being plugged into a phone's output ports (such as the headphone socket or USB port), or simply attached wirelessly, to provide richer controls and feedback.

## Design Challenge

Think of different materials you could attach to the back of your mobile (maybe a spongy one, or a putty style one) or that pulls up and over the screen (like a flexible, see-through piece of plastic). What sorts of gesture could these additions provide? How would you use them in your app? What forms of feedback could be displayed with them?

The previous two deformables separately provide additional surfaces to interact with the visual interface of a device. Somewhat further away from the production line are displays that combine these two elements in one. The *Tilt Display* (see Figure 6.7) consists of a series of display tiles, each of which can be tilted in multiple directions independently of each other. In the example shown below, as a video plays and the flower is seen to open, the tiles themselves unfurl like the petals of the daisy. The team responsible for the innovation also proposes less romantic uses such as a map display with tiles reconfiguring themselves to show the contours of the land.

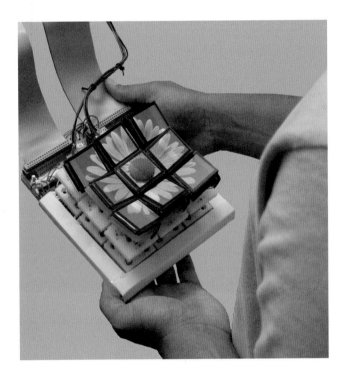

Figure 6.7 The *Tilt Display* prototype.

## Putting it into practice: Futuristic to feasible emotional communication

In this section we've encountered some inspiring but perhaps seemingly far-off technologies. There are two reasons we'd encourage you to keep reading about the visions coming out of research labs: firstly, you'll be prepared for the future that is emerging—start imagining apps and innovations you'll be able to create five years or so from now! Secondly, the types of interfaces and interactions they provide can be used to prompt novel approaches right now. Let's consider how that might work by looking at a seemingly strange and far-from-market mobile, and then see how some of its ideas might be articulated at the moment.

Fabian Hemmert and colleagues, in cooperation with Deutsche Telekom Labs in Berlin, think that ways we can currently emotionally connect with people remotely are too clinical: "poking" or "+1," sending a *WhatsApp* message and the like have a role, but they *"lack the capacity to give users a feeling of physical proximity."* To bridge the gap between a sender and receiver, they've been experimenting with "intimate mobiles." Two prototypes of these types of devices are shown in the following images. In the *kissing* prototype, the wetness of the kisser's lips activates fluid outlets through a semipermeable membrane on the receiver's device. Meanwhile, using the *whispering* prototype, when one person blows or whispers into the device, as if intimately communicating to a lover, the receiver's handset outputs gentle air streams!

Although these prototypes might seem very strange and, indeed, perhaps a little creepy, they do shake us from the conventional views about communicating

There's Not an App for That | Inspired by Materials

through our apps, which abstract intimacy from the physical to surrogates such as likes, pokes, or comments on photos.

So, how about taking this futuristic example and making something that keeps something of its charm using today's technology? Burberry, the luxury fashion brand, has made one such simple, yet delightful attempt.

The company teamed up with Google to produce a send-a-kiss mobile app. Download and try it yourself: you are invited to kiss your mobile screen; then, the imprint of your lips is used to seal an onscreen envelope which you can share in a number of ways, as the illustrations below from Simon's interactions with the system show.

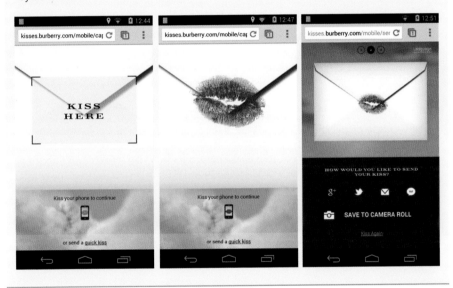

**Search for:**
*Burberry kisses*

## Resources

In this final *Opportunity* around touch and feeling, we stepped back to look at approaches and new interface technologies that might enable us to produce the richer, sense-ful interactions explored through our earlier meanderings around food, fashion, and fitness. We considered UI guidelines [1,2] and multimodality [3]; tangible interfaces [4,5,6]; *UltraHaptics* [7]; and deformable displays [8,9,10]. We ended with a kiss [11] and a pointer to an app [12].

[1] Android UI guidelines. 2014. Retrieved from http://developer.android.com/design/get-started/ui-overview.html.

[2] iOS UI guidelines. 2014. Retrieved from https://developer.apple.com/library/ios/documentation/userexperience/conceptual/mobilehig/index.html.

[3] Reeves LM, Lai J, Larson JA, Oviatt S, Balaji TS, Buisine S, et al. Guidelines for multimodal user interface design. Commun ACM 2004;47(1):57–9. http://dx.doi.org/10.1145/962081.962106.

[4] Cheng K-Y, Liang R-H, Chen B-Y, Laing R-H, Kuo S-Y. iCon: Utilizing everyday objects as additional, auxiliary and instant tabletop controllers. In: Proceedings of the SIGCHI Conference on Human Factors in Computing Systems; ACM; 2010. pp. 1155–64. http://dx.doi.org/10.1145/1753326.1753499.

[5] Hardy R, Rukzio E, Holleis P, Wagner M. Mobile interaction with static and dynamic NFC-based displays. In: Proceedings of the 12th International Conference on Human Computer Interaction with Mobile Devices and Services; ACM; 2010. pp. 123–32. http://dx.doi.org/10.1145/1851600.1851623.

[6] Ylirisku S, Lindley S, Jacucci G, Banks R, Stewart C, Sellen A, et al. Designing web-connected physical artefacts for the 'aesthetic' of the home. In: Proceedings of the SIGCHI Conference on Human Factors in Computing Systems; ACM; 2013. pp. 909–18. http://dx.doi.org/10.1145/2470654.2466117.

[7] Carter T, Seah SA, Long B, Drinkwater B, Subramanian S. UltraHaptics: multi-point mid-air haptic feedback for touch surfaces. In: Proceedings of the 26th Annual ACM Symposium on User Interface Software and Technology; ACM; 2013. pp. 505–14. http://dx.doi.org/10.1145/2501988.2502018.

[8] Tactus Technology. 2014. Retrieved from http://tactustechnology.com/technology/.

[9] Nakagawa Y, Kamimura A, Kawaguchi Y. MimicTile: A variable stiffness deformable user interface for mobile devices. In: Proceedings of the SIGCHI Conference on Human Factors in Computing Systems; ACM; 2012. pp. 745–8. http://dx.doi.org/10.1145/2207676.2207782.

[10] Alexander J, Lucero A, Subramanian S. Tilt displays: Designing display surfaces with multi-axis tilting and actuation. In: Proceedings of the 14th International Conference on Human-computer Interaction with Mobile Devices and Services; ACM; 2012. pp. 161–70. http://dx.doi.org/10.1145/2371574.2371600.

[11] Hemmert F, Gollner U, Löwe M, Wohlauf A, Joost G. Intimate mobiles: Grasping, kissing and whispering as a means of telecommunication in mobile phones. In: Proceedings of the 13th International Conference on Human Computer Interaction with Mobile Devices and Services; ACM; 2011. pp. 21–4. http://dx.doi.org/10.1145/2037373.2037377.

[12] Burberry Kisses. 2014. Retrieved from http://kisses.burberry.com/.

# CHAPTER 7

## Problem 2
## FROM HEADS DOWN TO FACE ON

## WHAT'S THE PROBLEM?

Most apps today require us to look down at the screen. This can lead to what's been called a stop-start form of living: we are drawn away from the action around us to complete a task on our phones. Breaking our flow is one thing; perhaps a bigger issue is that we are missing opportunities to use our devices to enhance our experience of the people and places around us.

## WHY SHOULD YOU TACKLE IT?

In the next sections we'll encourage you to think about the benefits of lifting up your users' eyes to look around them, to confront the world rather than retreat from it. There's a "utility" and an "innovation" reason to introduce this new thinking:

- You can keep your users in the flow of what they are doing if they don't have to stop or even pause to look down at their device.

- By getting your users to see the richness of the physical world around them as a toolkit for their digital interactions—a resource to create and share content as well as control services—you can weave physical and digital interactions together. It's not about augmenting reality or mixed reality, it's about making a coherent, immersive, singular reality.

# KEY POINTS

- Heads down is the default interaction style for mobiles. Users stare down at the screen while prodding and swiping.

- We are information omnivores and we are driven to consume and create content. It's not surprising then that heads-down screen time is popular—the screen offers a rich visual display that can communicate a great deal of content, quickly and pleasingly.

- Think instead of what face-on interactions could offer your users. Face on is about giving your users more of a chance to maintain eye contact with the world around them.

# Introduction

The time we spend interacting with our mobiles mostly involves heads down, necks bent in dereference, screen enraptured. While many tech researchers have persuasively argued for heads-up alternatives, and lots of prototypes have been created, heads down is still the norm.

For our second design disruption, we will look at how heads-down interactions might be diminishing user experiences, and where not just heads-up, but *face-on* designs might be better. We will explore why it is difficult to design effective face-on interactions, highlighting a number of prototype attempts. Importantly, though, we'll see why it is worth the effort, and how such a design standpoint could improve future user experiences.

# What is "heads down"?

Think about your usual posture when you are using your mobile phone. What's your body language like while you interact? Do you feel open and expressive, or are you more likely to be closed and withdrawn, looking down and completely focused on its screen?

Then consider the number of times you turn to your mobile to check email, send a tweet, or read the sports reports. In 2012, Lookout's Mobile Mindset Study sampled over 2,000 US adults, and found that 60% couldn't last an hour without checking their phones. Over 30% checked phones during meals with friends, or more dangerous situations, such as while driving.

Decades ago, TV shows and films like *Star Trek*, *James Bond*, and *Doctor Who* imagined a future full of fantastic gadgets—things you pointed with, manipulated, and felt reactions from. Devices that really were magical, despite some unusual uses such as killing Klingons. These devices helped fictional heroes probe, scan, and alter physical environments while tackling head-on the devious aliens and other monsters.

Meanwhile, the mobiles most of us carry tend to teleport us away from things right in front of our faces. Tapping on a map for directions while in the middle of a beautiful park just doesn't feel quite the same as looking around, asking for directions, or simply following your instincts to see where to go. Looking down at a device to scan restaurant reviews while

> *"Sometimes people signal their departure by putting a phone to their ear, but it often happens in more subtle ways – there may be a glance down at a mobile device during dinner or a meeting"*
>
> Sherry Turkle

There's Not an App for That | From Heads Down to Face on

in a busy tourist spot is so different to physically exploring the possibilities even with all the awkwardness and human interaction this might involve: dodging over-keen waiters luring you in, peering into a busy restaurant to see if there's a quiet table somewhere inside.

So, "heads down" breaks the link between the user and the people and places physically present. There's something special about seeing things with your own eyes, and about touching things with your own hands. Consider pioneering explorers—the burning human desire to reach unexplored jungles, the summit of Everest, or the surface of the Moon—in person. Director and deep-sea explorer James Cameron, on his recent journey to the deepest point in the ocean in a submarine packed full of display screens and digital technologies insisted that there was a window to see the view. He puts it bluntly: *"there is no way I'm coming down here to the deepest point in the ocean and not seeing it with my own eyes."*

## Built for better?

Evolution theory tells us that over many millennia, humankind has emerged from the swamp, our species adapting to ever expand the abilities to perceive and manipulate the environment. From slithering over the ground, we crouched, then stood tall to take the world in. From the postures we developed, to the Y vision cells spread around our retinas to acutely respond to peripheral motion, we are "face on" creatures.

While we are making the case for a return to the physical as a reference point for design, there are many people who disagree. They argue that we are in a transition

**Search for:**
*Kevin Warwick*

period between physical groundedness and digital primacy. That is, until now, humans have thrived through physical connectedness; in the future we'll become more and more digital beings (for the extreme outcome, think *The Matrix*).

Will humankind evolve further over time to retreat from the physical and embrace the digital? Or, do we designers need to rethink the tools we are developing?

## How did this happen?

We are voracious consumers of information, constantly craving new content. We are also highly social animals, wanting to know more about each other. The way these reflexes have played out in the digital era of course is a huge collective effort to index, map, and share all our experiences. Over the past two decades we've jumped at the chance to be able to absorb so much more of what's happening around us into our own already busy lives. As Microsoft Research's Richard Harper explains, in his book *Texture*, we complain about being busy or overloaded, but we're constantly looking for more ways to engage and expand our web of connections: *"we seem to delight in the experiences that new channels of communication afford."*

The physical world and the people actually around us may be absorbing and fascinating, but there's a near-unlimited sea of possibilities if we use our mobiles to connect. It's easy to see, then, how so many of us give in to the temptation to look down eventually, and after that it's hard to return to the less alluring local surroundings. Somewhat ironically for a device we still call a phone, its most heads-up basic feature—phone calling—is actually dwindling in usage, particularly amongst younger people. Other tasks have taken over, and these require more of our focus.

We look down at a screen because it allows us to absorb large quantities of information. Compared to other modalities such as audio or vibration, visual displays easily win in pure bandwidth (see the *Screens are effective* box for an example). Then there's the way a mobile's home screen can display many app notifications—new messages, status updates, breaking news, weather reports—all as eye-catching teasers. And once you've looked, it's tempting to dive in and drop out. Clearly, there's also the fact that websites, images, and videos just don't work well in any other modality. For all these reasons, it is a challenge to encourage designers to think about alternative approaches.

## Screens are effective

Try this exercise. Look at the mobile map below and summarize it verbally to someone standing next to you. Try to do this within 10 seconds.

Afterwards, show the screen to the person. What strategy did you take in your description? What did you miss? How did the visual display beat the verbal description? How did the verbal description beat the visual? Imagine building an app that verbalizes local descriptions: what would it be like?

For people with impaired vision, screen readers can help provide access. Looking into research that has been carried out to improve these services is an interesting starting point when thinking about how to present the richness of a visual display without a screen.

As an aside, take a look at the top of the display, too. There are five visible notifications (and often more in an overflow panel), each tempting the user to spend longer on the screen, to check calendar notifications, emails, and app updates. Things like these can encourage us to remain in the screen, even if we weren't planning to originally. A better way might be to only give notifications in this manner for key events, grouping lower-priority emails and updates into a single push when the user has already been using the device for some time.

## Face on

The "face on" design principle is about thinking how to create mobile devices, services, and apps that increase the chances people have to take in the people and places around them. A first simple step is to consider alternatives to screen-based interactions, reducing the look-down distractions involved in conventional everyday app use.

## We are not as aware as we think we are

Christopher Chabris and Daniel Simons devised a simple selective attention test that has since become famous for its straightforward but effective demonstration of attention blindness. If you haven't seen the video (or, if you have, its sequel) it's well worth watching it before you read the rest of this box.

**Search for:**
*Selective attention test*

The video starts with a group of six basketball players, three wearing white and three wearing black, passing two basketballs between them. At the start of the video the viewer is instructed to count how many passes the players wearing white make to each other. At the end of the video, the answer is revealed.

The task is quite simple, so you probably counted correctly. However, there's also an unusual event that you probably missed—midway through the play, another person, dressed as a gorilla, wanders across the screen, right through the middle of the players. In tests, around half of the people who watched the video didn't see the gorilla, despite it wandering in plain sight and even dancing for the camera.

After watching the video, think about the number of times you've experienced this sort of situation in the street, or in a restaurant—missing things until they're strikingly obvious—while focused on your phone.

An interesting example of how to replace a visual interface that has multiple layers of on-screen menu frustration has been provided in *BodySpace*, by Steven Strachan and colleagues, who used sensors in the device to determine the mobile's position relative to a user's body. This information was then used to access particular features of the application such as volume control. Further gestures with the device allowed the user to change settings, access content, and so on (see Figure 7.1). For example, a flick of the wrist at waist level increases or decreases volume; next to the ear the same gesture changes tracks.

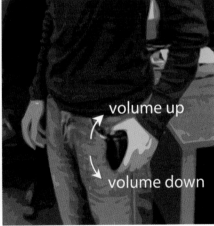

Figure 7.1 *BodySpace* aims to reduce on-screen menu frustration by using areas around the body to control the phone's functions.

Using this method of interaction means that there is no need to look at the screen for quick tasks that a user frequently performs. While perhaps not suitable for long and involved tasks, for short, recurring interactions, this method can be used to lessen the amount of attention that needs to be paid to the device.

## Design Challenge

When you read about research prototypes in this book, as well as using them as potential blueprints for your own work, challenge yourself to think of alternative or additional approaches.

So, taking *BodySpace*, at first glance, while making the point that gestures can be used to navigate menus and content, the approach seems, perhaps, overcomplicated. Today, we have volume rocker switches on the sides of our devices, and headsets with small controllers that can pause, skip, or replay tracks, without the need to take the phone out of our pockets.

But if we take the broader insight of BodySpace—using the user's body and how they gesture around it as a navigation tool—how could we go beyond these buttons to have a more fluid, simpler, interaction?

Maybe you've struggled to hit the right button on your headset wire toggle to take a call while listening to music? What if by simply grasping the toggle and moving upwards towards your ear the call is connected, but if you pull down, towards your pocket, the music keeps playing and the call is rejected? Or, when you do want to do something more complicated, like change a playlist, instead of having to fire up the app, look at the screen, scroll, and select, why not use different locations around your body as ways of jumping straight to the songs you want? Favorites next to your heart, upbeat running music on your thigh…

There's Not an App for That | From Heads Down to Face on

The BodySpace research prototype was created and evaluated long before accelerometers, magnetometers, and the like became commonplace in everyday mobile devices. Now, though, most smartphones have these and more sensors. Developers have used such features in lots of interesting ways: think of how you can shake your phone to undo a typing error, or how tilting the mobile during a gaming app can control a race car or a ball in a maze. There's currently little use of the techniques for off-screen interaction, though. One reason for this is that gestures can be difficult to learn, and hard to understand without feedback.

As developers we might be put off from using these more innovative techniques because we are tied into a "keep it simple" or "ease of use" mindset that measures success in the very short term. That is, we worry about interfaces that are not mastered immediately. However, there are many exhilarating, impressive skills that our users develop with longer, fulfilling periods of practice (playing a musical instrument, crafts, reading, or sports to name but a few).

## Design Pointer

To help users develop into beyond-the-visual virtuosos, you can introduce a gestural technique when they are looking at the screen, providing visual feedback to help them as they practice it, then allow themselves to wean off the screen as they become masters of the gesture. So, think back to the *BodySpace* example. As the user takes the device out of their pocket the range of gestures could be displayed on the screen with the one the system thinks the user is performing becoming more visually prominent as the device is moved: move the mobile up towards your heart and the favorites icon might get brighter and bigger, for example.

Helping people remain aware of the world around them is just the first step in achieving "face on" interactions, though. A grander challenge is thinking of ways to weave mobile interaction into physical experiences, enhancing or altering a person's experience of a place as they engage with it (see the *Enlivening interactions* box below for an example).

**Search for:**
*Zombies, Run!*

## Enlivening interactions

*Zombies, Run!* (and its sequels) is a highly popular app that cleverly adds to a runner's experience. As they jog round their daily routes, listening to their music soundtrack, they are led to imagine themselves as a hero of a post-apocalyptic world, devastated by a zombie attack.

The app adds in radio reports and challenges them to complete missions, with disturbing zombie grunts emerging through the sounds: slow down too much and the zombies catch up, and it is all over for the runner. Look at app store reviews and it is clear that many people have found the approach compelling, changing the way they see physical exercise and the routes they take.

While the runners do play the game by using their movements, there's room for further integrating the digital and physical interactions. For example, one reviewer noted that when they had to stop at traffic lights at a busy intersection, the zombies caught up and the game was over! Runners' actions are mapped to a digital world that they have to view on-screen. Making the actual run route the stage for the gameplay would be very challenging, of course, but would dramatically deliver "face on" play.

## So what's to be done?

For people without visual impairment, a screen is a compelling canvas for foraging for information; this keeps our users' heads down. How can we lift up people's eyes and still provide them with the connectivity and content they crave? Some possibilities are:

- Heads-up displays—either visual or conversational speech interfaces.

- Displays and devices that you only need to look at briefly or when there's something important.

- Designing for an ecology of devices, encouraging the user not to feel they have to do everything all the time on their mobile.

- Seeing the mobile as a pointer or wand to connect to the world around your users.

In the next two chapters we'll take this range of responses to consider two contrasting *Opportunities* for design:

- In your face technology

- In the world approaches

## Resources

Lookout's Mobile Mindset study can be found at [1]. Richard Harper's book on the future of communications is a compelling discussion on the effect of communications on our lives [2]. For an interesting article about how mobile phones are no longer mainly used for phone calls, see [3]. James Cameron's comments about the need for windows as well as screens are in an in-depth *National Geographic* feature article [4].

The *BodySpace* system illustrated in Figure 7.1 was developed by Steven Strachan and colleagues—the paper describing the approach can be found at [5]. Christopher Chabris and Daniel Simons' selective attention test was published in [6], and the video used for the experiment can be found at [7]. The game *Zombies, Run!* can be found at [8].

[1] Mobile Mindset Study. 2012. Retrieved from https://www.lookout.com/resources/reports/mobile-mindset.

[2] Harper RHR. Texture: Human Expression in the Age of Communications Overload. Cambridge, MA: MIT Press; 2010.

[3] Vanderbilt T. The call of the future. 2012. Retrieved from http://www.wilsonquarterly.com/essays/call-future.

[4] Cameron J. Pressure dive. 2012. Retrieved from http://ngm.nationalgeographic.com/2013/06/125-deepsea-challenge/cameron-text.

[5] Strachan S, Murray-Smith R, O'Modhrain S. BodySpace: Inferring body pose for natural control of a music player. In: CHI '07 Extended Abstracts on Human Factors in Computing Systems; ACM; 2007. pp. 2001–6. http://dx.doi.org/10.1145/1240866.1240939.

[6] Simons DJ, Chabris CF. Gorillas in our midst: Sustained inattentional blindness for dynamic events. Perception 1999;28:1059–74. http://dx.doi.org/10.1068/p2952.

[7] Selective attention test. 2010. Retrieved from https://www.youtube.com/watch?v=vJG698U2Mvo.

[8] Zombies, Run! 2012. Retrieved from http://www.zombiesrungame.com.

# CHAPTER 8

## Opportunity 2.1
## IN YOUR FACE TECHNOLOGY

### WHAT'S THE OPPORTUNITY?

In the last chapter we argued for a move away from heads-down screen interactions. An obvious solution seems to be to allow the user to access content and give commands without having to reach into their pockets, pull out a device, and look at a display.

Two technologies that are "in the face" of the user are heads-up, eyeglass style devices and spoken language systems.

### WHY IS IT ATTRACTIVE?

- Both of the technologies we look at in this chapter have the advantage of being accessible without having to fiddle with a handheld device. Simply tap or talk to interact. Being—to a large extent—hands-free, users are also able to engage with their digital services while carrying their baby, doing their shopping, or taking part in some active pursuit like running or cycling.

- Visual displays have the added benefit of potentially overlaying digital content directly on to the scene in front of the user. Need to see where to turn to get to your destination? There's an arrow in front of you showing exactly where. Why is that shop ahead being highlighted with a glowing border in your display? Maybe the retailer has a special discount for you.

- Speech approaches have—for now—a social acceptability advantage over heads-up displays. We are used to seeing people talking in public on their phones and via wireless headsets.

## WHAT ARE THE CHALLENGES?

- Eyeglass displays, even with styling, look geeky. Worse still, perhaps, they may force a further retreat into the digital, placing a bigger barrier between the wearer and the world.

- There are a wide range of privacy, social, and ethical issues that are being raised around the world.

- We think that the biggest argument against such technologies, though, is that most people will increasingly desire to feel less—rather than more—plugged into the digital world.

- Conversational interfaces are still not very robust, and despite the promise of improvement it is important to note that such improvements have been promised as just around the corner by each generation for many years.

- Even with human-like recognition and synthesis skills, spoken audio has an efficiency problem compared to visual displays. Bluntly put, you might have to listen lengthily to get the point—it is much harder to skip or skim speech than it is with written and visual content.

- Then, there's the special nature of speech. It is perhaps the most "exposing" and intimate of tools we have to communicate. We are happy using it to talk to other humans, our pets, and our God. But will we ever be truly comfortable talking to a soulless device?

## WHAT DO YOU THINK?

Before we jump into these points with more detail and illustration, what's your view? Think about the apps you use the most. How could they be used via a heads-up display or speech-only interface? How could you change them or ones you are designing to make better use of these technologies?

# Introduction

Heads-up displays (HUDs) have been in common use in fighter jets for many years: as well as flight stats like speed and altitudes, pilots can get on-screen guidance that appears on targets ahead of them. Less-lethal aids have also been installed and sold for car drivers: some high-end cars have them built in; for those on a lower budget, manufacturers have marketed adaptors for mobiles to reflect data onto the windscreen.

**Search for:**
*In-car head-up display*

The idea of having a wearable display has been around in research teams for many years, with pioneering research done by Steve Mann of Toronto University (Figure 8.1). Mann was, then, the fighter plane of wearables, and only relatively recently have commercial prototypes been considered, such as Nokia's eyeglass concept and, of course, the more svelte design of Google's *Glass* (Figure 8.2).

Meanwhile, speech-based systems have been the stuff of technology fantasies for a very long time—think back to Hal in the film *2001: A Space Odyssey*, first screened in 1968. Off-screen, speech systems for anything beyond dictation have been notoriously unreliable in most real-world contexts. With the launch of Apple's *Siri* and Google's

Figure 8.1 Steve Mann through the ages—a pioneer of wearables. From left to right: 1980; mid-1980s; early 1990s; mid-1990s; late 1990s.

There's Not an App for That | In Your Face Technology

Figure 8.2 Thad Starner, one of the tech leads of Google Glass and a scientist at Georgia Institute of Technology, modeling Glass.

voice input on mobiles, the time for speech input and output seemed to have come. Some users certainly find it useful when there is no other option, but the reliability and expressibility of such approaches compared with screen interaction still seems low.

Let's look now at both of these technologies to consider what they bring to address the face on disruption, and why they might not be the full answer.

## Surely heads-up displays are the answer?

Google's *Glass*, which launched with great excitement amongst early adopters in 2012, brings a screen directly to the eye of the wearer. Its design follows that of conventional eyewear, but gives the user a micro screen just above their eye line, similar to looking at a normal-sized computer screen from about two meters away.

Rather than having to look down at a phone, with Glass the display is always right in front of you where you need it. Its straightforward controls allow the wearer to interact via speech (saying *"OK Glass"* activates the recognizer), or by swiping a capacitive touch band on one side of the frame. It seems like there's no need to look away from the world at all. Perhaps we might just have found a solution to heads-down interaction's shortcomings.

The promotional videos for Glass show it as an omnipresent guide and assistant with everything the wearer might encounter—a virtual butler at your every beck and call. Need directions? Just ask Glass. Want to send a message to a friend? Just dictate and Glass will handle the technicalities.

What's really going in these contexts, though?

While it's tempting to see Glass as a successful effort to make heads-down interactions a thing of the past—with the screen at your eye there's no need to take your attention off the world around you—perhaps we are actually stepping further into the digital and away from the physical world. The device represents an impressive technological leap, but we want to suggest that the path it is forging is a distraction from alternative directions.

Recognizing some of the potential issues with the technology, Google published a set of Glass guidelines in 2014, including "don'ts." One was a warning not to "Glass-out" by overusing the device and "staring off into the prism for long periods of time"; another warns of being creepy "...aka, a 'Glasshole.'"

Scenarios for these heads-up displays and other wearables often include some very active pursuits, like running round a city. However, there is another possible future these ever-present helps might herald. In the Pixar film *WALL·E*, much of the action is set on a space cruise liner where all of the passengers' needs are met by technology. They travel around the ship on levitating chairs, a holo screen floating above their eyes; never having to move, they are all morbidly obese.

At Google's *I/O 2013* event, engineering head Vic Gundotra talked about the company's drive towards pushing the digital into the background: *"computers should get out of the way, so you can get on with the things that matter in life: learning, living, and loving."*

Despite such aims, it might be difficult for users to overcome the urge to see the digital as more important than the physical—after all, wearing a device and overlaying content in front of the world around the user suggests the world is somehow unfinished without the completeness brought by digital supplements. Heads-up displays frame the world as something to be computed, a resource that can enhance *the digital*. The digital is in view, removing the need to look down at a screen. Not only do we risk losing ourselves further in the digital, being drawn away from the world, we begin to see the digital as a better, easier to use reality.

## Design Challenge

What if some of the notifications or content you might get on a HUD were actually available via the physical environments you encountered? Think first about how everyday surfaces like walls or tables might be recruited to the task (see the image in Figure 8.3 of a system that can turn any surface into a multitouch display). Then, more ambitiously, what if materials like water or plants could present or manipulate your content (see the image in Figure 8.4 of the *Babbage Cabbage*)? These scenarios may seem far-fetched, but some of the ideas have already being prototyped in labs and in real-world contexts (see the *Another type of heads-up display* box for a large-scale water drop printer, for instance).

Figure 8.3 John Hardy's *Ubi displays* project creates touch screens anywhere.

Figure 8.4 *Babbage Cabbage*: plants that change color to represent changes in a user's social network, health, and so on.

## Another type of heads-up display

Matt visited the Olympic Park in London during the Games of 2012. The Olympics celebrates physicality, and the park's designers brought this perspective even to some of the digital elements in use at the venue.

Take the waterfall display, placed over one of the bridges near the park's entrance. Multiple ribbons of water acted like an old-fashioned dot-matrix printer, spelling out words in a deliberately slow manner. The display was physical, as much part of the environment as the bridge and the breeze that attenuated it.

## Is speech the answer?

A while back, if you saw someone walking down the street, angrily shouting and gesturing, you'd probably cross the road, assuming the person was a colorful, eccentric local character. Now, you would not give them a second glance: they are probably simply using a hands-free headset to communicate with a colleague, friend, or family member.

Advances in speech recognition, for input, and speech synthesis, for output, mean that in the near future the conversational partner might be a machine, not another human. Speech approaches seem to have two great advantages over heads-down methods:

- **Advantage 1:** Speech and audio input and output seems like an obvious way to deliver face on interactions, allowing, as it does, the ability to make requests and receive responses without taking one's eyes away from the view ahead. It also frees up your hands, allowing their use in other ways, be that carrying a bag or pointing or gesturing as another form of interaction with a mobile service.

- **Advantage 2:** There is also the further advantage over eyewear-based approaches that people are already happy to wear headphones—many of us routinely listen to music and audio on our everyday commutes or exercise regimes as well as chatting via hands-free headsets.

But, there are problems with speech that make it less attractive as the front-runner to move people away from heads-down mode.

## Technical and performance issues

**Accuracy:** The underlying technology for speech recognition is improving all the time with both better modeling of speech and greater data sets to train the systems. Recognizers also learn how an individual user speaks, leading to greater accuracy. However, in noisy environments, or if the user speaks with stops and starts (*"ums"* and *"ahs"* and the like), accuracy can decline and frustration increase. The natural reaction can then be to speak slower, more loudly or in discrete chunks—like talking to someone who cannot speak your language—and this can make the performance of the speech recognition system even worse.

**Inefficient interactions:** Unlike a visual display, audio has the drawback of being a linear medium: you can't easily get an overview of audio content. While there are some interesting techniques to skim and search audio, when you are mobile, unless you resort to screen control interfaces, it can be difficult to hear what you need without simply listening to the whole message.

To overcome the frustration of having to wait as content is played, spatial or 3D audio techniques have been developed. These can allow multiple audio sources to be placed in front of or even all around a listener's head. A number of studies have shown that people are capable of selectively listening to such concurrent streams, and additional interactive techniques have been created to allow a user to make one more prominent than another, a bit like maximizing or minimizing a window on a visual display. Such techniques, studied for many years in research labs, are gradually becoming viable in higher end smartphones.

**Search for:**
*Audioclouds*

**How does the user become a virtuoso?** One of the successes of touch screen devices from a user experience point of view is the sense of control and mastery of complex content and information spaces they can provide to the user. By touching, swiping, pinching, zooming, tilting, and so on, people can easily feel like they are information virtuosos.

Using voice to command and interact with a system does not currently provide the same sense of power and flexibility, and it is harder for a user to see the pathway that takes them from being a beginner to an expert user of the tool. One way to combine the attractive power tool elements of touch screens with the heads-up advantages of speech and audio is to allow the user to manipulate and select from audio sources by using movements of the head or by pointing with a finger to the requested sound source. A number of such multimodal approaches have been demonstrated in research prototypes.

## Bigger problems

Putting aside the expressiveness or otherwise of audio displays, there are several other barriers to this form of interaction becoming the first choice for face on interaction. That is, even if they were very accurate and elegant, they may not solve the bigger problems: how to avoid users being distracted by the digital and how to enhance their experience as humans, rather than leading them to feel like proto-cyborgs.

**Even if your head is up, it doesn't mean you're present**. Just because audio interaction methods reduce the need for a distracting engagement with an in-hand mobile, this does not mean that they automatically enhance awareness of what is going on around the user. A number of studies of vehicle driver distraction while using hands-free mobiles or voice-activated devices have provided some evidence of slower reaction times and reduced overall driving ability. This is caused by the need for the driver to divide their attention between the driving task and what should be the secondary task: the talking or device interaction. Researchers have suggested ensuring that any in-car devices using speech control should prioritize safety by allowing the driver to use cognitive resources effectively when needed. The system could, for instance, spot lapses in attention through, say, lane veering and both warn the driver and shut down access to some services during vulnerable moments.

These studies have focused on the way device interaction divides attention for the critical tasks of driving. There are less serious consequences of such attention deficits when walking through a park or sitting at a café table, of course. However, the research suggests that in these contexts too, just because there isn't an obviously obtrusive visual display in-hand, this does not mean this style of interaction is immune to the problem of pulling people back into the distracting digital.

**Speaking to a machine makes us sound like machines**. Let's return to the scene of the person walking down the street, talking over a hands-free headset. Assuming there's a human at the other end of the line, if you eavesdrop you'd notice the normal rhythms of a conversation as the two people deftly and often rapidly weave their words into each other's flows. Spoken language interfaces have improved over recent years, but there is still a long way to go. Currently, talking to a machine even in private sounds awkward and stilted, and this leads to discomfort—or embarrassment in public—a strong disincentive to use.

**Perhaps speech is a communication mode reserved for things that live?** Nearly 20 years ago, Byron Reeves and Cliff Nass wrote a book called *The Media Equation*, detailing research that shows that people treat computers and interactive media in similar ways to how they approach humans (e.g., being cooperative or polite, depending on how the interface is presented). In a later book, *Wired for Speech*, Nass and Scott Brave considered how voice-based interactions could be designed to exploit a user's inbuilt responses to spoken style, emotion, and so on to improve effectiveness.

This work and many follow-up studies certainly suggest that people will be able to become comfortable with speech systems as they become more natural if they *want to*; but perhaps, even then, they will not rush to embrace them. An open question, we suggest, is whether speech between a person and a device will ever feel "right" enough. Speech is a very intimate, personal form of communication that exposes us even when we are doing prosaic activities like completing a hotel booking. We give away our mood, our backgrounds, and even health status as soon as we start speaking. Obviously, it can be argued that talking to a machine instead of a human agent means that people would feel less under scrutiny; but, if our voices do express so much of who we are, why would we want to waste our breath on unfeeling, uncaring devices? Maybe we will always want to reserve spoken interactions for special categories of entity. As Richard Harper, a Principal Scientist at Microsoft Research's Socio-Digital Interaction's group puts it, reflecting on a conference panel session Matt was involved in:

**Search for:**
*Profharper*
*wordpress*

*"I began to think that perhaps there is something to do with the status given to speech that leads people to resist defiling it with the mere task of communicating with computers. Perhaps there is something about our capacity to talk with other people (and our Gods if we so choose) that we want to preserve as well as honour.*

*This lead me to think of Wittgenstein and his remarks that if lions could speak we would not find anything to talk about with them. In his view, our conversations are about our human experience; what it means and feels to be human.*

*And then, as I reflected on the tribulations that using voice-based dialogues with computing induce, how foolish they can make one seem as they force us to keep repeating words and phrases, I began to realise that this foolishness might be making us feel less human. It degrades our hopes for what we want to be: gifted with words and talk, talk that bonds us with each other (and for some, like Matt Jones, to their God)".*

**Richard Harper**

# Interacting with voice services without having to speak

In certain contexts, voice-based interactions are certainly beneficial, and often essential. Take, for example, the *Spoken Web*, designed by researchers in IBM Research Labs, New Delhi. The Spoken Web is a telephone-based service, designed to provide a voice-based analog to the Internet. Its primary usage is to help rural farmers connect with each other and with experts, and provide a voice message forum for communication. Importantly, the service can be accessed using any telephone—dumbphone or smartphone, or even a landline.

Watch people walking down the street talking on their phone, and you can easily see that they're immersed in the call while talking, in the same way we get immersed in the screen while looking.

The same distractions could also be a problem when people are interacting with purely telephone-based information systems like the *Spoken Web*. In collaboration with IBM researchers, we designed a way to extend the interactions possible with voice services, and reduce the heads-down attention needed.

During a call, the microphone on your phone picks up noises outside the conversation itself. While this can often be annoying while making a call, we used this property as a benefit, to allow detection of other interactions the caller makes with the phone. The *TapBack* system we saw in Chapter 4 lets taps and scratches on the back of the phone's case act as controls for the telephone service on the other end. So, for example, tapping twice could speed up the audio to skip past a section that you're not interested in. Scratching might add an audio bookmark to let you return to a particular point later. As the voice service provider handles recognition remotely, the interaction works on any phone.

What's the value of this type of "audio gesture" in the contexts you're designing for, to reduce the need to look at the screen? Could you add more interaction to your app by letting people interact with the entire phone, rather than just the screen? Recent mobiles are certainly capable of picking up audio interactions in real time.

- You could let people define their own touch or tap areas around the phone's casing, regardless of where the physical buttons are placed.

- A quick scratch on the back of the case while in a pocket could check for new messages, with the device responding with a vibration pattern to let you know the quantity and some indication of who they are from, thus removing the risk of becoming drawn into the screen.

## Why do we need to think of alternatives to these exciting technologies?

Our heads might be up, but with eye-based wearables and always-ready spoken dialogue services we are in danger of becoming even more digitally orientated than when we simply bowed our heads to the screens in front of us. Remember the title of Jaron Lanier's book we discussed in Chapter 1? It is *You Are Not A Gadget*: we need to think of interaction designs that recognize rather than reinforce this.

We've looked at two qualities of these "in your face" approaches that are problematic from our point of view:

- They are at the front and center of your life experience.

- They do not have the potential—as they are currently imagined—to match the virtuoso skills people have, and enjoy developing, as they manipulate screens of content with the swipes, flicks, and pinches on responsive touch screens.

Combining hand gestures, tracked by body-mounted cameras, might be a way to address the second stumbling block, but such gestures—as we will see in the next chapter—might be better allied to less invasive output modalities.

# Resources

Find out more about the Garmin in-car head-up display in the accompanying BBC News report [1], and John Hardy's *Ubi displays* at [2]. The research paper discussing the *Babbage Cabbage* technique, which engineered vegetables to show changes in a user's social network, health, and so on can be found in [3].

Google's *Glass* guidelines reminding people not to "Glass-out" can be found at [4]. Byron Reeves and Cliff Nass explore how we often treat computers like people in [5]; and, Nass, with Scott Brave, explores how voice-based interactions could incorporate natural responses in [6]. Richard Harper's reflections on voice-based dialogues with computers are at [7].

[1] Smartphone becomes in-car head-up display. 2013. Retrieved from http:// www.bbc. co.uk/news/technology-23226569.

[2] Hardy J, Ellis C, Alexander J, Davies N. Ubi displays: A toolkit for the rapid creation of interactive projected displays. Int Symp Pervasive Displays 2013.

[3] Fernando ONN, Cheok AD, Merritt T, Peiris RL, Fernando CL, Ranasinghe N, et al. Babbage cabbage: Biological empathetic media. In: VRIC Laval Virtual Proceedings. 2009. pp. 363–6.

[4] Glass Explorers 2014. Retrieved from https://sites.google.com/site/glasscomms/ glass-explorers.

[5] Reeves B, Nass, C. The Media Equation: How People Treat Computers, Television, and New Media like Real People and Places. New York: Cambridge University Press; 1996.

[6] Nass C, Brave S. Wired for Speech: How Voice Activates and Advances the Human-computer Relationship. Cambridge, MA: MIT Press; 2007.

[7] Harper RHR. Dialogues with computers? 2013. Retrieved from http://profharper. wordpress.com/2013/07/.

# CHAPTER 9

## Opportunity 2.2
## IN THE WORLD APPROACHES

### WHAT'S THE OPPORTUNITY?

Instead of providing an ever-present visual or audio heads-up display, here we look at two classes of technique that might allow users to be less in the digital and more in the world:

- **Peripheral methods**: The first group we'll look at promotes short, glanceable interactions, interrupting your user only when you need to, or ways of delaying interactions until a time when your user is more distractible.

- **Direct manipulation**: The second class of technique involves pointing and gesturing at the world to access and manipulate services and content. The ideas you'll see here are the most "face on" of the ones we'll see. As with all of the design provocations we're presenting, these are starting points for you to think about how to engage the user with the world around them, conducting the digital with their physical interactions.

### WHY IS IT ATTRACTIVE?

- The time users need to interact with a device can be reduced.

- The quality of the information or service provided can be enhanced with automatically summarized or chunked content.

- The pleasure of being able to develop dexterity on the small screen can be transferred to a much bigger canvas, seeing the wider world as a wraparound "touch screen" for interaction.

## WHAT ARE THE CHALLENGES?

■ Creating glanceable displays or services that only interrupt you when needed can rely on careful use of contextual and user data to predict what the user needs to know and how to present it. Errors can frustrate or lead to more heads-down interactions.

■ Even when simpler techniques are used (such as alert summaries in status bars) good content design is essential—too many items or too curt a summary again could be counterproductive.

■ Pointing and gesturing accuracies with current technologies are not yet as fine-grained as they need to be.

## WHAT DO YOU THINK?

To prime yourself for this chapter, think about these two questions and then read on:

■ Have you built any apps that include elements of content summary or glanceable updates? If so, what was your motivation: to reduce the time people needed to get what they wanted, or to tempt them in to interact further with your app?

■ Imagine your mobile as a magic wand. How could you use the world in front of your user to transform the way they interact with apps you've built using gestures and pointing with this wand?

# Introduction

In Chapter 7, we said that people have their heads down because they want to consume content, and the visual screen display is a large plate to serve up rich meals. We want you to look at the situation differently in this chapter by first thinking about how to move users away from high dining to smaller snacks. We'll do this by looking at three design propositions:

- Glanceable displays

- Apps that bite back

- Beyond the instant

But, in Chapter 7, we also pointed out that being "face on" doesn't mean we can't actively interact with our devices and services as we move through places and meet people. We'll be thinking about the mobile as a wand to explore these perspectives. The wand is a useful metaphor because it encourages us to think about the virtuoso dexterity in interaction we think is missing from other heads-up approaches and to imagine how wielding it might create dramatic transformations of both physical and digital experiences.

Wands might also remind you of the *Harry Potter* series of books. You might even remember putting your head down into each book as they came out and spending hours and hours reading them to the end. To close this chapter we'll think about how this sort of heads-down experience differs from many mobile interactions, and what we can learn from it.

# Weaning off heads down: Glanceable displays

As we noted earlier, wearable heads-up displays like *Glass* go further than just putting a screen in front of your eyes: they try hard to be an indispensable part of all your interactions with the world. The intentions are understandable, but the approach, rather than lessening screen interactions, is bound to increase them. After all, with a screen directly in your eye line, why wouldn't you consult it whenever you had the urge?

Another interaction technique, and one that shows more promise for weaning us off our screen dependence, is that of glanceable interfaces. There are two methods that can be usefully employed:

- Clever use of context data to work out what would be useful to show the user right now.

- Careful information design to succinctly present useful content.

## Using context data

Google's *Now* is an example of this first approach. It has a card-based display that presents content in bite-sized chunks, with a sophisticated machine learning backend that analyses users' habits and intentions in an attempt to optimize the content (Figure 9.1).

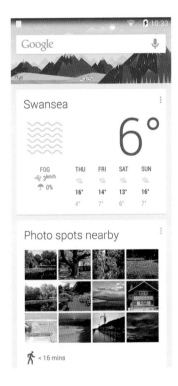

Figure 9.1 Google Now's card-based interface.

One of the key technical requirements for such an assistant is accurate context aware-ness. Context data that might be useful includes:

- Where the user is;

- The day and time;

- Who is close by;

- The weather;

- How fast or slowly they are moving; or,

- What they are traveling in (or on).

## Design Challenge

We've listed a few data items that could help apps accurately infer context. Can you think of others that could improve the apps you have written or have planned?

While knowing where a user is located is relatively easy, and this information can straightaway trigger the appropriate "weather" card, it is not always a straightfor-ward task to understand what a piece of content might mean to the user, or what their needs are at any given time. Take, for example, a *Now* reminder Simon recently received about a flight—it told him that the flight would depart the next day and caused a minor moment of panic as he thought he had overlooked a travel plan. The algorithm had picked up an email about a special offer from an airline's marketing department and turned this into a flight reminder. Or, take the commute tips Matt receives: despite always cycling or walking, the system automatically chooses a car route, helpfully analyzing in detail the traffic delays along the journey of less than one mile.

If you are planning to use context to collect glanceable chunks of content, it is important to design with uncertainty in mind, for example by:

- Cross referencing to a number of sources (checking a calendar entry as well as flight information in the first case, for instance);

- Giving some color-coded clue as to how certain the system is in making a prediction; and,

- Allowing the user to quickly dismiss or correct advice that seems unhelpful (as *Now* attempts to do).

Uncertainty and interaction is explored in more detail in Chapter 12.

## Careful information design

Using context to generate summary content is one way of providing fast access to content. Other glanceable interfaces take a different approach—rather than trying to intelligently extract from existing information and content, they simply condense it into microforms.

Figure 9.2 The *Pebble* e-paper watch. The watch pairs with a phone using Bluetooth, then displays alerts at a glance.

The *Pebble* smart watch (Figure 9.2), for example, is a wrist-worn e-paper display that synchronizes with a mobile to provide alerts and basic control of phone apps without the need for the wearer to use the phone itself. Clearly this approach has the potential to allow interaction in short bursts, rather than risking becoming enveloped in the screen.

**Search for:**
*Pebble watch*

Devices like this have been proposed before, Microsoft's *SPOT* watch being a prominent example that displayed content transmitted over the FM radio signal. Earlier attempts at these types of innovations failed to take off, and were eventually abandoned; but the ability to link small, power-light, wearable glanceable displays directly to a user's mobile may change the viability and usefulness of such approaches for mainstream users.

# Stop pausing and start peeking

Matt took this photo of a dramatic mobile service advert in Cape Town. It is advertising one form of information design aimed at quick glances for updates. The user can swipe a screen to uncover as much of their email list as they want. Other apps and operating systems have similar features. Can you think of other ways of doing a quick reveal and cover up of some key services?

# Design Challenge

There are a number of wearable devices designed to work in conjunction with fitness apps. The one shown below has a very lightweight set of inputs and outputs. There's a vibration motor that buzzes when targets are met (e.g., the goal of doing 10,000 steps a day), a set of five LED lights, and the user can get a status update or change modes by tapping the front of the bracelet.

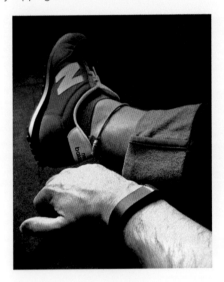

Imagine you were creating a wearable computer that could only display LED lights (up to five LEDs, each with different colors) and that could vibrate in different ways (up to three different ways). Design a prototype that someone could use to get fast prompts (to look at something in their vicinity) *and* updates (about something happening on their phone). They should be able to glance at the wearable to get all the information they need to decide what to do (e.g., whether to look around to spot a poster, or take their phone out for more information).

Glanceable strategies can be applied to apps (see the box below to try this yourself). One approach can be to use on-screen icons that show a smaller overlay with, for instance, the number of messages the user has received since they last checked.

# Glanceable travel apps

Lots of airlines and land-based public transport services have apps. Imagine you were booked to take a journey today on one of these services. What would be helpful to have at a glance as soon as you selected the app? What would get in your way and make you spend longer interacting with the device than you needed to? The screen shots above show some example app designs to help you think through even better solutions.

## Apps that bite back

Mobiles spent a lot more time in people's pockets or bags before they became "smart." Before the smartphone, the device had to draw attention to itself by ringing or making a noticeable alert noise when a text message arrived. As we noted earlier, people now need little excuse to reach out to their mobile and to begin interacting.

Perhaps, though, it is worth considering how to design in such a way that apps or services only intrude when there's really something special to say. Pushing this idea to the limit, you could build an app that called you or sent a text message. If you use push notifications or update indicators, you might reduce the number or frequency with which you use them, waiting for some threshold of activity before alerting the user. For an app, when the user starts it up, if there's nothing much new, the first screen could be presented in a muted, deactivated style, using, for example, grey coloring and recessed button styles.

of any types of apps where the designer really wants to keep people engaged? What about games? Even in these cases, is there value in providing a spectrum of hyperactive to ambient interactions?

---

# Beyond the instant

In the last few pages, we've been arguing for designs that reduce the overall time spent interacting with mobiles, so that any digital interactions enhance, not diminish, our users' experience of the people and places around them. We've talked, then, of the value of glanceable styles and how to encourage interaction only when there is something worth doing on the digital.

To further encourage shorter, more efficient mobile interactions, a number of mobile service providers have begun to think about how to provide a user experience that spans all the computing devices a person might work with before, during, and after being mobile. Clear examples of the value of this are the way search engines can suggest keywords when mobile based on searches done earlier on, say, the large-screen home computer, and the automatic upload of photos to the cloud from a mobile, allowing more sophisticated editing, tagging, and commenting when back home.

Nicholas Carr's book *The Shallows* explores how constant access to all the world's information might be affecting the ways in which we think. His argument is that we're becoming creatures of breadth—with short, scanning information browsing habits—rather than real depth. In his words, *"the Internet is making us stupid."*

While we're not sure the future is quite as bleak as Carr makes out, in our own work we've explored the value of lessening the impact a constant connection has, by postponing mobile searches to later, more appropriate moments. The *Laid-back search* tool tries to prompt more reflective, slower ways of searching than simply answering every query immediately.

Its design is simple: searches that are conducted while mobile are stored, rather than queried. Afterwards, search results and the results pages themselves are presented for the queries that were made on the mobile. The benefit here, then, is twofold:

- There is an immediate and tangible restriction of the temptation to leave the physical for the digital: no results are given, so there is no reason to keep using the device.

- There is also a delay in the fulfillment of those temptations we have to look up every query at all times. As Carr argues, part of the problem is the lack of focus on a single thing: we skim and search for short snippets at the expense of deeper understanding. Delaying the result might dampen this expectation, then, and leave us resorting to thought and reflection instead.

**Search for:**
*Slow technology*

# Direct manipulation and the power of the wand metaphor

There are other ways to address the heads down disconnect rather than trying to move interaction to intermittent glances, delayed interaction, or other low-attention methods.

A team from Telecommunications Research Center Vienna have been exploring the possibilities for more direct manipulation of geolocated information. Rather than prodding and pinching a touchscreen, they wondered whether it might be better to use the phone as a pointer to explore the world. Their *GeoPointing* design took inspiration from the magic wands of fantasy and made the interaction a reality: use the phone to point to a historical site or famous building and their app retrieves its Wikipedia article automatically (Figure 9.3).

Figure 9.3 *GeoPointing*: The mobile phone as a magic wand for spatial interaction.

The design was particularly effective for the same reason that pointing to items on a screen is effective: direct manipulation for selecting objects is more immersive and satisfying than, say, browsing an overhead map view of an area.

In our own work we explored how this metaphor might be combined with the *Laid-back search* design discussed earlier. The *Point-to-GeoBlog* system used quick point-and-tilt gestures to both select a place of interest and fire off a series of search queries to be browsed through later. Afterwards, when the user returned home or had stopped at a café for a break, they could open up a browser and see the routes overlaid on a map, with markers for the places they had pointed to, and a selection of the most relevant search results displayed for each point.

We conducted a trial of the *Point-to-GeoBlog* design, and found that it was used not just for building up a collection of searches about nearby locations, but for expanding existing knowledge about familiar places. For example, one participant discovered a new route to work; another found a local business that she later used instead of an out-of-town supermarket.

Pointing-type interactions are slowly gaining popularity in current apps. For example, the *Layar* or *City Lens* augmented reality browsers can show information about nearby shops, tweets, or points of interest. Similar apps exist for other uses, including star charts, designing buildings, or games. Just like the augmented reality concepts for Google *Glass*, these apps use the phone's camera to provide an image of the scene in front of a user and then overlay content such as pointers to geo-relevant photos, articles, or social content as the device is panned around.

One thing that all these type of apps tend to miss, however, is that the focus on the screen diminishes the experience of discovering things in the wild. Rather than a smart helper to answer queries, the screen in front of the real object is more like a barrier that is held in front of your eyes, directly in front of the object you're interested in.

## Design Pointer

In the *Point-to-GeoBlog* approach we combined the wand metaphor with the delayed interaction we talked about a little earlier. If you want to use the wand metaphor for real-time control of content and services, think carefully about how not to break the spell of face on interactions when you do so. So, how can you combine the wand approach with glanceable approaches, or with no-screen outputs such as audio or vibrotactile output?

## Design Pointer

Current technology means that the level of granularity you can achieve with geo pointers is lower than you might like—you want to be able to point at a tree but you get the whole wood, instead. While waiting for accuracies to improve, you can enhance the user experience by using some filtering techniques. For example, list the objects most likely to be of interest to the user based on their prior history, friends, or popularity so that items with more tweets or Wikipedia content related to them are the most likely pointing targets.

# When heads down works

Matt has a young daughter, Rosie, who loves reading. So much so, she wanders around the house with a book right in front of her nose. She reads while brushing her teeth, reads at family supper times, and even reads while practicing her gymnastic forward rolls. Meanwhile, her two brothers spend a great deal of time focused on the small screens of their smartphones.

After a recent parental attempt to draw these teenage sons back into to the world—to play chess, to make origami models—one of them retaliated, asking why we didn't take Rosie's book away, hiding it like we do with their devices. After all, as the eldest pointed out, she spends even more time with her head buried in her book than they do with their gadgets.

It's a good question, as many of children's questions are, but there are a number of interconnected differences that make us more comfortable, as parents, with the reading habits of Rosie:

- **Persistence**: Each time you pick up a book, you return to a set of characters, places, and story lines that you grow to understand, and, in the case of many highly successful books, love to immerse yourself within. In contrast, one of the reasons why smartphones have become so addictive is the range of services—from email to social networks—that offer the unexpected. Swiping the unlock screen can feel like pulling the lever of a one-arm bandit, excitedly waiting to see what treats will appear in your inbox or newsfeed. Books offer a reassuring stability; smartphone services a dynamic change.

- **Progression**: With most books, there is a clear progression from the beginning to the middle and final resolution. You journey with the author, and even when there are twists and turns or meandering passages, there is a sense of direction and destination. Jumping from app to app or page to page on your mobile offers, rather, divergence: an unending set of possibilities, seductive yet perhaps ultimately leaving the sessions on the device without a sense of achievement or progress.

- **Commitment**: Smartphones are attractive because they are ideal time killers to use in the "dead" time—on commutes, while traveling, or at a spare moment in breaks at work. Instead of being a distraction, books require focus and commitment. Rather than killing the already dead time, they can fill our imaginations with thoughts that give us insights into what it means for us to be alive ourselves.

So, how can we use the qualities of book reading "user experiences" to improve the apps we write? First of all, with book-based ones (and purpose-built e-readers), perhaps we should resist the temptation to build in all the interactivity that can be easily added: the tweeting of passages, the automatic summaries, the links to other works. Hide these away, and allow the linear, comfortable rhythm of reading to be at the fore.

Then, what about others, ones not designed for reading texts? Here are some starting points, for you to think about next time you begin to plan out your app or service:

## Design Pointers

- Aim for a persistent, stable, experience. One that allows the user to anticipate what they will see and do, picking up where they left off last time.

- Consider leading the user on a journey, the app and service having a crafted narrative. Sometimes, fewer branches and options will be better.

- Help the user to commit and focus on what they are doing with your app or service.

# Facing up to reality

We began in Chapter 7 with a design *Problem*, considering what "heads-down" interaction is, and what the drivers to it are, contrasting the retreat to the digital with the opportunities for encouraging our users to experience life "face on."

In the first *Opportunity,* two seemingly obvious technologies for this face on form were discussed. While heads-up displays and speech and audio interactions appear to hold some promise, we explored reasons to be skeptical about their ability to engage rather than distract.

Here, then, as starting points with perhaps more potential, we've suggested the value of designing for more focus on the world. We saw how glances and just-in-time interruptions can be used in simple ways with current apps and services, and may be even more potent an approach in conjunction with wearable devices like smart watches. Finally, in viewing the mobile as a wand, something that is held and pointed more than it is looked at, we've illustrated how you might strengthen the awareness of physical senses in the user experiences you develop.

# Resources

Nicholas Carr's book *The Shallows* [1] is a wide exploration of the ways in which the Internet is changing the way we think and behave. The *Laid-back search* system can be found in [2]. A summary of several elements of *GeoPointing* work is in [3], and our *Point-to-GeoBlog* work is in [4].

[1]  Carr NG. The Shallows: What the Internet Is Doing to Our Brains. New York: W. W. Norton & Company; 2010.

[2]  Jones M, Buchanan G, Cheng T-C, Jain P. Changing the pace of search: supporting background information seeking. JASIST 2006;57(6):838–42. http://dx.doi.org/10.1002/asi.20304.

[3]  Fröhlich P, Baillie L, Simon R. Feature: realizing the vision of mobile spatial interaction. Interactions 2008;15(1):15–8. http://dx.doi.org/10.1145/1330526.1330534.

[4]  Robinson S, Eslambolchilar P, Jones M. Point-to-Geoblog: Gestures and sensors to support user generated content creation. In: Proceedings of the 10th International Conference on Human Computer Interaction with Mobile Devices and Services; ACM; 2008. pp. 197–206. http://dx.doi.org/10.1145/1409240.1409262.

# CHAPTER 10

## Problem 3
## FROM CLINICAL TO CLUTTER

## WHAT'S THE PROBLEM?

The apps that we use are neatly designed, efficient at what they do, and quickly lead us through our daily tasks. But, in accepting an efficiency-led approach to mobile user experience, are we removing the "spice of life"—its messiness, ambiguity, and disorganization? We'll encourage you to think about the benefits of designing for less rigid interactions, contrasting "clinical" design with "clutter" thinking.

## WHY SHOULD YOU TACKLE IT?

Clutter—mess, complexity, vague ordering, and the like—is a part of life that humans have evolved to exploit and enjoy. There are several reasons to design in a clutter-orientated way:

- Coping with complexity, managing when there's disorder, or making one's own sense of it is something we find highly rewarding.

- While there are obvious benefits to focusing on "ease of use," the friction provided by clutter in real life helps us keep our grip, stopping us from skidding out of control.

- Personal expression and creativity are better supported in contexts that are more loosely constrained.

# KEY POINTS

- Our mobiles and digital tools have long been designed to be "smart"—this is the dominant approach to interaction and there is surely value in efficiency and tidiness that users appreciate.

- But, there is also great value in allowing for the smartness of *people* that can work effectively with complexity and uncertainty.

- We can make apps and services that aim to preserve and exploit some of life's untidiness, disorganization, and ambiguity.

- We'll begin to think about how apps and services might find ways to *support* clutter, rather than fighting it.

# Introduction

Bill Gates, the cofounder of Microsoft, once wrote a book titled *The Road Ahead*. In it, he explained in detail his vision of a "friction-free" future, where the world was cleared of the delays, complexity, and imperfections that had hindered us so far. Everything we desired would be perfectly customized to our needs: future computers would be used to ease our journey through life wherever possible. Though the main goal in Gates' view was to improve business and trade efficiency, the friction-free aim applied not just to commerce, or to tedious tasks that might be automated; he imagined that whenever and wherever we might encounter a situation in which computers could help, they would.

*The Road Ahead* was published in 1995. Now, Gates' friction-free vision is increasingly true, especially for mobile life. Today's search, mapping, or sharing tools aspire to tell us everything we need to know, at any time, leaving us never unsure, never lost, never alone. To a certain extent, these tools are now starting to meet needs we didn't even realize we had.

Take Google's popular mobile search tool *Now*, for instance, that we encountered earlier in Chapter 9. Leave it running in the background for a week or so and its activity recognition components begin to learn your patterns of behavior. Sensors in your phone track your position, pace, and movements. Your emails and calendars are monitored for appointments and events. Streams of context-sensitive information are gathered from online sources and mined for relevance. Then, the app begins to offer information that you might find useful, such as highlighting delays on common journeys, reminding about appointments, or offering entirely unprompted directions to new places that your interests and previous behaviors suggest you would like. All of this behavior is automatic, with no need for user interaction or instruction.

## Design Challenge

In Chapter 9, we said that services like *Now* might be able to reduce the amount of heads-down interaction by providing glanceable information. Here, though, we are less positive about it, worrying that its automated approach can take away our initiative.

Designing is all about trading off. What do you think is more important: quick access or a greater feeling of autonomy? How does *Now* attempt to ensure the user feels in control of what they receive? How could the design be improved?

Smart systems like this are just a small part of the mobile future. Think now about mobile search. Being able to access encyclopedic knowledge on demand has transformed the way we think about information. No longer do we need to remember a query for later; now we can simply pose our questions to the cloud whenever we have a thought. Future devices will let us access this information in easier ways, too.

One computer science researcher has taken this to an extreme: Professor Kevin Warwick at the University of Reading has had a series of tiny chips surgically implanted into his arm. The first let him control doors, lights, or heaters when nearby; a second allowed him to move a robotic arm mimicking his own arm movements. The most recent versions allowed him to communicate with his wife with a simple touch of his arm.

**Search for:**
*Kevin Warwick implants*

## The quest for cyborgs

HCI researcher Christian Holz and colleagues have been taking the idea of implanted interaction technology to one potential conclusion. Their starting point was a realization that people often feel so dependent on their mobiles that the devices seem like an extension of their physical bodies. Holz and colleagues proposed to physically realize this dependency by implanting electronic circuitry directly into our bodies.

Their implant concept is not just a simple passive tag, or even a thought-controlled chip, but an active interface, with buttons, sensors, and other ways of manipulating and receiving feedback from the device. Human skin is relatively thin in certain places on our bodies: because of this, buttons and touch sensors, LEDs, and tactile feedback motors can work directly through its surface.

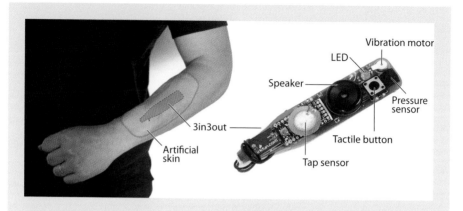

The researchers began by attaching their *3in3out* circuit board to participants' arms, and covering it with artificial skin. By trying this simulated implant in several everyday scenarios, they explored how people might interact with these sorts of implanted interfaces in the future. In general, people who tried the circuit board on their own arms found it easy to use, and could both give input to and receive output from the device. More interestingly, people who used the chip also didn't report anything more than a few curious looks from other people who saw them tapping and prodding their arms.

Clearly this approach is taking user interfaces to the extreme. Before dismissing it as science fiction, though, imagine what it would be like to live with this type of device. Think about what you would design if when your user touched on a specific part of their forearm it could feel and operate like a standard button:

- What digital interaction would you associate this physical action with? Perhaps sending a tweet about their current location or what they are up to?

- Perhaps another region of the user's body might provide a touch area that acts as a remote control for the other technology around them?

- Consider the other devices and services that would have to be designed to support the scheme: at night the user would lie in a bed with a special charging circuit built in to the mattress that wirelessly powers up the various chips around their body parts.

The box above explores a possible future for this type of implanted computer system. Imagine the next generation of mobiles where, like this design, a small implant means that there is no need to type, touch, or even speak; just think. We'll clearly be faster, smarter, and more efficient.

Take a step back, though, and consider what this ubiquitous smart behavior means for our core, human lives. Of course, it seems quite comforting to have access to an intelligent digital assistant—something that is always doing its best to keep us up to date, on track, and on time. Who wouldn't want a smart companion that they can rely on to help them keep ahead of their ever-increasing and complex workload and personal life?

But, are we, in the drive for perfection, losing some part of what makes us human? While we are becoming digitally perfect, from a physical, human point of view, we often feel a lingering sense of loss. Where is the expression, the variety, or the emotion in a smart, overly organized digital life? The small things that make us human are maybe gradually slipping away, being rationalized and ordered out of reach, and our expected future digital lives are in actual fact becoming clinical and detached.

## Design Challenge

What does the research into implanted interfaces mean for the future of humans and machines: will we all become digitally augmented cyborgs? There is a clear desire for more natural interaction with our mobiles. But, what ways can you think of that achieve a similar level of naturalness without having to implant our mobiles into our bodies?

There are hints of an answer to this question with devices such as the *Nike+* sensor, available for many years, which attaches to your shoe to track your running performance. Maybe, then, rather than implanting circuit boards, we could wear augmented clothing, where your jacket senses a flick of the wrist (return back to Chapter 4 for a more detailed exploration of clothing and the physicality and fashion of interaction). Or, like the *Intimate Communication Armband* prototype built by Enrico Costanza and colleagues, muscle tremor detectors could allow you to almost imperceptibly interact—one flex of your bicep and your mobile is under your control.

With wearable devices we can dress for high-tech interactive action, but when we want to return to really natural interactions, we can take them off, free again to fend for ourselves, exposed by being digitally naked.

# Ordered chaos

While the trend in mobile design is to "tidy up" the messiness, taking away the uncertainty, let us think now why a more cluttered outlook might be helpful. To begin, we'll take a look at a number of "clutter" examples, drawn from both the physical and digital worlds.

## Physical clutter

Towards the end of 2012, Simon and his friends Jen and Patrick decided to try to complete a large jigsaw puzzle. So, a *6,000-piece* puzzle was ordered. Opening the heavy box there was a powerful sense of the challenge to come—a huge heap of tiny shapes was completely jumbled, and the task we had set ourselves looked impossible. Finding and connecting the edge pieces was achieved relatively quickly, but as more and more fragments slowly slipped into place there was an overwhelming sense of foreboding, and the realization that we had taken on a very large and daunting endeavor.

The puzzle took up an entire dining table, and for 11 months it was an ever-present reminder of the challenge we had set ourselves. There are no cheat codes for a jigsaw: the only options are to complete it or to give up. At times, then, it was also a clear reminder of our lack of progress.

When you work on a jigsaw puzzle you can easily feel that you are part of the process—you sit down or walk around to get a better angle; strain your eyes and your arms to find and reach pieces; search the scattered mess of shapes or the tiny solution picture on the box; or riffle through the pieces that have been connected. We invented systems to keep track of all the parts as we divided and conquered, stacking boxes and boards around the room to separate colors and types and similar shapes. We were free to split out smaller segments individually, grabbing a handful of pieces to explore whether they fitted together. Sorting approaches were tried and then discarded as we experimented with various ways to tackle the challenge.

Figure 10.1 The finished product: 6,000 pieces of clutter.

Completing a big jigsaw puzzle is a long project, and not one to be recommended to others lightly. But there is something in the slow, steady chipping away of the process: that building sense of accomplishment as another piece pops into place, and the finished picture takes shape before your eyes. Collaboration is key, and it is more fun to work together on particular areas. After the puzzle is completed it feels like a real success—you might frame it to show off the effort you put in (see Figure 10.1), or take pictures to show friends and family.

As this experience illustrates, these elements are a key part of the puzzle process as a whole. The physical clutter of the jigsaw is clear, with its piles of disorganized pieces. But, still, the overall goal is to sort these messy heaps into a tidy, arranged, interlocking whole. The mess involved, then, is an essential part of the process of the puzzle.

Think about how it might have felt to solve the challenge of the jigsaw puzzle with some sort of digital agent pointing out potential solutions. It would certainly have been significantly faster! But, some of the enjoyment and eventual satisfaction would undoubtedly have been lost. When the last tiny piece dropped into place for us there was a huge sense of relief, of fulfillment, and of pride.

The disorganized pile of jigsaw pieces that are eventually made up into the completed picture are a good example of physical mess, but also of how space that might look cluttered to a casual observer can be neatly organized to another. The systems of sorting and organizing puzzle pieces that puzzlers devise can be scattered, but effective. The experience as a whole also shows the value of uncertainty and complexity: while the challenge was high, this aspect was part of the overall enjoyment and satisfaction of completing the puzzle.

Compare this feeling to the currently dominant digital ways of interacting, where, say, a navigation app might take you directly to the place you need to be, rather than letting you explore and experiment, or social media posts inadvertently announce an important life event (such as a friend's marriage proposal) before the people involved can tell you personally.

Digital systems often take away complexity, then, with the goal of improving efficiency. Later, in the *Opportunity* chapters that follow, we will see how systems that allow us to choose our own levels of efficiency or variety can be both effective and enjoyable. In the same way as the jigsaw puzzle, a concrete goal is still achieved, but the flexibility and looseness given during use can ultimately improve and enrich the user experience.

# Nostalgic design

In promoting the recluttering of our lives with digital content spilling out into the physical, you may think we are being too nostalgic, harking back to what feels like a more meaningful time in the past.

Being nostalgic might not be a bad thing, though, and in designer circles there's a growing interest in such perspectives, as we found when we interviewed Haian Xue of the Aalto University School of Arts, Design and Architecture in Finland.

Nostalgia is a positive emotion that comes from reflecting or being reminded of something from one's past or from the past of a culture or community you belong to. There's evidence that not only do people feel good at the time of a nostalgic encounter, but that it can also have deeper effects on well-being.

Haian and his colleague Martin Woolley from Coventry School of Art and Design in the UK have carried out research to understand how designers are recruiting nostalgic elements into their new designs. In one case study they interviewed a team from the renowned Ziba design consultancy that had been asked by TDK to reinvigorate their brand.

TDK was a company synonymous with music recording in the 1980s and 1990s. They produced high-quality cassette tapes that were rugged and robust. Paul O'Connor, creative designer of Ziba, tells of how when TDK approached them, their design team felt a nostalgic pull that informed their ideas: *"The designers on the project team grew up in the 80s and early 90s, so the name (TDK) brought a flood of memories, of unwrapping a fresh cassette in front of the stereo, crafting a mix-tape for some road trip, some friend, some girl."*

With this perspective, the designers went onto propose a range of audio devices that combined the best of digital and analog, calling their range *Digi-Log*. The devices included boomboxes like the ones seen carried in the city streets in the 1980s; heavy, large—real statements of technology.

Describing the value of such a nostalgic outcome, O'Connor says: *"Digital allows you to have access to a lot of things, makes things very easily acquired, but at the same time you are compromising the tactile interaction you used to have. So our original hypothesis was, because TDK's most reminiscent connection was from this era when people still touched, felt and interacted with things, we needed to make a connection to that, you know, former experiences and memories that we all have, and try to mix it with, in some interesting way, the digital experience we have today."*

- What are you nostalgic about? Do you miss the clutter of CDs or music cassettes now that all your music is streamed or stored on a single device? Are your bookshelves bare now that all your reading matter is downloaded to your e-reader? What could you design to connect to these positive emotions rooted in your past?

- Can you think of ways that app designers have recruited nostalgic perspectives into their work? Instagram and other photo filtering apps are obvious examples. What other approaches are there?

## Digital clutter

Let's turn, now, to digital examples of clutter. Groups of human-computer interaction researchers have for years been trying to incorporate more human, messy behaviors into our digital lives, exploring the value of digital support for easier interactions. Take Alex Taylor of Microsoft Research, and his colleagues. They've looked at how smart homes can be more than just sterile, organized, and lifeless digitally dominated spaces. Taylor describes several designs that they invented, where the key to each is the starting point that the term "smart home" itself is misleading.

Figure 10.2 Left: Physical kitchen clutter. Right: A digital fridge design—browse photos, look at the weather forecast, or view your calendar on your fridge.

The researchers' prototypes take inspiration from messy physical situations and aim to, rather than digitize and organize everything, bring digital advantages to existing physical objects. As a prime example, they open our eyes to the humble fridge door. Instead of substituting the flat, dull metal surface with a digital alternative (e.g., a display), their starting point was that rather than being lifeless, the fridge door is already a display: *"fridges may be dumb, but the artefacts that are attached to them are not."*

The kitchen scene in Figure 10.2 (left) might look messy to a casual observer, but woven into the clutter is a "smart" working area of notes and reminders, plus a spatial record of family history. The fridge in particular is a family noticeboard where both adults and children can leave notes and reminders, or display achievements for everyone else to see. As well as being the main source for food and nourishment, then, it is also, almost by accident, a social networking service for the home.

These various forms of communication are a long way from the types of digital kitchen display concepts that have been proposed recently (e.g., Figure 10.2, right). The predominant aesthetic seen in these smart fridges is similar to that seen on mobiles or tablets: apps and widgets that can be placed on a grid over the surface.

In contrast, Taylor explains how the Microsoft group created objects that built on the concept of the fridge door as a display, designing, for example, digital augmented fridge magnets that would glow when moved, or could store a short audio clip by the family member who placed the object on the door. Another idea aimed to extend the status of the fridge as a noticeboard, and allow remote viewing of the lists and reminders that are placed on its surface.

Figure 10.3 The Whereabouts Clock.

The approach seen in these concepts involves embracing the physical clutter of items, rather than trying to bring order to the fridge door. A further design by the same researchers is the *Whereabouts Clock*, shown in Figure 10.3. At its heart this system is a digital representation of where family members are geographically located over time. But, rather than a map or a precise street plan of exact locations, the display clusters the family into three simple categories: home, school, and work.

The display is always on, and accessible at a glance, but it is purposefully vague about people's actual geographic locations. According to the researchers, this provided a number of benefits beyond the coordination and location awareness commonly associated with location-based systems. Families using the system talked about the sense of connectedness and identity that they felt, and the "social touch" that the clock gave over previous traditional map-based designs.

## Design Challenge

The jigsaw puzzle, *Whereabouts Clock,* and digital fridge magnets we've just seen are not mobile apps. However, they are all useful pointers to the value of mess-orientated or less-prescribing technology designs. How might you bring mess, uncertainty, ambiguity and human-orientated "smartness" to your app design? Can you see how such design approaches could enhance the sense of satisfaction, achievement, and connectedness in interactions?

## So what's to be done?

There's obvious value in efficient, clever digital services that make our lives easier. With this being the point of many apps, perhaps it is too late to undo the emphasis on phones being "smart"? While most people might be designing for clinical efficiency, there are clear opportunities for alternative thinking that could give your apps a unique edge.

In the next two *Opportunity* chapters, we will focus on two viewpoints that will provide you with new ways of looking at human-app interactions: *messiness* and *uncertainty*. In both cases, the aim is to get you thinking about how to support more variety, diversity, and creativity for your users to exploit and enjoy. It is time to revel in rather than rationalize clutter, seeing how apps with such a clutter-orientated interaction design can free users to act in effectively personal ways, having fun as they take their own initiative.

## Resources

We begin by revisiting Bill Gates' vision of friction-free life in his 1995 book [1]. Christian Holz and colleagues' implanted user interfaces are in [2]; possible alternatives to implanting chips into our bodies are given by Enrico Costanza and colleagues in [3]. Haian Xue and Martin Woolley's work on nostalgia and design can be found at [4]. Alex Taylor and colleagues provide an overview of their work on realizing the smart elements of homes without covering every surface with a screen, including their smart fridge magnets and the *Whereabouts Clock* [5]. The team at Microsoft Research have done lots of research on clutter [6] that strongly inspired us to think about moving mobile designs from a clinical perspective.

[1]  Gates B. The Road Ahead. New York: Viking Books; 1995.

[2]  Holz C, Grossman T, Fitzmaurice G, Agur A. Implanted user interfaces. In: Proceedings of the SIGCHI Conference on Human Factors in Computing Systems; ACM; 2012. pp. 503–12. http://dx.doi.org/10.1145/2207676. 2207745.

[3]  Costanza E, Inverso SA, Allen R, Maes P. Intimate interfaces in action: Assessing the usability and subtlety of EMG-based motionless gestures. In: Proceedings of the SIGCHI Conference on Human Factors in Computing Systems; ACM; 2007. pp. 819–28. http://dx.doi.org/10.1145/1240624. 1240747.

[4]  Xue H, Woolley M. The charm of memory: Examining nostalgic experience from a design perspective. In: Proceedings of the 4th World Conference on Design Research. 2011.

[5]  Taylor AS, Harper R, Swan L, Izadi S, Sellen A, Perry M. Homes that make us smart. Pers Ubiquitous Comput 2007;11(5):383–93. http://dx.doi.org/ 10.1007/s00779-006-0076-5.

[6]  Swan L, Taylor AS, Harper R. Making place for clutter and other ideas of home. ACM Trans Comput Hum Interact 2008;15(2):9:1–24. http://dx. doi.org/10.1145/1375761.1375764.

# CHAPTER 11

## Opportunity 3.1
## INSPIRED BY MESS

## WHAT'S THE OPPORTUNITY?

By messiness we mean the opposite of the tidy, techno-centered, clinical look and feel of many apps. In contrast, we'll look at ways to exploit mess creatively. The mess we use can be digital but we will also see how to use the rich complexity of the physical world around us.

Messiness is uncommon in current mobile apps. However, it is a useful notion to provoke approaches that might allow your users to feel more at home with your designs.

## WHY IS IT ATTRACTIVE?

- The world is full of mess. Take a look around your own home or the homes of your friends. You'll probably see coffee tables with piles of magazines, shelves full of photos, and sofas colonized by multiple cushions.

- Mess in our physical lives allows us to express ourselves creatively.

- Instead of making us less efficient, messiness can help us be more effective, e.g.:

  - Allowing us to organize in highly personal ways, making resources easier to find and use.

  - Enhancing productivity by building in redundancy—having lots of pens scattered round a room, for instance.

  - Allowing us to experiment or "mess around" to make sense of possibilities.

## KEY POINTS

- A tidied, clinical design is promoted by current mobile guidelines and templates.

- Tidy thinking is not always best.

- Replicating some of the physical mess we experience can help us become more adept at using our devices.

- Clutter around us—the panoply of physical objects that fill our spaces—can be recruited as platforms for novel mobile user experiences.

## WHAT DO YOU THINK?

- Have you designed apps or services with "messy" interfaces? How did this affect the design process—was it a hindrance, or did it free you from the existing conventions?

- Think about the apps that you use every day—perhaps you read and organize email, manage calendar appointments, or simply browse the Web. Where do the current designs allow you to be *messy* in your interactions? Where are they lacking in this respect, and how might you redesign them to work more like the clutter-ful physical world we live in?

# Introduction

There are people who abhor mess and work hard to keep their homes and offices tidy and ordered. Mobile user interface components and design guidelines seem to have been created with these people in mind. So, our mobiles tend to be designed with a narrow focus on order and tidiness—designs are driven by a philosophy that neater and cleaner is better.

However much we might like the idea of tidiness and simplicity, striving for organization, the fact is that life is messy and complex. As Paul Dourish and Genevieve Bell explain in their book *Divining a Digital Future*, scratch the surface, and the seductively shiny veneer peels away to reveal a more gritty reality:

*"[...] the practice of any technology in the world is never quite as simple, straightforward, or idealized as it is imagined to be. For any of the infrastructures of daily life — the electricity system, the water system, telephony, digital networking, or the rest — the mess is never far away. Lift the cover, peer behind the panels, or look underneath the floor, and you will find a maze of cables, connectors, and infrastructural components, clips, clamps, and duct tape."*

**Paul Dourish and Genevieve Bell**

What Dourish and Bell touch on is that life works *because* of mess, not in spite of it. Instead of focusing on "tidying away" in app design, let's think about how being less than perfectly organized might be beneficial, both in making our users more effective and letting them be able to express themselves as individuals.

# Designing for messy organization

Since the early days of the graphical user interface, one of the core ideas running through our interaction with technology has been that of the office desktop. The desktop metaphor began in early computers and continued through PCs and laptops; to a certain extent, it has also been inherited in our mobiles.

We are intimately familiar with key concepts such as organized folders of items, a "desktop" space where files or application icons can be stored, and the "trash," where you put things that you don't need any more. The neat list of app icons on a mobile screen, similarly, is like the pen pot, which you reach into every so often to get the tool you need.

When you sit at a physical desk, though, what do you see? Looking at the desk on which this paragraph is being written, there is a fairly clear area that houses the keyboard, but surrounding this is a more messy, personal collection of other items that have been—or will be—used at some point, kept ready at hand:

- Piles of documents stacked in a seemingly ad-hoc way;

- Sticky notes and reminders pasted around the screen and the desk surface; and,

- Collections of personal mementos: reminders of the world outside work, of our family and friends.

In contrast, our computer desktop, app screens, and information organizing structures prod us towards layouts and orders that are not our own. Many users try to fight against this. Take Jen, one of our friends. She used to keep all her digital documents in a seemingly scattered way around a work folder. She had purposefully turned off the system's automatic sorting into alphabetical, date, or size order; instead she preferred to do the arranging herself. To anyone else the positions looked entirely random; but to Jen her documents were carefully filed spatially—with a glance she could go directly to the right position and open a file just as quickly, if not faster, as had they been sorted alphabetically.

But, the system fought back.

After a recent software upgrade, she opened her work folder to find out that the update had helpfully ordered her files into alphabetical order. No longer were they arranged in the previously messy fashion; now they were tidy and neat. While the new software had intended to clear up the mess and make it easier to find items, it actually had the opposite effect and, obviously, Jen didn't like this.

There are several good examples of systems that attempt to recruit some elements of the messiness and customizable layouts of physical spaces. *BumpTop*, for instance, developed by researchers at the University of Toronto, is a replacement for the standard app and file interface (Figure 11.1).

Figure 11.1 *BumpTop's* 3D layout customization. The user can organize the layout in flexible ways to fit their view of their content, contacts, and resources. Objects can be pasted around the 3D space, mimicking physical mess.

It allows unrestricted layout organization, and quick ways to browse through content. The interface can also be controlled by finger gestures that work particularly well on a mobile screen, e.g.:

- Circling a group of documents to cluster them together; and,

- A quick flick gesture to browse through a pile.

As the figure opposite illustrates, the design adds an appealing 3D perspective to the visualization and, to provide a personal touch, mementos can be displayed around the screen's edges, in the same way as you might pin up family photos around your physical space.

Search for:
BumpTop
prototype

## Design Challenge

*BumpTop's* gestures are more expressive and physical-world orientated than the standard pinch-to-zoom or swipes we are used to deploying. Can you think of other on-screen gestures you could implement to deal with content in a more natural way? Imagine your emails were visualized as a pile of letters in your hands: what gestures could you use to simulate quickly sorting through them, getting an overview, and spotting the ones you want to tackle first?

## Clutter customized to place and purpose

The sort of clutter you have around you when you work is probably different both in composition and organization to that in your kitchen, lounge, or bathroom.

In contrast, on the whole, the way mobile apps and services organize content is deliberately place and purpose independent. Useful apps like *Dropbox* let us remain coordinated and pick up where we left off, regardless of where we are. Similarly, our photos, browser tabs, email views, and app layouts are usually independent of the places or task context. Indeed, orthodox thinking says that there is a great benefit in

**Search for:**
*Productivity Future Vision*

having everything available anywhere for anytime: take a look at Microsoft's recent *Productivity Future Vision* concept video that extols the value of this sort of approach.

But, what if you designed interactions so they *were* bound by places or purposes: your content views, workspaces, and apps changing depending where you are or what you are doing? At home relaxing versus in the office working; traveling for business versus traveling for leisure. Think about designing so your users can pack and organize their mobiles as if they were packing a bag for different purposes or destinations. One possible implementation of this notion is discussed in Chapter 4, where interchangeable phone cases are used to switch contexts.

## Designing for messy interaction

A neat and tidy grid or list of items is often an easy way for users to interact with content. A grid of photos, for example, or a list of email messages can be effective at giving both an overview, and an easy way to select items for more detail. But grids and lists are not always the most satisfying ways to present content—sometimes it can be worth exploring less rigid options.

Take, for example, the *StoryBank* system, which was developed by Matt and colleagues to display digital stories made by villagers in Budikote, a small community in rural Karnataka, India (see Figure 11.2).

Figure 11.2 *StoryBank's* animated collage display.

Rather than a standard thumbnail grid, the design used a simple animated collage, where each story appeared at the back of the pile, and slowly grew larger as it made its way toward the front.

This design had two benefits:

- The constant rotation of content made sure that no explicit interaction was needed to see any of the stories: while the display was a touch screen, it was also situated in a community center, so it was important for it to also be an ambient display—gently but persistently displaying the community's stories.

- The approach also made sure everyone's story was at the top of the pile at some point, so there was no unintentional preference for one person or group's creations.

While the ambient, collaging approach was seen to be effective, the design team also made sure that people could get to a particular story more directly. As the image shows, at the left of the screen is a filter panel for broad story categories, and at the bottom right is a selector panel, where entering a particular story's code loads it into view straight away.

## Design Challenge

How could you use collaging in your app designs? Maybe a simple application would be in mobile photo browsers. Retelling a story from your day, or recalling holiday snaps with friends could involve passing around your phone with a photo collage, rather than huddling around as you flick through each one. What about using it to access other forms of content?

Before digital photography became the norm, we used to hand out photos around groups, able to share images with everyone by passing them to each other, or, if necessary, spreading out all the prints on a table and looking together.

Andrés Lucero of Nokia Research Centre and colleagues have been investigating how to digitally replicate the ways in which we used to share photos with others. Their *Pass-Them-Around* system replicates the metaphor of sharing paper photos between a group, allowing individual browsing or owner-led discussions, with photos being flicked from one user's device to another's.

Beyond exploiting the paper photo metaphor, the system also enables the combination of multiple displays to view larger versions of photos; like spreading out printed photos on a table as we used to do. So, groups can gather together to enjoy a collection all at once (see Figure 11.3).

Figure 11.3 The *Pass-Them-Around* system.

Let's move away from photo viewing to other forms of interaction. Again, as we look at these examples, notice how the messy interaction design perspective relaxes some of the constraints that can stifle expression and creativity.

Lancaster University researcher John Hardy has written in depth about his year-long experience with a projected desktop. Not satisfied with a plain workspace, Hardy built his own above-desk projector system that extended his screen onto the surface of his desk. Infrared-tipped pens let him "draw" on the surface, and various interactive tools he developed sat side by side with the usual desktop clutter, such as mugs and bits of paper. As he explains, the experiment was useful in several ways:

> "Part of the value of being able to creatively arrange your working environment stems from epistemic actions: the act of modifying your environment to put yourself in a better position to think, solve problems, and extract information from your surroundings. The desk expanded the palette of such actions, allowing me to mix the physical and digital, juxtapose items, and play with layouts by changing position, size, colour, and orientation—with the layouts all remaining in view and sharable with those around me."
>
> **John Hardy**

As Hardy found, the modification of the environment to allow creatively laying out his workspace was a valuable part of the system. Clearly, though, the design is impractical for mobile purposes—it consisted of a bulky wooden frame to hold the projector above the space, various cables, and an infrared detector strip appropriated from a Wii game console. In contrast, mobile projectors (also known as pico projectors) are available as peripherals or built into phones and we've explored using them as a messy tool for creativity.

*PicoTales*, for example, is a projector-based storytelling tool. As can be seen from the images in Figure 11.4, the interface is particularly freeform and basic. To tell a story using the system, the user holds a mobile phone in their hand and draws a simple

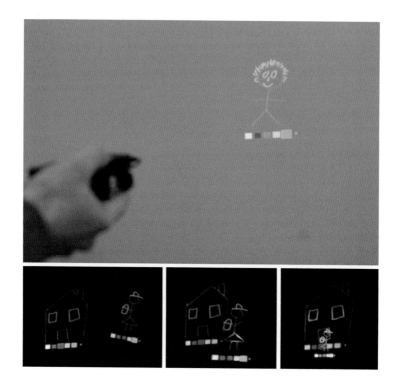

Figure 11.4 *PicoTales*: Pico projectors for interactive sketching. Top: Projecting a simple sketch onto any surface. Bottom: Multiple participants can sketch and animate together to tell a story, with the movements and audio automatically brought together afterwards into a video.

sketch on screen. Then, the sketch is projected on to any nearby surface, along with those of other people using the same app on other phones. The sensors inside record the movements made by the phones, and afterwards, the app creates a video that replicates the projected story, also including the audio (such as a narrative) that was recorded at the same time.

PicoTales is not intended to be a fully featured, highly efficient drawing tool. Instead, it is designed as a playful interactive experience, where sketchy drawing and similarly sketchy movements became part of the storytelling.

There's Not an App for That | Inspired by Mess

# Designing for mess media

Let's return to our friend Jen, who we met earlier as she fought with a tidy desktop design framework. She's a fan of keeping scrapbooks recording her trips and holidays. As Figure 11.5 shows, they are often an eclectic collection of photos, tickets, trinkets, sketches, and other memorabilia. Each book is a rich collection of memories, and it is clear just from a glance that these were action-packed events, purely from the number of items that stick out of the pages.

Figure 11.5 Jen's scrapbooks.

Recently, due to a lack of time, Jen has started using a digital scrapbooking tool. She uploads her photos to the online service then drags and resizes to arrange them into a preset layout. By doing so can quickly archive her memories of a trip. When the book is complete, she receives a printed copy in the post within a few days.

## Design Challenge

The digital scrapbook service that Jen uses is clearly faster and more convenient then collecting and collating physical memorabilia. However, the physical way of scrapbooking offers richer ways to present events.

How could you design an app that better captures the creative mess of the physical version? Perhaps, for example, you could give items a 3D feel with visual design and pop-up or fold-out interactions. What else could help enhance the experience?

---

At least Jen creates physical books of her memories. For many of us, our digital experiences are trapped on our personal devices or shared in a virtual space such as a social networking service. Meanwhile, back at our homes or in our offices, we signal what we've been up to family and friends in physical ways (see the image in Figure 11.6, of Matt's office noticeboard, for example).

Figure 11.6 Signaling experience through physical clutter.

The Microsoft Research team we met in the previous chapter examined the ways people use mess to usefully communicate and coordinate with each other. Inspired by their studies, they created a design concept bowl to contain clutter, as shown in Figure 11.7. When people come home, they can drop their phones and other digital devices along with other clutter like keys into the bowl. The content on the mobiles is then set free and displayed around the interactive edges of the container.

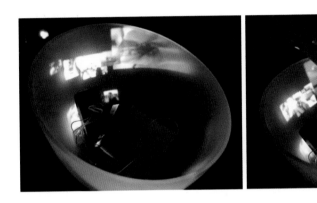

Figure 11.7 Microsoft Research's *Augmented Bowl*.

## Design Challenge

When we stick up pictures or souvenir objects around our office, we obviously think carefully about what we are saying about ourselves to others. How would you feel about using the *Augmented Bowl* in your office? What controls would you want (on the mobile or the bowl) to protect your privacy or to present a certain side of your life? How could you make these controls lightweight enough so that the simplicity of the concept isn't broken by the user having to manually do too much filtering or weeding of content before it comes visible?

The mess media design of the *Augmented Bowl* requires an additional physical object and wireless infrastructure. Think about how to use the ideas it expresses in terms of making the user's life visible in a casual way on the mobile's screen. When your user is at home or in the office, and the phone is put down on the kitchen table or filing cabinet, perhaps it could switch to being an augmented bowl itself.

# Mess and creativity

When you are a child, a lot of creativity is very messy: think finger painting or cooking with flour and icing spilling everywhere. These experiences, like so many in childhood, are optimized for flexible, personal expression and experimentation.

But mess as an effective mode for learning and creativity isn't confined to our early years. If you can't remember your childhood messiness and are of a certain age, you might wistfully reflect on the fun you had in changing the sound of vinyl records by playing them on the wrong speed setting.

To help people understand and use a technology effectively or idiosyncratically, a useful design principle, then, is to promote messing around and messing up. Some interactive systems have explicitly tried to bring such experimentation to the forefront. So, the *reacTable*, a table-based music device, uses algorithms to generate sounds based on where and how plastic blocks are placed on the table. Each block represents a different instrument or control. Users create music by experimenting with different layouts and positions, forming their own connections between items or simply adjusting their proximity to create a huge range of sounds.

Another design that embraces such messy experimentation is *Dirti*—in which any liquid or granular material is used as an input device by placing a camera under a semitransparent container to detect the density of the materials it contains. So, a terrain modeler might scoop out mud or clay to shape the landscape they were designing. In another guise, the system's creators use the system to let children experiment with an iPad via a container of grains (see Figure 11.8).

Figure 11.8 Dirti's tangible interface.

## Design Pointer

Allow experimentation, and consider the playful ways that users might want to interact with your designs. Constraining your app to what you as a designer see as the "right" way to do things can dampen the excitement of an experience and limit users' creativity.

## Using clutter in the world

Up to this point we've been thinking about how physical mess in the world might inspire us to add mess as a feature of app interfaces. Off screen, we are surrounded by all sorts of clutter in many of the environments we encounter. Let's think, then, about better using this mess in the world to enhance the user experience.

To start you thinking, we'll take a look at some ways we've been exploring this perspective in regard to a very pervasive physical clutter: paper. Despite the long-hoped myth of a paper-less world, paper-based magazines, leaflets, advertising flyers, books, posters, and the like surround us in many messy ways. The tenacious way this media has clung on despite all the advances in digital technology suggests it will be around for sometime to come.

In our work, with our colleague Jennifer Pearson, we have been looking at ways of using paper-based clutter in three ways:

- For output: As canvasses to messily spread out digital content in the world;

- For input: As surfaces to capture freehand pen-based scrawls; and,

- For interaction: As signposts in a mobile indoor navigation aid.

## Output: Spreading digital content onto paper objects

Our first design in this space—the *AudioCanvas* app—uses physical leaflets, posters, and other pieces of paper for interaction with a mobile. AudioCanvas documents are ordinary pieces of paper with the addition of QR codes in two of the corners. These codes can be printed directly onto the item or attached to any object (for example, imagine a noticeboard with the two codes pinned in the corners).

The system works in the following way, as illustrated in Figure 11.9:

- Take a photo of the object and scribble with your finger on any part of the image.

- Record an audio comment and it is then saved to the cloud service.

- When someone else takes a picture of the paper display, they can touch where you left a comment and hear what you recorded earlier.

The paper display might be a fixed object like a newspaper or a leaflet, but it could also be more like a noticeboard or the fridge display we talked about in the previous chapter. New items could be pinned to it and the additional items can then become hooks onto which additional audio content can be attached with the physical and audio space becoming more and more cluttered (see Figure 11.10).

There's Not an App for That | Inspired by Mess

Figure 11.9 *AudioCanvas*: Take a photo of a tagged object or document, and it becomes an interactive canvas with audio hotspots. The QR codes in the two corners identify the object to the service and allow the app to accurately compute the coordinates of any touch on the screen, requesting the correct audio content associated with this location. Scribbling on the photo adds further audio.

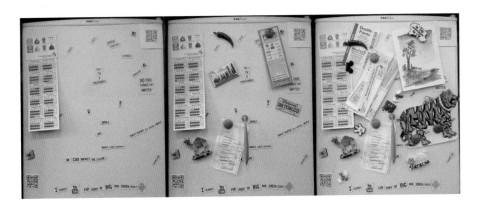

Figure 11.10 *AudioCanvas* allows physical clutter to be added or removed from the space. Here, a fridge door is used as an ad-hoc noticeboard, with both physical and audio content changing over time.

# Input: Scrawling ticks on paper

Our second example is the *TicQR* prototype that processes pen ticks people make on paper to enter data into a mobile app. It can be used flexibly for different types of content as the images of newspapers and shopping lists in Figure 11.11 show.

Figure 11.11 TicQR in use capturing marked items on paper lists. In the first example, the app retrieves digital content associated with the news and advertising items ticked by the reader; in the second case, a shopping order is captured from a list.

TicQR is able to preserve the most useful aspects of mess found in physical spaces, but can then take advantage of powerful mobile processing to integrate with digital services:

■ Think about the way a group of flat sharers could prepare the weekly shopping list. A wipe-clean TicQR list can be stuck to the fridge door and the friends can tick things needed as they think about them over the week; they could edit each other's choices, too. At the end of the week, one of the friends uses the app to take a photo of the list; it generates an order and sends it to the retailer automatically.

■ Or, what about all of those takeout food menus that come through your door and end up stuffed into your kitchen drawer? Your friends are over and you want to choose a meal together so you pass round one of the menus and everyone ticks off what they want to eat. Take a picture with TicQR and the restaurant is sent your order.

# Interaction: Using visual clutter for mobile indoor navigation

Take a look around any supermarket or bookshop. The visual clutter of marketing and packaging bombards our eyes. One of the most obvious elements as we get closer to a display of products is barcodes.

A research team in Nottingham argues that the ugliness of barcodes filling our spaces should be rethought by making the codes more aesthetically pleasing. To this end, they worked with artists to cleverly incorporate identifiers within beautiful illustrations on restaurant menu cards and plates that they call *Aestheticodes* (see Figure 11.12).

Figure 11.12 *Aestheticodes* on a plate. The dots on the flower encode an identifier in similar ways to a barcode. A mobile app can scan and convert the image quickly into the corresponding code.

Instead of hiding this "ugliness" away, though, we think the real beauty of barcodes is that they are so obvious and visually accessible to users. Barcodes, of course, are used primarily for product identification at the point of sale or checkout, but this is a rather uninspiring and unimaginative use of such a ubiquitous and clearly visible tag.

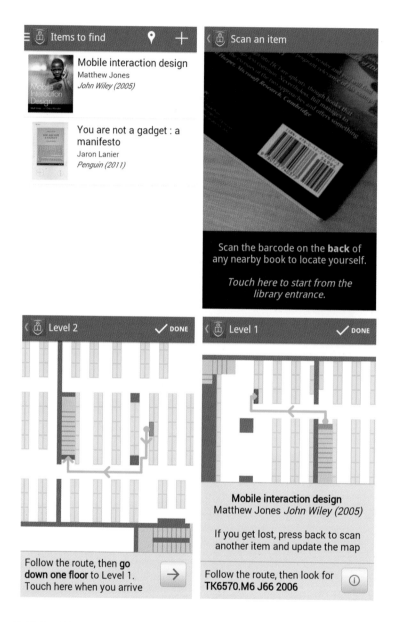

Search for:
BookMark
Swansea

Figure 11.13 *BookMark*: Appropriating barcodes to aid interaction. Scan any barcoded book, and the app can generate a map to any other book in the space.

There's Not an App for That | Inspired by Mess

We looked at barcodes from a new angle, then, taking advantage of the fact that they are easily recognizable, and the items that they are printed on or attached to are often associated with a specific location in places like libraries or shops.

As a first prototype to explore our ideas, we built the *BookMark* app. It is a navigation aid for people to find their way to any item in a library simply by scanning any other item. In the app, barcodes are seen not simply as book identifiers, but as huge numbers of tiny signposts to other barcoded items. Because library books are organized on shelves that are held in stacks and so on, knowing that you are near a particular barcoded item can both locate you in a physical space, and help guide you to any other item. Figure 11.13 illustrates the app.

## Appropriating clutter in the future?

We were able to appropriate the clutter of barcodes for two reasons:

- Barcodes are visible and highly recognizable. The first machine-scannable barcode design used ultraviolet ink, invisible to the user so as not to detract from product packaging. This approach failed, though, partly due to the code being hidden from the person scanning. The type of information piggybacking adopted by *BookMark* would not have been possible if not for the visual properties of the barcodes themselves.

- Barcodes are based on an open specification that allows people like us to write programs to decode them.

In contrast, more recent digital-physical tag designs, such RFID and NFC, are by default generally hidden from view, which greatly reduces their appropriability. Furthermore, some of these tags are proprietary and cannot be read in an open way.

# Beyond paper: Physical clutter and voicemail access

We've focused on using the clutter of paper. As we saw in Chapter 6, there have been lots of inspiring examples of how to use other physical objects as interaction devices.

A key point in all this is to find ways to let the digital spill out freely into our physical world so that we can see it and touch it. Try to think of ways of releasing it from the structured menus, grid views, and search result lists that constrain it under the screen. Give it a cluttered, physical form to make it easy to manipulate, visualize, and access.

An early idea that articulated this vision was the *Marble Answering Machine*, proposed by Durrell Bishop. Before we had mobile apps, or even mobile phones at all, Bishop was thinking about how voicemail is typically an audio-only interaction, and how odd it is to listen to a message so disconnected from the person who is speaking.

**Search for:**
*Marble Answering Machine*

Bishop's concept was to use a series of physical marbles that were identified by a smart voicemail machine. When a new message is received, a marble appears in the machine's tray. On arriving home, the owner picks up a marble from the tray and places it on top of the machine. The associated message is then played automatically.

The collection of received message marbles could be arranged in any way the user wanted, however. In Bishop's concept video, the user places them into various bowls to save for later or to give to others. Marbles for messages that have been dealt with are simply put back into the machine. Those that need further attention can be placed into a noticeboard slot, with room for notes to be written alongside.

Today's mobile visual voicemail services go some way to dealing with the frustrations in accessing and processing audio messages. What added benefits does the physical approach with lots of small glass balls scattered in bowls bring?

# Tidying up

We hope that you feel challenged to *relax* your design perspective. Instead of defaulting to highly organized, uncluttered displays, think how you can allow your users to mess up their space to make themselves more at home and more productive.

Conventional interface design promotes clear paths to meet a goal. Of course, this is important in many situations, but think too about how to provide more sketchy direction to your user. Let them fiddle, experiment, tinker, and mess around with the possibilities.

The original motivation for us to think about messiness in the interface was the messiness in the world. We've also seen how we can not only be inspired by the physical resources around us in our digital designs, but recruit the clutter around us to enhance our interactions with apps and services.

## Putting it into practice

Take a look at an app you are currently creating and answer these questions:

- What messy organization of content do you promote?

- How can your users express themselves in terms of the visuals or interaction?

- Are you providing sloppy ways for the user to interact? Perhaps a casual flick or riffling though content?

- How have you used messiness to communicate content?

- Can your user easily experiment with your app to get a sense of what's possible? Can they disrupt your well-thought-out plan for their interaction to configure things in idiosyncratic ways?

- In what ways are you using the physical clutter around your users to enhance mobile interaction in the app?

It could well be that your current app does none of these things. That's fine, of course, as clinically tidy, efficient approaches are often useful. But, next time you embark on a project, pause to consider the opportunities you've overlooked in the past.

## Resources

Dourish and Bell's exploration of the mess of ubiquitous computing as it has turned out can be read in [1].

Physical representations of voicemail [2], photo sharing [3] and desktop objects [4] remind us of how important the ability to customize our own interactions can be. Other ways of bringing physical items into our mobile interactions can be found in [5] and [6]. Also related is our look at appropriating everyday objects as scattered signposts for navigation [7].

John Hardy has written in detail about his experiences with a projected desktop [8]; our playful *PicoTales* system is in [9]. Tangible performances and interactions are illustrated by the *reacTable* [10] and *Dirti* [11].

[1] Dourish P, Bell G. Divining a Digital Future: Mess and Mythology in Ubiquitous Computing. Cambridge, MA: MIT Press; 2011.

[2] Bishop D. Marble answer machine. 1992. Retrieved from http://vimeo.com/ 19930744.

[3] Lucero A, Holopainen J, Jokela T. Pass-them-around: Collaborative use of mobile phones for photo sharing. In: Proceedings of the SIGCHI Conference on Human Factors in Computing Systems. 2011; ACM; pp. 1787–96. http://dx.doi.org/10.1145/1978942.1979201.

[4] Agarawala A, Balakrishnan R. Keepin' it real: Pushing the desktop metaphor with physics, piles and the pen. In: Proceedings of the SIGCHI Conference on Human Factors in Computing Systems; ACM; 2006. pp. 1283–92. http://dx.doi.org/10.1145/1124772.1124965.

[5] Robinson S, Pearson J, Jones M. AudioCanvas: Internet-free interactive audio photos. In: Proceedings of the SIGCHI Conference on Human Factors in Computing Systems; ACM; 2014. http://dx.doi.org/10.1145/2556288.2556993.

[6] Pearson J, Robinson S, Buchanan G, Jones M. TicQR: Flexible, lightweight linking of paper and digital content using mobile phones. In: Kotzé P, Marsden G, Lindgaard G, Wesson J, Winckler M, editors. Human-Computer Interaction – INTERACT 2013, vol. 8120. Lecture Notes in Computer Science; Springer Berlin Heidelberg; 2013. pp. 220–8. http://dx.doi.org/10.1007/978-3-642-40498-6_16.

[7] Robinson S, Pearson J, Jones M. A billion signposts: Repurposing barcodes for indoor navigation. In: Proceedings of the SIGCHI Conference on Human Factors in Computing Systems; ACM; 2014. http://dx.doi.org/10.1145/2556288.2556994.

[8] Hardy J. Experiences: A year in the life of an interactive desk. In: Proceedings of the Designing Interactive Systems Conference; ACM; 2012. pp. 679–88. http://dx.doi.org/10.1145/2317956.2318058.

[9] Robinson S, Jones M, Vartiainen E, Marsden G. PicoTales: Collaborative authoring of animated stories using handheld projectors. In: Proceedings of the ACM 2012 Conference on Computer Supported Cooperative Work; ACM; 2012. pp. 671–80. http://dx.doi.org/10.1145/2145204.2145306.

[10] Jordà S, Geiger G, Alonso M, Kaltenbrunner M. The reacTable: Exploring the synergy between live music performance and tabletop tangible interfaces. In: Proceedings of the 1st International Conference on Tangible and Embedded Interaction; ACM; 2007. pp. 139–46. http://dx.doi.org/10.1145/1226969.1226998.

[11] Savary M, Schwarz D, Pellerin D, Massin F, Jacquemin C, Cahen R. Dirty tangible interfaces: expressive control of computers with true grit. In: CHI '13 Extended Abstracts on Human Factors in Computing Systems; ACM; 2013. pp. 2991–4. http://dx.doi.org/10.1145/2468356.2479592.

# CHAPTER 12

## Opportunity 3.2
## INSPIRED BY UNCERTAINTY

## WHAT'S THE OPPORTUNITY?

In the previous chapter we argued for recruiting notions of messiness into our designs as ways to move away from always creating apps that stifle a user's own creativity, self-expression, and choice.

In this chapter, we look at how not providing the perfect answer to a user can lead to fulfilling mobile experiences. Location-based services are an important class of mobile apps, and we will be focusing on them to illustrate the value of less precise or ambiguous forms of human-app interaction.

## WHY IS IT ATTRACTIVE?

- Your users can be freed from their reliance on devices, and allowed to explore their surroundings using their own initiative, instead.

- There's no need for uncertainty to be the only way of interacting—you can let your users pick and choose what works best in each scenario.

- Navigation is a key candidate for uncertain or ambiguous interaction, but there are many other areas in which these techniques might be beneficial.

## KEY POINTS

- Developing systems that support both exact instructions when needed, and uncertainty in interaction when appropriate can be difficult. If you cannot allow the user to switch modes quickly and seamlessly, there is a danger that you will confuse them. Rather than freeing them up you might overload them and this may lead to frustration.

- It can be tempting for users to take the easy way out, "switching off" and choosing the prescriptive option. How might your designs prompt people to explore, instead?

## WHAT DO YOU THINK?

To get yourself thinking about the examples in this chapter, first look back to a recent time in which you used a navigation system either while driving or on foot. Did you feel reassured and aware of your surroundings? What would have happened if your device's batteries ran out, or the navigation system failed? How could you redesign the system to improve your personal experience; and, how could you transfer your learning to your own apps that are trying to help your users?

# The thrill of not being sure

The field of human-computer interaction has long been focused on creating the best, most effective, and easy to use interactive devices. Many of its core aims have been expressed in sets of guidelines or implications for future designs. Take, for instance, the many models of interaction that have been published, several by key figures in the field.

Usability expert Donald Norman, for instance, frames the thought process of a user during a task as "seven stages of action," covering the steps from forming a goal, specifying and executing actions, through to evaluating the outcome. Models of interaction like these have at their core a goal—a concrete statement of what needs to be achieved. Norman himself acknowledged the potential for goals to be vague or not well-formed. But most designs follow guidelines such as these rigidly (even if only accidentally). So, tasks such as search work best when you know exactly what you're looking for, and navigation apps are best when you know where you're heading.

Life, on the other hand, is uncertain. Being lost can be an adrenaline rush; making our own way is often exciting rather than unnerving. Risks can thrill, exhilarate, and even become addictive. A surge of fright leads to relief when sticky situations are avoided, and our emotions are mixed in deeply with so many of the things we do.

# Uncertainty at the heart of enjoyable experiences

Simon is a keen rock climber. To the uninitiated, rock climbing seems like it is clearly a sport with high levels of risk and danger involved. To the climber, there are two risks at play:

- **Physical**: The danger of the climber injuring him or herself. Despite what television and films portray, this risk is actually reasonably minimal for the majority of climbers. Those who take part as a casual hobby, and aren't pushing the boundaries of human capability, are in relatively little danger.

- **Psychological**: That of not succeeding. In essence, this is the core challenge of the sport for some, and a key part of why Simon climbs. As we saw in Chapter 5 with the visceral, pleasurable experiences of taking part in physical activities, this forms part of the thrill of the sport. The aim, then, is to try a difficult challenge, and see whether it is possible to succeed.

While midway through a challenging climb, it's often difficult to see where to go, to know what is the correct sequence of moves that will help you slowly inch your way to the top. Climbing at times feels like a difficult combination lock that must be solved. To open up the sequence of moves that is needed can be very difficult, and at times incredibly frustrating. But this is part of the enjoyment of the sport. In essence, it feels fantastic to push yourself to the limit, uncertain about whether you will succeed or fail: a moment of delight when all goes to plan, or a moment of panic as your hands and feet slip away from the rock on failure.

Contrast this uncertain experience with the systems illustrated above. These conceptual designs were for a suite of digital tools that could be attached to a climber's equipment, giving them a constant update on environmental conditions, and indicating where to go next. So, as the left image shows, the climber's harness not only attaches them to the rope, their partner keeping them safe from below, but, a screen at waist level also points them to where to go next, amongst other functions, keeping them safe from above. Magnetized metal bolts in the rock provide a guide to the system about where the designated route should take the climber: there is no danger of veering from the correct path. Other, even more helpful systems have been proposed where, for example, the clips attached to the rock could point the way to the next handhold (right image), and a watch would suggest exactly which body part must be moved to each precise part of the rock to ensure success.

## Design Challenge

At first glance the system shown in the *Uncertainty at the heart of enjoyable experiences* box above seems very useful. But, by removing the element of surprise, and the uncertainty about where to climb, is the system perhaps merely turning a deeply physical and immersive outdoor sport into a sterile gym-based experience?

What do you think: has this design tamed the activity, or does it show potential to increase enjoyment and immersion, too? How could you use improvements to efficiency in ways that preserve the physical thrill?

In our own work, along with colleagues at Microsoft Research, we've considered ways to support uncertainty in digital interactions. Think for a moment about when you last tried to find out the answer to a query that you weren't able to clearly describe. In this case it's difficult to look up the answer straight away using a search engine because it is very hard to form a suitable question (Figure 12.1).

The *Questions not Answers* prototype took a different approach to search—its purpose was to display other people's questions, rather than answers to your own. In the design, then, people saw an overlay of other search queries on a map. The thinking was that showing queries in the context of locations could help the user get a sense of the places and people around them. There was no filtering or interpretation

Figure 12.1 Sign spotted on a church building in Swansea, early 2014.

of these searches—users could stare at the sometimes strange and eclectic set of terms appearing before their eyes and make their own sense of what was going on. In a city center trial, people found that it was useful and interesting to see the queries around them. Furthermore, they spoke of how the queries around them gave a better sense of place.

## Design Challenge

Providing other people's questions as search cues works well for location-based search. Search queries of other people are also interesting in aggregate—see Google's annual *ZeitGeist* feature, for instance.

Aside from search, what other apps might this type of approach work for? For example, would it be helpful to see the physical routes that other people have taken as they move through a location? Or, could you use the density (or scarcity) of social media as an interaction cue?

**Search for:**
Google
ZeitGeist

# Illustrating the value of uncertainty: Navigation without navigating

Look at the navigation screen in Figure 12.2. See how the path offered is a strikingly clear line: a direct instruction that this is the way you should go. Consider how the directions tell you precisely where, and after how far, you must turn left or right; the first step in the directions even urges us to *"use caution"* as walking directions are still unpolished.

Now remember how you approached this task before always-on mobile navigation was possible (assuming, that is, that you read this book before such a notion appears quaint!). You might have had a map, or a vague idea of where to go. Maybe you would have had to ask a bystander for help.

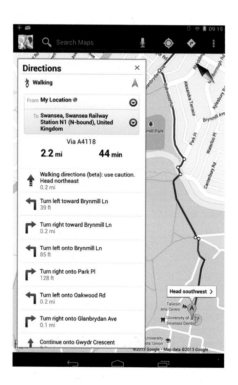

Figure 12.2 Google maps, showing walking directions.

Regardless of the source, these navigation cues would have been merely a guide, a suggestion you were free to ignore, and you'd have been able to vary the chosen path if you wanted to. In actual fact, on the particular route shown in Figure 12.2, a few meters from the suggested path, is a beautiful botanical garden. If you were using the mobile mapping tool, would you have been looking around, seen the sign, and decided to walk in and take a look, or would you be focused on the directions, and on getting there in time?

## Design Challenge
### *Other than the orthodox?*

Matt was walking through central London, near the popular tourist area of Covent Garden. Suddenly he heard a strange mantra: *"anyone lost, or in need of information."* Looking around he saw a bowler-hatted man standing near a tree, a bag of maps at his side. Over and over again, the man called out, in the exaggerated vocal style of a British street newspaper vendor: *"annnnnyoneeeee loooost, or in need of informaaation."*.

It was delightful, a little eccentric, and so different from the other source of direction Matt had at hand—a map app.

Can you think ways of disrupting other well-worn design frameworks to bring a smile to your user's face?

The three of us—along with colleagues—have been thinking about different approaches to pedestrian navigation for over a decade. Rather than coming up with new ways to bring ever more precise instructions into the device, though, we've been trying to allow, or even prompt people to experience more of the world while they navigate.

*Ontrack*, for example, helped people reach a destination by panning the music they were listening to in the direction they should travel. In trials of the system, it worked well at getting people to their destination with just music to navigate. But the full potential for new navigation approaches like this is perhaps shown by the experience of one participant, who spent a long time wandering around in a seemingly undirected way. Afterwards, when asked about this behavior, the participant saw it not, as the researchers initially did, as a failure to navigate effectively, but as a pleasant experience of being gently guided by the prototype and savoring the feeling.

Think, now, of how this attitude to navigation might have affected a recent journey you've taken. Did you experience your surroundings, or were you aiming to get from A to B without hassle? Of course, there are times and places where you are in a hurry and need straightforward directions, but at other times it might be quite pleasant to experience the world, heads up, in the same way as this participant did.

## Design Pointer

Giving rigid, efficiently direct directions to a user can be a perfect fit in many cases—when we're in a hurry, or in an emergency, for example. However, providing your users with more flexible help can let them truly embrace their surroundings.

More recently we've been thinking about navigation that is even less restrictive. Look back to the navigation instructions in Figure 12.2. The chosen path goes straight through a public park, but offers no hint that there are many other routes you might take. Using the current mobile system, you might take another path if you dare, but the device will put all its effort into getting you back to the "correct" route as soon as it can. How might this design be adapted to allow more exploration and flexibility, but still make sure you reach your goal?

One of our designs uses gentle vibration from the phone to guide you towards your destination. Point casually in the general direction of your goal and your phone vibrates; point away and the vibration stops. Rather than just simple direction cueing, though, we were careful to give the user a sense of the freedom they had to explore, of the potential to take control of the route and engage with the world rather than the

There's Not an App for That | Inspired by Uncertainty

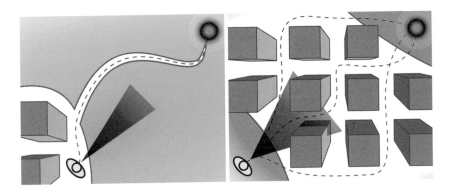

Figure 12.3 A more exploratory approach to navigation. Left: a narrow vibration area indicates that there are few path choices available. Right: a wider zone hints at the possibilities for exploration.

phone. So, the area that the vibration was active in expands or contracts based on the number of path choices around where the user is standing. When the choice is small, feedback is a narrow area; when there are many paths a wider area vibrates (see Figure 12.3).

We trialed this new system in the same area that is shown in the traditional map in Figure 12.2. Like *Ontrack*, it was effective in getting people to their destination. But people using the system were able to use their own intuition and instincts to decide which of the many path options to take. We also found that people enjoyed the experience and felt that it was good to be able to explore—they were able to combine both the technology and what they could see in the environment to pick a path. They were reassured by the vibration, but not controlled by it.

These examples illustrate how sometimes it might be better not to give a full, precise, and direct picture on a screen of what the device might think people want to do. While there will of course be situations when accuracy is vital, as designers we should design to make the most of the flexibility, adaptability, and uncertainty that people oftentimes enjoy.

In our navigation system we used vibration feedback. However, it would be equally viable to present the information on an easily glanceable screen-based display, with a narrow or wide arrow displayed that points in the approximate direction, for instance. Using a display would also work to provide a quick summary of social media posts related to the area, helping the user find new "hot spot" places to socialize or explore, perhaps.

In all of these cases, what's important is that we're supporting the ability of users to let go of the device's control and look around to decide what to do or where to go for themselves.

## Finding your own way

We began in Chapter 10 by looking at ways to move away from more rigid interaction designs. In the past two chapters we have seen how both messiness and uncertainty can benefit our users in ways that you might not expect. For example, navigation seems an ideal candidate for visual, screen-based instructions—following a route is simple when looking at a screen. However, embracing other senses and ways of giving feedback can let our users feel less intruded upon. Imagine you're exploring a beautiful foreign city—would you prefer to be given exact instructions, or be given the freedom to explore, but safe in the knowledge that you could find your way eventually?

The best way to go forward is to use these examples as starting points for your own design thinking. One way to start could be to think about your own usage of these tools—use a navigation device in a place that you already know very well, for example. What do you see around you that isn't expressed on the screen? What is on the screen that prompts you to look around? (Figure 12.4). After this, reflect on your current designs regardless of whether they are for location apps or other services, and list the ways in which you could support your users in flexibility and exploration by giving them less, not more, information.

Figure 12.4 Driving out of Gregynog (the place we begin our exploration of performance in the next chapter) our navigation system wants us to drive through a locked gate. The real route is to the left. Sometimes it is best to find your own way...

## Resources

One future without the uncertainty of rock climbing is given in [1]. Our work on navigation without the need to know exactly where to go is manifested in various articles, including the *Questions not Answers* technique [2], *Ontrack* [3], and a summary of several tactile-hinted exploration approaches [4].

[1] Schöning J, Panov I, Keßler C. No vertical limit - conceptual LBS design for climbers. Inst Geoinformatics 2007.

[2] Jones M, Buchanan G, Harper R, Xech P-L. Questions not answers: A novel mobile search technique. In: Proceedings of the SIGCHI Conference on Human Factors in Computing Systems; ACM; 2007. pp. 155–8. http://dx.doi.org/10.1145/1240624.1240648.

[3] Jones M, Jones S, Bradley G, Warren N, Bainbridge D, Holmes G. Ontrack: Dynamically adapting music playback to support navigation. Pers Ubiquitous Comput 2008;12(7):513–25. http://dx.doi.org/10.1007/s00779-007-0155-2.

[4] Robinson S, Jones M, Williamson J, Murray-Smith R, Eslambolchilar P, Lindborg M. Navigation your way: From spontaneous independent exploration to dynamic social journeys. Pers Ubiquitous Comput 2012;16(8):973–85. http://dx.doi.org/10.1007/s00779-011-0457-2.

# CHAPTER 13

## Problem 4

## FROM PRIVATE AND PERSONAL TO PUBLIC AND PERFORMANCE

### WHAT'S THE PROBLEM?

*Performing* is a part of everyday life—we are used to taking part in interesting scenes played out while we socialize, work, and relax. We interact *publicly*, together, sometimes in loud, extravagant ways, sometimes more subtly.

Today's mobiles, in contrast, are *personal* technologies that were originally designed for *private* interactions.

### WHY SHOULD YOU TACKLE IT?

Many current apps can turn us from being performers to being spectators, drawn to the periphery. Even when we want to be in the thick of the action, interacting with our devices can break the flow. There are opportunities, then, in ensuring that our designs accommodate the performances of everyday life.

Instead of simply designing to get out of the way of performances, there are also exciting possibilities to use mobiles as props and platforms for public, visible, and engaging social interactions.

# KEY POINTS

- We perform together, taking on different roles depending on context.

- Our apps are good at helping us tell our stories or have fast back-and-forth banter with *remote* partners.

- What makes them good for these sorts of interactions can result in users being drawn away from engaging with other people who are in the *same* place.

- Designs to keep people in the flow of togetherness can bring improvements.

- Interesting new ideas for togetherness through spatial social interaction are emerging from research labs.

# Introduction

Every year we take our final year undergraduate students to a beautiful historic country house—Gregynog—set amongst the rolling hills of mid-Wales. As well as it being an opportunity for the students to give presentations on their software design projects and hear research talks, it's a lovely way for our community to build relationships and understand each other better. And an important way these essentials happen is, of course, through play and being playful, together.

After the serious business of the day, the "pub" in the house is the stage for large and smaller group gatherings:

**The pub quiz**: A team of five or six cluster closely around tables while the quiz queen (as she styles herself) challenges them with questions that range in topic from brainy to banal. Mobiles are banned, with anyone daring to even touch their handset being publicly censured by loud calls and pointing fingers from the other teams. Not that many people are tempted to turn to Google or Bing: much of the fun in the game is seeing what your teammates know; not being sure of what the right answer is; or, even wittily thinking up an answer when you know you don't know the correct one.

The banter within the small teams plays out to the larger group, too. An answer spoken too loudly leads to the rest of the group collectively (and exaggeratedly) "ssshing"; conversely, synchronized silence can help the group, perhaps, eavesdrop an answer from a team nearby. Then, there's the shouted red-herring wrong answer, spoken out purposefully in the hope that another team will overhear and write it down.

**Small group games**: Later, the bigger group breaks into smaller clusters and chats, drinks, and plays a variety of games. Two stuck out the last time we were in Gregynog—an oversized version of *Jenga*, and an hour-long magic trick. *Jenga* is a game played with a stack of wooden bricks. In the Gregynog version these are large, each the size of a TV remote. When it is his or her turn, a player has to remove a brick, using just one hand, and place it on the top of the pile. At some point, the tower becomes highly unstable and a great fall ensues (as Figure 13.1 illustrates).

Both the player whose turn it is and the others watching are involved in a very engaging performance. Taking out a piece is acted out in many amusing ways: in intense concentration; teasingly, with pieces being prodded as the others look on nervously; or with powerful flair as a block is bullishly pulled in one movement. The audience provides encouraging or discouraging noises and gestures as potential blocks are tested; and, when the tower falls, there's a great shared moment of calamity and laughter.

Figure 13.1 The tower falls as the group performs: laughter, comments, and drinks pulled away just in time.

The group pictured in Figure 13.1 then went on to spend over an hour joined in a piece of impromptu magical theatre involving a deck of cards. The two protagonists sit opposite each other in the photo. The trick was simple: Matt shuffled a pack and then spread the cards face downward in front of Liam, who was then asked him to pick up a card and show it to the table. Matt then picked up another card, seemingly at random, which was higher or equal to Liam's card. This was repeated nearly 50 times, to Liam's disbelief. Three of the group saw what Matt was doing, and went on to collude with him by distracting the others at strategic moments or pretending to give Matt clues when none were needed. Others around the table were equally perplexed, though, and carefully studied the cards for trick marks or other hidden indicators, adding to Liam's confusion.

From the pub quiz to the magic trick, friends were fully immersed in a shared activity, having an opportunity to publicly express emotion and play out different roles or even be different characters (Matt is not known as a magician outside that co-created, spontaneous moment, for instance).

## Design Pointer

Think about the performance aspects of the vignettes above. Some of the elements we see are:

- People enjoying being fully together, in the moment;

- How the sense of togetherness is shaped in a dynamic, lively way;

- The importance of spontaneity and improvisation;

- The use of simple formats and interactions to platform the performances; and,

- The role of lightweight props as part of the performances.

Before we go further, consider some popular apps that might be used in social settings when people are together: *WhatsApp*, *Instagram*, web search, and so on. What aspects of their designs fit with the contexts we've seen? How could their designs be better shaped by further thought about what it is like to be really together, performing?

# Together moments

Gregynog is a particular place with a particular purpose, but it helps us illustrate common activities seen in many other places and times. There are a multitude of occasions when we come together to do something familiar that has a "script" with roles and narrative, but that also facilitates novelty and improvisation.

There are props and forms of gesture and language—some created specifically by the group over time, others more widely shared. Consider these three occasions that illustrate a spectrum of group interactions ranging from all-involving to near silence.

## Many-to-many performances: The festival dinner

For us, in the UK, a major festival meal is the Christmas Dinner, commonly consumed on December 25th between 1 p.m. and 3 p.m. (after which people leave the table to watch Her Majesty the Queen give her Christmas message on TV).

The table is festooned with the best cutlery, candlesticks, holly, and tinsel, and each place has a cracker (a brightly decorated trinket-filled tube that is pulled open with a bang). With plates bursting with food—some, like Brussels sprouts and red cabbage, hardly seen at other times in the year—the meal begins.

Crackers are pulled and each person has a go at telling one of the—usually awful—jokes they contain, pulls on a flimsy paper crown, and trades the novelty gift—perhaps a plastic ring or a pair of flimsy nail clippers—with their neighbors. The actors have their costumes and lines. People remember previous years—the Christmas pasts—and remind each other of all the good, bad, and interesting that family life involves.

As the meal progresses, and the first plates are cleared, games are played, charades being a favorite. A little later, the Christmas pudding—a dense fruitcake—is doused in brandy and set alight, paraded to the table with hearty singing.

## One-to-many performances: Fireworks

Just over a month before Christmas, we in the UK celebrate bonfire night—the night in 1605 when Guy Fawkes and his fellow conspirators were caught laying down gunpowder in the Palace of Westminster, in readiness to blow up the parliament when the King was in attendance. While many people do go to organized, large-scale events, there is still a strong tradition of doing it yourself in your back garden. You can buy boxes of neighborhood-friendly—that is, less noisy and dangerous—fireworks to set off in front of your family and friends.

Again, there are props, a script, and roles to be played out. First, give the sparklers—long sticks coated in aluminum that fizz with fire when lit—to the party. Watch as they trace light shapes in the air, perhaps spelling out their names. Responsible adults repeat the familiar *"be careful"* and *"don't touch the hot end"* to the youngest ones, and teenagers taunt their parents with daringly close encounters with their siblings.

Then, it's on to *"stand well back"* as one of the party takes on the role of lighting the main fireworks. Each one is carefully placed and then lit with taper. As the fuse spits sparks, there's the mock panic run back to safety, and the anticipation of the audience. As the firework phuts as it shoots toward the sky, they speak out the lines expected of them, like *"oooh,"* *"ahhh,"* or *"that's a nice one,"* to please or tease the firework master.

## Quiet performance: At a movie

From the dinner table with its free-for-all interaction, to the fireworks show with its one-to-many, firework-lighter to audience interactions, let's look in at one last together moment. But, this time, while there are lots and lots of people together—maybe several hundred—they sit, on the whole, in silence. Perhaps, though, these people have the profoundest of shared experiences.

They are sitting through a movie that is touching their emotions deeply. Matt can still remember the feeling of being in a cinema in Cambridge, in 1994, watching *Schindler's List*, the story of Nazi brutality contrasted to the heroism and humanity of Oskar Schindler, who worked to save Polish Jews from death. At different points in the film, the audience's silence held sadness, tension, anger, and joy. Occasionally a quiet sniff or murmur from someone led to tears, or a nervous cough would hang in the air. And, then, as the movie closed, the credits watched to the end, the lights now up, the audience sat in shock, quietly.

## Design Challenge

Think about the deep connections and audience "interactions" during the cinema event described above. In what ways could mobile user experiences lead to such reflection and emotional impact?

In this sort of movie, there's no tweeting, texting, or checking of email. Not only is using a mobile in a cinema difficult—your neighbors will be annoyed and the owners may evict you—but there's an alternative technology, the large screen, that engages you. It moves you not in 140 characters or small bursts of content, but through a long—and, as in *Schindler's List*—perhaps painful narrative that demands attention, even when you want to look away. You certainly connect with others watching with you, though; not by sharing your critiques or comments from your mobile, but in the sighs, coughs, and silences.

## Design Challenge

Think about a together moment you've recently experienced, for example a large family get together or a Halloween party:

- What were the "scenes" of the performance—its beginning, middle, and end—and how were transitions made between them?

- What roles did you observe?

- What props were needed to keep the action flowing or inject more interaction?

Did you use your mobile during the event? If so, did you use different apps at different points, or when you were playing different roles? How many times did your app usage push you out of the action? How did it enhance your experience?

Imagine a new form of mobile technology that could have really added to the performance. What would it be? How would you and the others around you interact with it? What would it help you do?

# Gathering around big technology makes us feel less small

As we saw above, movie theaters, play houses, and concert halls are ways for lots of people to come together, to sit usually amongst many strangers, but to feel connected. However, most people spend more time in front of a television than the performers' proscenium.

In a fascinating research paper from a team at Fudan University, Shanghai, the authors uncover the uptake of Internet TV watching in China. The appetite for watching what they call "new media TV"—that is, TV that is Internet accessible on PCs, tablets, and mobiles—is voracious, with the main service, *PPTV*, having in 2013 over 200 million subscribers.

Most of the people they interview, who are the younger generation, say they rarely sit down to watch "old TV." This finding is in line with other studies that have shown that teenagers and young adults gravitate to online watching, finding traditional TV too inflexible.

When the researchers asked about the occasions when these digital natives do sit down with the old technology, they find the experiences are seen as deeper, more emotional, or higher quality than when they are plugged into their own, new media devices.

So, the team saw that people wanted to gather for big live events like sports or public parades, one of their respondents noting the impact of the larger display on such viewing: *"The good thing about it is, since the screen is bigger, um... it feels more immersive and attractive than the smaller ones."*

While this form of watching is perhaps motivated by practicalities—broadcast TV for live events in China is higher quality than streamed, and screens in sitting rooms are bigger—the interviews also highlight emotional pulls to shared experiences.

Several people talked about using the old TV as a way of accompanying others—what was on the TV at the time being less important than who was on the sofa. Others were nostalgic about a past when they did watch together and made opportunities to recreate those special feelings from the past:

*"It has been rare for me to watch TV anymore since I went to college… So that kind [of] feeling, like watching TV in a stealthy way as what we did when we were kids, is gone. When I got home and watched TV in my fresh and sophomore years, I felt so good about it even when just watching ads. It was very satisfying, so TV watching has become a sweet childhood memory."*

## Not everyone has together moments

We are very conscious in writing about the fun of being together at Christmas, the fireworks party, or music events, that there are lots of people who would crave such company but are left lonely. In the West, for example, with an aging population and the increasing fragmentation of families, with children moving far away from the homes, there's the significant, silent sadness of the elderly.

Here it seems that there is great role for designing to overcome loneliness. Current mobile-based services can provide connection, of course, but the mainstream ones like Twitter, Google+, or Facebook have, perhaps, features that can have an adverse effect on isolation of these types of people.

So, imagine you are an 80-year-old, housebound, and you see all the parties, holidays, and sports others are up to on Facebook. How does that make you feel? It might be like Christmas Day every day, but not in a good way—the awareness of your alone-ness heightened. What if you comment on lots of posts and hear nothing back, like this man, Eddie, who, *"…initiates communication by sending messages to others or commenting on status updates…constantly trying to stay aware of others and stay connected"*, but his *"…communication is most often not reciprocated by his family members"*?

How could we do better, then?

The *EATProbe*, developed at Georgia Tech, was used to look at how to support people who live on their own and often eat alone. The researchers were motivated by the importance of such commensal—eating together—activities for bonding, creating identities, and other social gluing. While cooking, a user could glance across at a touch display and see the status of a small group of their similarly "home alone" friends. Each person could set their own status to be one of six, from *"no status"* to *"eating in – cleaning."*

Three features of the probe stick out in terms of helping to increase connected-ness rather than amplify the loneliness:

- The smaller, focused group each person connected with is important; everyone in the mini social network could empathize with each other's experience of eating alone.

- The background, ambient nature of the display, the tablet perching in the kitchen rather than actively held in a hand, anticipating a response, takes the pressure off people feeling they should interact or worrying why no one has responded.

- Finally, because the status updates were around a specific, usually time-constrained occasion, the researchers saw that it could help friends coordi-nate. Knowing you are doing something at the same time as someone else can promote other forms of interacting (like phoning them at the end of a meal), or just allow that sense of "accompanying" we touched on earlier to grow. Status updates asynchronous to your real life, in contrast, could make you feel you've missed out, or are not part of the party.

# Performance at the periphery

While people tend not to take out their mobiles during a movie or live theatre, as we've seen in other parts of the book, from elections of popes to romantic dinners, the mobile often makes an appearance. Apart from *disconnecting* by doing nonevent things, like checking their emails, what are people up to when they tweet, post a picture, and the like in these situations?

Often, they *are* caught up in some form of performance, connecting, showing off, empathizing, and playing roles with others. But these others are not physically with them; they are not at the same event or in the same place.

Let's return to the sitting room and TV viewing. Three computer scientists from Lincoln in the UK have done an analysis of what has been referred to as "sofalising"—the use of Twitter or some other social media when watching a TV show.

**Search for:**
*Sofalising*

The research team applied computer algorithms to analyze nearly 20,000 tweets during two popular BBC TV shows. One of them, *Question Time,* is a panel show where politicians and other notables answer topical questions posed from the live audience. The other, *Strictly Come Dancing*, is rather more fun and lighthearted—at least to us. Again, it is a live show where celebrities are paired with professional ballroom dancers and compete over several weeks to woo the judges and voting public, hoping to win this glamorous talent contest.

These two distinct formats produced patterns that had similarities and differences in those tweeting from home:

- In both shows, people connected to the guests using their Twitter IDs and by retweeting celebrity posts, the researchers suggesting that this allowed people to increase their visibility and status within the network of tweeters.

- Viewers also sent in their own opinions and comments, and had back-and-forth interactions with other people watching. The dance show led to more of the first sort of tweet, the panel show more of the second.

In reflecting on the results of this social network analysis, the researchers also noted the interesting way small groups of tweeters form subnetworks in the big network graphs. As they put it, *"The metaphor of inviting someone to 'share your sofa' through tweet mentions and retweets is a compelling one."*

## Design Challenge

The researchers in this tweeting study were led to wonder how to design a service in a way to better support such sofa sharing. What would you do? How would you invite a group of fellow tweeters (or other social service users) to join the conversation and then experience the banter in a richer way than is currently possible?

Harvesting and analyzing posts on a large scale is very much in vogue for those interested in understanding and designing for the increasingly mobile-mediated digital socializing at or about events. In another study, by a group at Microsoft Research and Rutgers University, different types of event were considered: from a big musical festival—*Bonnaroo*—to mass media events (like a *WikiLeaks* breaking news story).

This time, the team wanted to know if they could identify variations in what "ordinary" tweeters did at the event or from the comfort of their homes, compared to journalists, bloggers and big organizations:

- They found that there was a higher proportion of interaction from ordinary tweeters in events they could directly relate to, like the musical festival, and more from the professionals on the mass media events.

- The ordinary individuals asked more questions in posts than organization tweeters did.

- These individuals also used more emotional and personal language like *"awesome," "us,"* and *"excited."*

What both of these studies and many others show is:

- Many people do enjoy and find meaning in jumping in and out of the digital—connecting with remote others—when doing something else, like partying or watching a show.

- The activity allows people to express their emotions and provoke and contribute to discussions.

- It also helps them feel part of the event by being with others in the cloud, even getting "close" to the main characters such as the dancing show celebrities, who are all chatting about the same thing.

People do connect and perform via devices, then, expressing themselves in diverse ways. The problem we want you to think about is that they are doing this at the cost of the performances they could be having with those right next to them. Think, then, about the people they are actually with—the ones sitting down next to them on their sofa, the dog on their lap, or those friends chatting around the table with them at the pub.

## Design Challenge

How might we design services that support people when they are performing together, in situations like the "together moments" we sketched earlier?

## Alternative perspective

While we've just looked critically at apps that push a person out of the local action, there are other ways of looking at what's going in a more positive way:

- People mix private and public activities in many ways successfully: think of a group of friends sitting together for brunch on a Saturday morning. Some may be browsing magazines and newspapers, looking up from time to time to chat.

- People can bring their interactions with remote others into a local performance—reading out comments from another tweeter to their friends sitting next to them, for example.

Our aim is not to stop people doing things that they are enjoying or find useful! What we do want you to think about is where current designs interrupt or don't fully fit in to something that could be even more fulfilling. We also want to stimulate more adventurous uses of technologies to support performances when people are physically together.

## Leaning in

In the last section, the "sofalising" performances we considered might make the user feel they are in the thick of the crowd in the cloud, but in terms of those around them, they *lean back*, out of the action, to compose a picture or tweet a message.

The first straightforward way of promoting more of a *lean-in* design attitude, where mobiles push us to the center of the action close by, rather than driving us to the periphery, is to reduce the amount of time it takes to complete the mobile action.

Think of a simple case: how many times have you had to wait while a friend fiddles with their phone to find the app, start it up, open the camera, adjust the filters or the flash, and then take that *spontaneous* moment? Picture the frustration of one of the party round the *Jenga* table, described earlier, desperately trying to get the camera set up for the tumble and missing it by milliseconds, only able to take the less dynamic picture of the clutter of blocks on the floor. It's hard to convince the party to play it again, just for the photo.

The eyepiece wearables like Google's *Glass* offer one answer—just tap the side of the glasses or say a command and the moment is captured. But in Chapter 8 we've already considered some of the problems of such in your face mobiles. Other wearables, like smart watches with built-in cameras, might be better, as not only are they less obtrusive than eye-based devices, but the time to lift up your wrist to frame and take a photo should also be shorter than with a pocketable mobile. However, the quality of the resulting shot might be lower either due to the precision of the watch's camera or the ability to frame the photo in a satisfying way with the relatively impoverished "viewfinder" likely available on such devices.

In Chapter 9 we also discussed using context awareness cleverness to give glanceable *outputs*, the device anticipating what you might want to see and thereby reducing interaction time. Similarly, we can envisage the device anticipating what you want to *do*.

So, imagine picking up your phone and the camera is already active—when you hold it still the picture is taken and then automatically sent or uploaded. Such automated interactions are attractive, but in designing them it is important to make sure users are fully in control of what is going to be done in autopilot mode, and that they are quickly able to preempt and take back control if they want. In the following box there are some other examples of how anticipating interactions with apps can improve user experiences.

## Strategies for speeding up app selection

People have lots of apps on their phones. In one study published in 2013, the average number found on participants' devices was 177. With more and more apps, and higher spec devices, this number is likely to grow dramatically over the next several years.

There are a number of approaches that can be easily implemented by handset providers. Some are automated—like making sure there is a quick way to see the most frequently used or most recently used apps. Users themselves can also be given tools to organize apps into useful groups and screens.

A team from Carnegie Mellon University has investigated a sophisticated predictive approach to try to beat these conventional methods. They deploy three types of input to work out which apps are most likely to be needed and to then display these on the home screen. The categories of input are:

- **User related**: Ranging from GPS to get a fix on the user's current location to what's in the user's schedule and call or SMS log.

- **Environment related**: From sensing what the battery status is, to the availability of networks and amount of light in the environment.

- **App related**: What the user is currently doing, and what apps are in the background.

By using information about what apps the user actually selects in these different contexts, the researchers were able to train a predictive model to make a guess about what would help the user as they take out the mobile.

Their experiments show that their approach is 8% more accurate than the second-most accurate strategy (organizing the home screen by using data on the most frequently used apps). While 8% does not sound a great improvement, given the number of times people take out their phone to select an app every day, the reduction in hunting time this brings can significantly improve overall user experience.

This study acts as a reminder of the value of not overlooking changes that can make incremental differences: designs that make small positive differences in interactions that happen lots and lots of times might have more substantial impacts than the grand schemes we might be more attracted to as designers.

# Leaning in to research discussions

One of our colleagues, Emma James, has also been thinking about how to keep the flow of a group performance while exploiting the advantages of mobile technology. Her interest lies in research and learning interactions—think about the group discussions that lecturers might have with students or a research team might engage in over coffee, or a workgroup brainstorming some new product.

One of her systems, *Audio Gift*, is aimed at helping groups of people chatting together to tag and take bits of the conversation they think are interesting and useful to review later. Take a look at the image below that illustrates the interactions:

- Each person in the group is wearing a bracelet that contains a touch and gesture sensor.

- When one of the friends hears something they think might be important, they gesture, putting the hand out into the center of the group (highlighted, lower left).

- This gift-giving results in a snippet of the recent conversation being made available to all of the others round the table.

- Anyone else, triggered by this visible, obvious action, might take the content for their personal collection. They do this by tapping their bracelet, as the highlight in the lower right picture illustrates.

- Later on, individually or together, they can listen to the bits of conversation that were collected during the chat.

A system like Audio Gift could be implemented simply by using Bluetooth to connect wristbands to users' mobiles in the same way popular fitness bracelets such as *Fitbit* communicate with phone apps. In another of Emma's prototypes, though, everything is done on a standard mobile phone itself. Called *Moments*, it is a group discussion tool, designed to make the mobile always ready to capture anything someone thinks is important:

- Placed face down, when the phone is picked up (detected using the proximity sensor), the system immediately begins recording audio and video.

- When the phone is put down again, recording automatically stops.

- A filmstrip view accessible from the app shows the different research moments that have been captured, and provides easy ways for any of these to be shared by email or social network.

Simple capture tools like Moments using lightweight interactions and video with audio have three advantages over other approaches such as text or speech dictation:

- Firstly, the combination of images and audio make them potentially useful in a range of situations—from meetings talking about a physical object like a prototype product to those discussing written documents. Textual notes—be they typed or dictated—involve a lot more effort to explain some rich object or complex idea.

- Secondly, the combination of video and audio provides contextual metadata that a person can use later to interpret the actual reminder or note that was recorded. So, if you are capturing a discussion about a new product you've designed, for example, the recording may also show who is sitting round the table, what time of day or year it is, and even the mood of your fellow workers.

- Finally, firing up a keypad on the app, or speaking out a note in a mechanical machine voice, are sure ways of interrupting the flow of the group conversation.

## Design Challenge

There are many note taking and reminder apps, such as Google's *Keep* (below).

Use your favorite one next time you are in a meeting or socializing. How does its design keep you in the flow of the activity, and in what ways does it push you to the periphery?

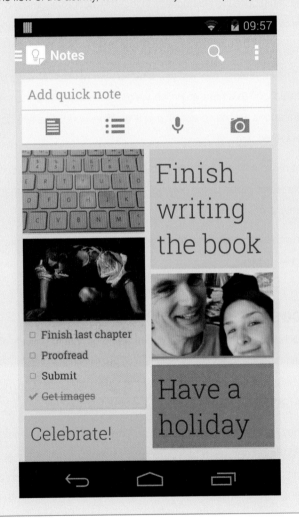

# Out of the shadows and onto the stage

In the last two sections we've seen:

- The ways mobiles currently support together performances for people who are *not in the same physical location.*

- How we can reduce the interruptions in together performances by designing to keep the user in the sorts of dynamic flows we sketched in our example together moments.

Now it is time to go further. In the next two chapters we will look at ways of extending the fulfilling interactions that happen *online* via mobile devices to enhance the physically together performances we are so adept at in the *offline* world. The two design *Opportunities* we'll explore, then, are:

- Ways to make mobiles become part of existing performances (such as dinner table parties or group game playing) rather than a technology that simply captures what is going on.

- Using mobiles to create new forms of social performance that are extravagant and highly visible.

# Resources

We've been talking in this chapter about encouraging people to actively engage with each other when they are together. TV watching used to be one of the core ways families and friends socialized together, and we looked at how digital practices might be affecting this; for the background see [1].

Not everyone has people close by, though (like Eddie, who we met earlier [2]), and we looked at the *EATProbe* approach to reducing social isolation [3]. The paper also has some interesting insights into the value of services that provide focused social networks. The *New Yorker* article [4] illustrates why these approaches may be better than systems that tell you about all of your contacts, regardless of your context.

The first approach to increasing social interactions we called *leaning in.* We gave several examples of speeding up interactions [5] and making them as lightweight as possible [6].

[1] Wang Q, Ding X, Lu T, Gu N. Digitality and materiality of new media: Online TV watching in China. In: Proceedings of the SIGCHI Conference on Human Factors in Computing Systems; ACM; 2012. pp. 347–56. http://dx.doi.org/10.1145/2207676.2207724.

[2] Karimi A, Neustaedter C. From high connectivity to social isolation: Communication practices of older adults in the digital age. In: Proceedings of the ACM 2012 Conference on Computer Supported Cooperative Work Companion; ACM; 2012. pp. 127–30. http://dx.doi.org/10.1145/2141512.2141559.

[3] Grevet C, Tang A, Mynatt E. Eating alone, together: New forms of commensality. In: Proceedings of the 17th ACM International Conference on Supporting Group Work; ACM; 2012. pp. 103–6. http://dx.doi.org/10.1145/2389176.2389192.

[4] Konnikova M. How Facebook makes us unhappy. 2013. Retrieved from http: //www.newyorker.com/online/blogs/elements/2013/09/the-real-reason-facebook-makes-us-unhappy.html.

[5] Shin C, Hong J-H, Dey AK. Understanding and prediction of mobile application usage for smart phones. In: Proceedings of the 2012 ACM Conference on Ubiquitous Computing; ACM; 2012. pp. 173–82. http://dx.doi.org/10.1145/2370216.2370243.

[6] Thom E, Jones M. Give and take: Audio gift giving to support research practices. In: CHI '13 Extended Abstracts on Human Factors in Computing Systems; ACM; 2013. pp. 235–40. http://dx.doi.org/10.1145/2468356.2468399.

# CHAPTER 14

## Opportunity 4.1
## MOBILES AS PROPS

## WHAT'S THE OPPORTUNITY?

Instead of seeing mobiles as things that get in the way of or simply record performances, let's look at how they can facilitate socializing together.

## WHY IS IT ATTRACTIVE?

We are used to and effective at recruiting all sorts of "to hand" objects to support our social performances. Some are designed for specific types of interaction (such as the cards and *Jenga* bricks we saw in the last chapter). Others are imaginatively appropriated—for instance, we pick up salt and pepper pots and serviettes to explain a historical battle over a family meal, and arrange shells on the sand to spell our friends' names.

Almost everyone has a mobile—it is natural, then, to think about how they might be used to support together performances.

## WHAT ARE THE CHALLENGES?

People are protective of their mobile phone: just ask someone to let you use their device and see their response. So, designing where mobiles are collectively passed around or put together is a challenge. However, with multiple shared tablets and other devices beginning to be seen in some people's homes and offices, this may be less of a problem in the future.

## KEY POINTS

- Mobiles can be used to support the sorts of together moments we discussed earlier, acting as conversation starters and as props that lead to enjoyable interactions including storytelling and playful teasing.

- People can collaborate by connecting their mobiles together for shared interactions.

- More adventurously, seeing mobiles as shared rather than individual resources leads to interesting new forms of interaction.

## WHAT DO YOU THINK?

Can you think of a situation where you have used your mobile as a key prop in a performance you've created with your friends or colleagues? Was it a one-to-many performance with you using the mobile to orchestrate a display for your spectators, or was it a many-to-many event with the whole group using your mobile or their set of mobiles together?

# Introduction

The motivation for the sorts of techniques we saw at the end of the last chapter is to speed up interactions, promoting the user to return to action as quick as possible, fully involved rather than a spectator.

What about using our mobiles as part of a together performance as illustrated in the *Capturing the moment together* box below?

## Capturing the moment together

The rise of the "selfie," pictures taken of groups with one person—usually the one with the longest arm—holding out the camera, illustrates a case where one mobile can be used together in a fun, engaging way. In the picture above, as Simon held out his arm, the rest of us squinted at the screen, adjusted our pose, and gave instructions to Simon to better orientate his picture.

Moving from one phone to many, a number of researchers have been looking at how spectators with camera phones can capture performances together. One group from Sweden investigated the *Instant Broadcasting System*, a tool that allows a team of amateur camera operators, each with their mobile phone, to stream video to a vision mixer operator (VM) who selects and mixes views to create a live broadcast. This collaborative video can be streamed live over the Internet or, in the case of their study, beamed to a large public screen at the event.

The prototype studied by the researchers allowed the VM to communicate with their three camerapeople by text messaging, asking them to, for example, take up new positions for the broadcast. The VM could also send buzzes to any operator, activating their camera phone's vibration motor to prompt them to action. When an operator was "on air" a little red dot appeared on their display.

During the trial, held at a Swedish music festival, the red-dot lightweight way of communication between the VM and camerapeople was preferred over the more intrusive text messaging. This is not surprising given what we've been saying elsewhere about keeping people focused on the action rather than having to attend to some task that isn't what they are there for (such as checking what the VM is saying to them via text message).

Reflecting on their study findings, the researchers had two further insights that can help us think about how to design technology aimed at groups wanting to create an experience together:

- The first is that unlike professional camerapeople, the amateurs were there to enjoy themselves, and so any interactions with the mobiles should enhance that enjoyment rather than simply be optimized for the best, shared performance.

- Secondly, unlike professionals, there were times when members of the group got bored with what they were being asked to do by their VM, or simply wanted a break from being a cameraperson. Just as with some of the together moments we saw earlier, like the family dinner or the magic trick, we should think about building mobile props that can be put down or withdrawn from without this choice by one or more people destroying the dynamic of the group.

## Putting it into practice: The app for conferring

Patrick Oladimeji and Jennifer Pearson from Swansea University built a prop to encourage people to confer more at conferences. Built for a key human-computer interaction conference attended by around 3,000 people, the design riffed off the fun of selfies and a popular game, *Bingo*.

The image below illustrates the interaction—before the conference the user can enter nine names of people they want to catch up with at the event. When they meet them they take a selfie. Whenever the four corners, a horizontal line, or the whole grid is completed, the user is rewarded with an app animation. Users can also share the photo grid easily across their social networks.

**Search for:**
*CHI Bingo*

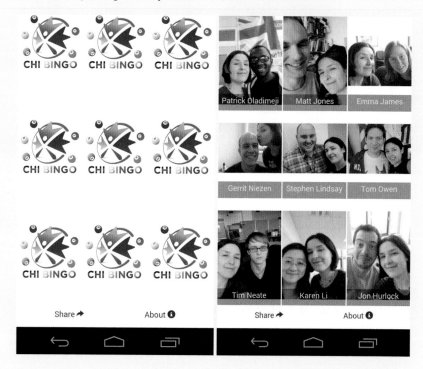

In the past, it was common to see people asking strangers to help them take a picture. The bystander would be handed the owner's camera and some good-natured banter would ensue as the co-opted photographer would try to figure out how to use it. The picture would be taken with smiles and thanks, and possibly reciprocation, with the bystander now posing for their own snap.

As we saw above, now, groups or individuals stand together while one holds their mobile phone at arm's length and the picture is grabbed in a split second. No interaction with others needed.

Of course there is nothing to stop people still handing over their mobile, but this is less likely both due to the ease of framing a selfie, and the special status of mobiles—handing over a camera is one thing, your mobile, another.

How could you design to reintroduce friendly stranger interactions? What if they took a photo of you with *their* mobile, and it was quickly sent to you (and deleted from their device)?

---

Let's return to two of the together moments we used as starting points at the beginning of the last chapter—the block game of *Jenga* and the magical fun centered around the pub card game. In both of these cases, there was a collection of relatively simple objects—wooden blocks and 52 playing cards—that were props for subtle, rich performances.

The games, of course, had a structure and purpose, but their value was also in the way they facilitated chats, laughter, side discussions, and the like. These side effects were, perhaps, more enjoyable than the actual games themselves.

Both of these activities *anchored* the socializing, too: holding the group of friends together but allowing some to bob out to the periphery of the activity, to return later. So, when we engage in this sort of fun, sometimes we can be really focused on the action in front of us; at other times we might sit back and take in the scene or chat to someone next to us.

## Design Challenge
### *Inviting interaction*

There are props that are placed in our shared spaces to entice us into engagement and social connection with others. So, along the seafront in Swansea, Simon and Matt's hometown, the local council recently installed an outdoor gym—every 10 meters or so, there's a piece of equipment that can be swung off, cycled, or pumped. Lycra-clad serious types compete, but young children and their parents have fun too as they playfully mimic the keep-fit professionals.

These props don't demand interaction actively, but because of their accessibility and clever placing, successfully tempt many people in for laughter. How could a mobile service prompt people to pick it up and use it as a prop for socializing together?

## Design Pointer
### *The prop principles*

- Design to make your mobile service unobtrusive: let it be less important than the people and social interactions it facilitates.

- Design in a way that your mobile service can be an anchor to a social setting, holding the group together but allowing people to drift away and back to the action.

# Designing to encourage people to use their mobiles together

To help us think through what such mobile services might look like, let us take a look at some prototypes built by researchers where devices takes on similar roles to the playing cards and *Jenga* blocks.

We've already encountered one of these systems briefly—the *Pass-Them-Around* photo sharing prototype. We used it to inspire thinking about the value of messiness or clutter in design through the use of multiple devices (see Chapter 11).

Pass-Them-Around is actually part of a bigger picture, being just one of the applications the Nokia researchers built to explore what they call a *Social and Spatial Interactions* platform. They sum up the trend that motivates their work by saying, *"In this paradigm shift, collocated users engage in collaborative activities using their devices, thus going from personal-individual towards shared-multi-user experiences and interactions."*

With the application, groups sit around a table each with a mobile in hand. The design metaphor is that the mobile they hold is a stack of individual photos: the users each grasp a set they want to share, much as friends in the past might have done with printed pictures, newly out of their mail-delivered envelopes.

Riffling through the photos on their devices, one user can perform a flick gesture on the touch screen and the photo slides across to their friend's device. (This works by employing a sophisticated positioning system built into each mobile that allows a device to know how it is orientated relative to others.)

The system also allows a more controlled passing around of photos where one user shares their set of photos by first sliding a photo to the person next to them, who then passes it on to the adjacent user's device, and so on. This process is very similar to one physical photo being handed round a group of friends to enjoy in turn.

**Search for:**
*Social and spatial interactions*

## Putting it into practice

The *Pass-Them-Around* prototype requires sophisticated ways of sensing where one device is positioned relative to the other using custom-built hardware. But work Gary did with a colleague a few years before the Nokia prototype shows that it is possible to build engaging photo sharing services with simpler, commercially available technologies.

In that system, a set of Personal Digital Assistants was connected over a wireless network. (This work was done a while before touch screen smartphones emerged commercially.) With the devices synchronized, the screens were shared, allowing anyone in the group of friends to broadcast the photo or image on their device to everyone else.

A user could become the ringmaster, or firework lighter, to use the analogy of another of our earlier together moments, by using a "floor control" method. We tested three different policies or methods to pass control from one user to another:

- **Using a direct token:** To take control, a user would request the control "token" from the person currently holding it. They kept control until it was given up.

- **The three-second rule:** The user with control would lose it if they did nothing for three seconds. When the floor was free, the first user to do something on their device would then be able to take control, losing it themselves if they were idle for three seconds.

- **No rule:** Everyone could interact at the same time.

The most effective protocol was the first one, with its explicit token. In the second case, we found that people did not know who currently had control, and ended up asking each other who was in charge and then requesting control. In this case, then, people re-created the direct token approach, manually. The third case invariably ended in chaos, but was also seen as the most fun!

We'll return to both the Pass-Them-Around prototype and our photo sharing system in Chapter 17. There, we move to consider how these shared interactions not only

There's Not an App for That | Mobiles as Props

illustrate a refreshing perspective, bringing messiness and performance to mobiles, but also promote an outward looking, less me-focused view on interaction.

As you read through this book and encounter inspiring or provocative new ways of looking at interaction, don't be put off if some of the prototypes involve new forms of hardware and software. Rather, think about how to implement some of them now. The flicking gesture of Pass-Them-Around is very neat, but our simple, more computer-centric token request approach worked well too.

## Design Pointer
### Simple forms lead to imaginative uses

LEGO—the toy that consists of small colored bricks—is a famous example of a prop that is very simple but can be used to create a multitude of diverse constructions. Similarly, playing card decks, such as the ones we used in our magic performance, have been appropriated for countless types of games varying in complexity (and, like LEGO can be used in the challenge of building card houses).

In a recent road trip taken by Simon, Matt, and five others, traveling in two cars, we used *WhatsApp* to create a fun shared game. Although we were journeying in convoy, there was competition as to who would arrive first. The passengers in one car teased those in the other and vice versa via a WhatsApp group, sometimes with attached photos, or using the shared map feature. When one car was out of sight of another, one group bluffed the other by sending comments or media that suggested they were somewhere further on than they actually were in the journey.

Like LEGO and the cards, one of the reasons why services like WhatsApp have been so successful is that they let users imaginatively adapt them to a myriad of purposes. Contrast this with, for example, more constrained services such as Google's now retired *Latitude*.

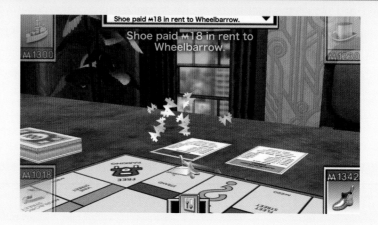

Board games are great family and group fun of course, but they are bulky, and if you are traveling it's hard to take lots of them with you. With mobiles like tablets, there's a solution—you can buy digital versions of the many popular ones, such as *Monopoly*.

While well designed and effective, without the physical elements, some of the aspects of gaming performance are lost. Matt can remember the fun he had, as a boy, hiding his money on his lap, tricking his brothers that he was bankrupt when he actually had two $500 bills still in play!

How could you enhance such tablet games by combining them with each player's mobile phone? Are there any other ways you could bring back some of the performance aspects of the traditional board game?

# Designing as if mobiles were public rather than private devices

In both of the photo sharing systems we've just seen, groups of friends hold onto their own devices, but see them as part of a collective resource. As we discussed in Chapter 11, the *Pass-Them-Around* prototype has other features that promote the shared surface perspective. Friends can, then, put their devices side by side to create a larger, collaborative screen.

But what about going even further, and getting people to really let go of the personal attachment to their mobile? What about getting people to think of their devices as really like the photos you pass around on paper; the playing cards you sometimes hold close to your chest and at other times throw down in front of others; or the *Jenga* blocks you push, pull, and place in the center of a shared pub table?

## Design Challenge
### *Can I use your mobile?*

What was your reaction when someone last asked you if they could borrow your phone to search for something, look up a map, or even send an email from your account?

If you are like us, you might have hesitated, even if the person asking you was a close friend. Do I want them seeing what I was last searching for or what's open in my browser windows? What if they see my other friends' instant messages?

What features would you add to your mobile device or app to allow it to be quickly switched from private to public mode?

A team of researchers from the UK and Denmark are exploring this freeing design notion, exploring what they call *Scrap Computing*. They want to see what sorts of services and apps might develop if you view tablets and phones as you would scraps of paper. Things you are happy to pick up, use, and then put down, share, and pass around.

To begin their exploration they carried out a study with family groups, getting them to play the game of "consequences." It's a simple and charming game, often played at those significant family together times we mentioned earlier, like the Christmas meal.

Each player has a piece of paper and begins by drawing a head of an imaginary person. They then fold the drawing over and pass their paper on to the person to their left or right. All other players do the same, the papers circling the group as the game unfolds. In the next round each player draws a body, adding to the picture without seeing what the head looked like. The game continues until the character is complete. At this point the papers are unfolded and there's usually a lot of laughter.

The researchers built a tablet app that facilitated the same interactions. Instead of the drawings being passed virtually, though—like with, say, popular networked games such as *Draw Something*—the actual tablets were handed over, in the same way as scraps of paper are.

As this was a scientific study, the team compared the user experiences of using paper and their scrap computing system. The tablet system was seen to be similar to the paper version in that it could be used in a way that did not disrupt the flow of the game (compare this to the sometimes clunky intrusions mobile interactions bring to social settings). They also found, though, that the drawings created on the tablets were richer in both originality and cohesiveness—the pictures made more sense—than those sketched on paper (as judged by experts).

Why was there more creativity? The researchers put this down to the mode of drawing on the tablet compared to the paper—people created with their fingers on the screen instead of pens and pencils on the paper. Finger painting, suggest the researchers, is a very unconstrained form of creativity that we learn to love early on as young children and continue to enjoy, say, when we as adults draw on steamed-up windows.

The increased cohesiveness of the pictures on the tablets might be explained by the "digital traces" each user left as they passed the tablet onto the next person. These allowed others to see what colors or line styles had been previously selected. In addition, unlike with the paper version, where folding was not always neatly or consistently done, the system always ensured that there was a small bit of the previous drawing visible.

The consequences game and scrap computing ideas we've just encountered highlight the benefits of providing "digital traces" to give hints to others about a previous user's intentions where devices are shared.

Look around your home at the scraps of paper lying around on kitchen tables, stacked in piles or stuck on a fridge door. In a shared home, what are the paper trails that help us make sense of these shared interactions: the handwriting, perhaps, the color of the ink, or even the paper chosen? Are things on the top the most important or recent? Is that piece of paper left by the kettle, the first thing you see as you prepare breakfast, something to pay attention to?

How can such shared physical information help us to think about what we might build into our scrap computing applications to support implicit between-person communication, especially in a world where there may be many "house" rather than "personal" mobiles lying around the home?

# From one precious personal device to multitudes of utensils

Go into your kitchen.

Just maybe you can find a special mug or eggcup—given to you when you were a small child—that *only* you use. Less likely, but possible, you'll open your cutlery draw and pull out the egg top cutter that your family think is an eccentric implement but for *you* is the only way to open the shell and expose the yolk. In contrast, most of the implements in our kitchens—from cutlery to cups, bowls to breadboards—are collectively used at our everyday mealtime performances.

We are sure to have personal devices at least in the mid-term future. However, they might be increasingly seen in the same way as we see that special eggcup or idiosyncratic egg-opener in the kitchen: something that is of sentimental value or particularly of use just for us. Meanwhile, we will see a multitude of nonpersonal devices scattered round our homes that might become ours for a moment, connecting to our personal or shared content through a cloud.

As designers we should start to anticipate a future where there are many mobile gadgets around our workplaces and homes, thinking of services that might be choreographed across them, and the forms of interaction that are going to deliver rich user experiences.

So far, we've seen how one person's device can be used by a group of people to have fun through the selfie. We then moved to look at examples where several personal devices are used together as a platform for social interaction. Finally, the tablet game we just considered helped us shift towards this utility view of mobiles, where together performances can be constructed by nonpersonal groups of devices.

The *Siftables* research team at MIT have taken this view a lot further by exploring what you can do if you have tens or hundreds of small displays that can be scattered in front of you or a group of your friends. Each of these Siftables is networked to the others, and can react to how it is placed relative to the rest.

The researchers have thought of lots of ways such a collection could be deployed in useful and playful ways. For example, instead of having to sort your photos on the small touch screen of your phone—tricky to do as an individual user, but even more unsuited to group interaction—why not use the Siftables? Each Siftable could show one picture, with the physical clustering organizing the digital albums, and with lots of people able to pick up, move, and group at the same time.

The Siftables research was commercialized as *Sifteo* cubes. Designer Roy Martens has used these to consider how multiple devices might interact with the music streaming service *Spotify*. In his concept prototype, illustrated below, there are a number of networked cube Sifteos that connect with the service and the portable loudspeaker (shown in the top left of the image):

- One cube—the one being held in the left hand in our picture—is the control cube. The user can scroll through the service's functions using the cube's touch screen.

- The other cubes can be used to represent playlists, artists, friends, and the like.

- Connecting a playlist (like "chill out," below) to the control cube starts the relevant music playing.

- Meanwhile, selecting the "similar artists" function on the control cube and then physically connecting several other "artist" cubes in sequence to it allows an interesting exploration of how one artist's music relates to another.

- In another interaction, shaking a Sifteo shuffles the music in a pleasingly direct way.

**Search for:**
*Roy Martens*
*Spotify*

There are clear practical benefits to making the digital physical in these ways. While it is exhilarating to think we have access to a seemingly infinite collection of photos or music in the cloud, it can become overwhelmingly frustrating to get, find, manip-ulate, or share. Multiple physical containers can alleviate the complexity, exploiting the abilities we've already touched on in Chapter 2 as adept physical beings.

However, there are other benefits too in terms of our desires to express who we are and to engage each other in social performances. Shelves full of books, DVD collections, photos on the sideboard, cushions on the sofa. In the physical world we have countless ways to signal our tastes and many props to launch chats and fun. While our collections and games are locked away in our personal devices, we'll continue to lose these starting points for together interactions. Reorienting to collective, shared, or utility devices scattered round our homes and workplaces is a good and exciting place to begin designing for a richer shared future.

## Design Challenge

Consider the two scenarios illustrated below. In the first, a group plays together on their networked handheld devices. In the other, a group has fun solving a shared crossword.

What's lost and gained in terms of social interaction in both cases? How could the game playing UX be enhanced by thinking about the crossword socializing and vice versa?

# Supporting role to leading actor

In this chapter we've looked at using mobiles as props in familiar contexts when groups come together for fun or work. Two types of interaction were explored:

- **Collaborative:** One or more people in the group use their mobiles as part of the together performance.

- **Collective:** Mobiles are seen as shared, public resources to be picked up and used by any of the group, as if they were playing cards or other "commodity" props.

In the next chapter, we turn to consider how mobiles can play a much bigger part in our performances, creating, in fact, new forms of socializing and public interactions.

# Resources

From getting the mobile out of the way, we moved to think how it can be a prop for socializing, helping people participate in another activity in a new way. Our examples included a novel mobile videoing method that a group of friends could use together to capture a shared experience [1]; prototypes that involved passing content or mobiles around in a group, moving us to think beyond individual use [2,3]; and how taking the ideas to the extreme with lots of small mobile devices—like the *Siftables*—could change how we interact together with content and tasks [4].

[1] Engström A, Perry M, Juhlin O. Amateur vision and recreational orientation: Creating live video together. In: Proceedings of the ACM 2012 Conference on Computer Supported Cooperative Work; ACM; 2012. pp. 651–60. http://dx.doi.org/10.1145/2145204.2145304.

[2] Lucero A, Holopainen J, Jokela T. Pass-them-around: Collaborative use of mobile phones for photo sharing. In: Proceedings of the SIGCHI Conference on Human Factors in Computing Systems; ACM; 2011. pp. 1787–96. http://dx.doi.org/10.1145/1978942.1979201.

[3] Yuill N, Rogers Y, Rick J. Pass the iPad: Collaborative creating and sharing in family groups. In: Proceedings of the SIGCHI Conference on Human Factors in Computing Systems; ACM; 2013. pp. 941–50. http://dx.doi.org/10.1145/2470654.2466120.

[4] Merrill D, Kalanithi J, Maes P. Siftables: Towards sensor network user interfaces. In: Proceedings of the 1st International Conference on Tangible and Embedded Interaction; ACM; 2007. pp. 75–8. http://dx.doi.org/10.1145/1226969.1226984.

# CHAPTER 15

## Opportunity 4.2
## EXTRAVAGANT COMPUTING

### WHAT'S THE OPPORTUNITY?

Consider designing for truly public interactions with technology: think about outputs that are available to more than just the user—such as large-screen video and loudspeaker audio. What could you do with clearly visible inputs—expressive hand, head, or even full body movements?

### WHY IS IT ATTRACTIVE?

People express themselves in many ways publicly—it can be part of their own identity display, or as part of group togetherness. Mobiles will increasingly be able to process expressive gestures and other forms of "natural" user interface, and to use resources to publicly display outputs.

### WHAT ARE THE CHALLENGES?

People may be embarrassed and not want their interactions overheard or observed. Some cultures will be more accepting than others, and what is meaningful in one locality could have a very different interpretation in another. Such social and cultural aspects, along with technological challenges in implementing the schemes, make this area rich for further research and commercial innovation.

## KEY POINTS

- People are adept at public display through their nondigital accessories, gestures, and social interactions.

- Technologies such as projection, large screens, and embedded audio speakers could be used as stages for users to connect their mobiles to.

- Some forms of public interaction have been shown to be more embarrassing than others. Careful design can limit these sorts of negative effects.

- We illustrate the ideas with a case study of work that attempts to enable users to bring visitor attractions alive, together.

## WHAT DO YOU THINK?

Walk down your local main street and try this experiment.

Imagine you want to raise the volume of the music you are listening to. While walking, lift your hands up in front of you. Repeat this a few times when you pass others. How did you feel? What was their reaction?

Now repeat the experiment, but do it while sitting opposite someone on a metro train or bus. What differences did you notice in your feelings and the responses of others?

# Introduction

In the 1970s and 80s boomboxes—portable cassette tape music players—were "big": both in popularity and dimensions. Carried aloft on the shoulder of the owner, perhaps, or set down on steps in a neighborhood, this was visible, extravagant technology with something to say.

Early brick-style mobiles exposed the user and the devices they were carrying to the others around them. While the boombox was a token of coolness, though, the nonusers who saw the technology as pretentious and unnecessary viewed the early adopters of mobiles with somewhat pitying eyes. Indeed, one British television comedian, Dom Joly, made his name by wandering around the streets holding a hugely outsize mobile and shouting, *"I'm on the phone."*

Over time, and increasingly so, both music players and mobiles have retreated, tortoise-like, pulling in their visible elements into the protective cloaks of invisibility—their owners' clothes, or tucked into the ear.

In this chapter, we look at what might happen if mobiles, in conjunction with other technologies, are brought back into the open again. Instead of being props to existing social performances, such as the ones discussed in the last chapter, our focus here is to consider new forms of social interaction these extravagant uses might afford.

# The boombox reimagined for the 2010s…

One mobile handset manufacturer has experimented with encouraging users to unplug their personal headphones and share their music with those around them. The system allows one person to take control of everyone else's mobile music player, effectively broadcasting music to these multiple speakers.

One of the commercials to promote the service begins with an excited basketball crowd pounding their feet together in anticipation of a big match. In contrast, the home team sits quietly in the locker room, fidgeting.

One of the team is listening to a track, trying to zone in, as athletes do before an event. Looking around, he realizes that the prematch nerves are getting to his teammates.

He opens up the broadcast app on his phone and soon the others are using their mobile to connect to the music. Suddenly, the room is filled with a pumping beat, the team is energized, and they flex and punch the air. Their on-pitch performance is primed.

Search for:
S4 group play advert

## The view from an artist: *"Shouldn't you call it Baroque computing?"*

When Matt described the notion of extravagant computing to an artist colleague, she said it reminded her of the values behind the Baroque movement in art, architecture, fashion, and culture that developed in the 17th and 18th centuries in Europe. It was all about drama, display, and detail (see the image above). The Victoria and Albert Museum in London had a major exhibition in 2010 about the movement, titled *Style in the Age of Magnificence*. It's a nice phrase: how can we design a mobile digital world for a new age of magnificence?

**Search for:**
*Baroque V&A*

## Small screen, large screen

A few years ago, there was some excitement around the novel user experiences that pico projectors might bring. Some handset developers began to market mobiles with these very small output devices built into them. The uptake from consumers was low, though, and for now the pico-projecting mobile is likely to remain a niche interest.

The reasons for this initial failure range from technological—they could not project brightly, and battery life was an issue—to alternative devices that made one of their key use cases obsolete. In much of the marketing around the projectors, a businessperson was shown either using the projector to give an impromptu café-based presentation or to pass away lonely hours back at the hotel catching up on a box set of TV episodes. With the rise of tablets, both of these rather uninspiring uses of the technology were better met with the superior displays and battery lives of their successors.

Technology will improve over time, with the output capacity of projectors and the battery life both increasing steadily. What are needed in addition, however, are some more imaginative, compelling reasons to entice users to push their digital interactions out into the physical world, for new together performances.

## Projected performance

Researcher Karl Willis, from Carnegie Mellon University, and colleagues at Disney Research, have been exploring more fun uses of pico projection, particularly for games. Their *SideBySide* design uses invisible infrared markers projected at the same time as the image to allow a group with pico projector phones to interact with their projections together.

The team have demonstrated several application designs using the system. In one, for instance, each person controls a boxer, ducking and diving by moving the projected image, and only able to throw a punch when in range of the other player. Another design, shown in the following image, puts one player in charge of an angry gorilla, challenging them to resist capture by the other player's rescue plane, which tries to trap the animal in a net.

The *Projected performance* box above illustrates one example of what could be achieved with pico projectors applied to mobile gaming. We saw another possibility in Chapter 11 with our *PicoTales* system. Bert Bongers, a designer and artist from Sydney, has been investigating an alternative use, deploying portable projectors as art installations. In his work he uses larger projectors, showing what mobile-based devices could achieve in the years ahead when technological issues have been addressed.

With the projector held in his hands and the supporting gadgetry carried in his backpack, Bongers embarks on what he calls videowalks. Each videowalk is a journey through a neighborhood during which he projects images—both still and animated—aimed at provoking a response from passersby and an audience that wanders with him.

## Principles for new performances: Surprise with juxtaposition

In his videowalks, Bongers sets out some principles for successful, audience-engaging performances. He argues for clever juxtaposition of physical and digital elements, creating a narrative between the environment around us and the content we can conjure up from our devices.

- Overlay rich digital textures onto bland structures—e.g., on an iron-clad corrugated structure, project the complex, multimaterial façade from a Gaudí building.

- Change colorless regions with vibrant displays—e.g., a grey wall becomes a tree with a colorful parrot.

- Add dynamics to a usually still space—e.g., project a fast movement through a tunnel onto a well-manicured lawn.

Transforming spaces in this way can also be done with other forms of output. Bongers' backpack also holds a loudspeaker, and as he walks around, similarly intriguing and provocative sounds are played (the parrot, for instance, squawks loudly).

Turning away from visuals and sound, a team at Disney Research has shown how the way surfaces feel can be changed not by projection but by what they call "injection."

Their system, *Revel*, does not alter the things the user touches; rather, they trick the user's brain into perceiving a texture that isn't there. The system works by applying a harmless electric current to the user via some device (for example, a mobile phone) that the user carries. This current interacts with the object being augmented, or, to be more precise, with the special coating applied to the object that allows for an electrostatic charge to be generated when the user touches it. When a surface is touched, a visual tracking system recognizes the object and the device creates a signal that causes a different texture to be felt. So, as an example, a smooth teapot can feel like it has a wavy, ceramic pattern.

**Search for:**
*Revel programming touch*

## Design Challenge

If walls, displays cases, furniture, posters and even another human's skin can be augmented with haptics, what sorts of together performances might we create? Take a look at the *Revel* video to kick-start your ideas.

---

While waiting for portable pico projectors to reemerge into the consumer landscape, there are alternative display technologies that can be commandeered in combination with the mobiles users carry. The *MobiSpray* prototype illustrates how performers can use their mobiles as virtual spray cans, coloring buildings using large, high-powered projectors.

The performance begins with the actor putting on a costume and positioning himself on a small podium in front of a public building. He then gestures with his phone as if he was sketching a picture with the building as a canvas. As he moves the phone, a powerful projector near him projects his virtual spray painting on to the building, following the

Figure 15.1 *MobiSpray*: Large-scale performance with projected spray paint.

paths he creates (see Figure 15.1). So, the overall performance—by a developer who styles himself as MobiLenin—brings together visible, crafted gestures with the stunning projected visuals that these create.

The system is at the extreme end of the performance spectrum: it moves the user's actions very much away from being private and almost invisible to being obvious and expressive; and, the outputs move from being trapped under the glass of their own personal device to being out there in the physical world for others to spectate.

## Putting it into practice

Live sharing startup Togeva has created a series of apps that can be used to provide similar small-screen to large-screen expressions to those created by MobiLenin. One of them, *Graffito*, is a service that can allow groups of people who are, for example, enjoying themselves at a club, to create colorful canvases that are displayed on large-screen displays or projections in the venue. The following image shows the app's interface—a simple sketching tool, the output of which can be projected on a screen. As more and more drawings are added, older ones fade away, giving new drawings a chance to be seen.

There's Not an App for That | Extravagant Computing

## Self-expression and embarrassment

As you think about these extravagant, public, highly visible forms of mobile-mediated interactions, you may be worrying about whether people will feel comfortable and really enjoy such exposure. To allay this fear, consider first evidence that people do express themselves in nondigital ways:

- People clearly are sometimes happy to make a statement. Firstly, there's the things they wear or carry in public. As researcher Linda Candy notes, people have always signaled the "tribe," mode, or mood they are in by their fashion choices. Sometimes this is blatant, as in the case of the business suit or Goth garb; other times it is subtler, with jeans being worn with different stances. The things people accessorize their outfits with can also be used as part of this personal performance. This might involve the coolly elegant wave of a cigarette holding hand, or the gentle swinging of a handbag.

- Then, there is the freedom afforded by being in a group—a small group of friends or a larger crowd. Researchers from Sweden studied how groups in a sports bar gesture dramatically and react as a live sports game is shown on the big screen. Their study highlights how even the less extrovert among a group can be drawn in to the performance. Incidentally, the fieldwork also illustrated how everyday extravagant gestures can be a problem to high technology. In this case, the jubilant movements by the fans might cause interference with devices like smart TVs that are also controlled by waves and pokes.

Turning to gestures people might make with mobile devices, a number of researchers have used the classification proposed by researchers at the Mixed Reality Lab in Nottingham, UK to explore the notion of embarrassment (See the *Different types of performance* box, below).

# Different types of performance

When we interact with a technology, there are the manipulations we make—such as pointing with our mobiles at a notice board—and the effects, such as a video connected to the poster being played. Thinking about these manipulations and effects and their visibility to bystanders allowed researcher Stuart Reeves and colleagues to classify gestures into four groups:

**Secretive:** Both the manipulations and effects are hidden to those around you. This is the default mode in most mobile apps.

**Expressive:** Both the manipulations and effects are exposed to bystanders. For example, your phone is on the café table; it rings, you pick it up, stare at the screen, and then swipe to answer the call to talk.

**Magical:** Your phone interactions are hidden but the result is public. For this case, think about connecting your mobile to a loudspeaker via Bluetooth. Everyone can hear your music choices, but they are not necessarily part of the small-screen browsing and searching of tracks.

**Suspenseful:** The inverse of magical, where the gesture is visible but the result is not seen. For example, imagine grasping your mobile tightly and then doing a throw gesture to post a geo-tagged comment onto a building in front of you.

In one of these studies, a team from Bristol University showed participants videos with different types of gestures relating to the classification. They were then asked to rate how they would feel doing such a gesture in public. The results showed this group would be uncomfortable using suspenseful gestures but that the others were more acceptable.

The problem with the suspenseful performances is that the individual would be exposed doing something—perhaps something strange-looking—with no context for bystanders to understand what they were up to. Magical gestures, although creating a public output, do not shine a spotlight on an individual, as their manipulations are hidden.

This sort of study, as the research team point out, can be useful when prototyping ideas for gestures before releasing a product or service. They also note, though, that when a new approach becomes publicly available a complex set of forces can actually determine its social acceptance or otherwise. Early adopters might experiment, happy to look strange or act oddly (think Google *Glass* and the other heads-up displays coming to market) while late adopters wait for the technology to both improve technically and become more of a norm. This normalizing can be influenced by marketing, high-profile users, exposure of the technology in films and TV, and so on.

The Bristol study illustrates a quick and relatively cheap way you might develop gesture-based elements of your new mobile apps and services. One of its drawbacks, though, is that it asks participants to *think* about how they would *feel* performing a gesture in front of others. How would they actually feel when they were out and about in public?

To look at this question, a group from Glasgow University built a working mobile prototype that allowed users to browse through speech-synthesized news feeds. They could control the readout by rotating their wrist (to go to the next or previous story) and by shaking it (to select items from a menu and move up and down the story hierarchy). In terms of Reeves' gesture classification, all of these were suspenseful performances—an observer could see the manipulation but not the effect.

## Design Pointer

We usually design for our "users." How could you take account of the bystanders and, as the Glasgow researchers put it, *"design for strangers"*?

## Alternative perspective

It is easy to get very excited about the power of the sorts of gestures we've been discussing. If you want to read more about them, it's worth taking a look into "natural user interfaces."

Don Norman, one of the founders of the field of human-computer interaction, warns us, though, that there are lots of open design questions to tackle before these gestures reach their full potential. These range from coping with cultural differences (a wave in one context can mean something very different to a person from another culture) to providing the sorts of cues and hints as to what actions are possible (think about the how-to instructions that are springing up to train people to use "natural" interactions—see the following image).

**Search for:**
*Natural user interfaces are not natural*

*"Gesture and touch-based systems are already so well accepted that I continually see people making gestures to systems that do not understand them: tapping the screens of non-touch-sensitive displays, pinching and expanding the fingers or sliding the finger across the screen on systems that do not support these actions, and for that matter, waving hands in front of sinks that use old-fashioned handles, not infrared sensors, to dispense water."*

**Don Norman**

As with the video study, the researchers found that participants were uncomfortable doing the gestures when they were observed. However, the discomfort was only in the context where they were on display to bystanders over a longer period of time—e.g., sitting opposite someone in an underground metro train. They did not report feeling awkward when interacting with the service while walking. During these periods, they encountered many bystanders, but each of these would only be aware of the user for a very brief period.

# Case study: Hafod world heritage site

This detailed case study illustrates two of the more extravagant uses of mobiles we've been discussing, and provides a more in-depth look at the range of user experiences possible when thinking about performative interaction.

## Context

Over the last few years, we, led by researcher Liam Betsworth, have been working with a range of other stakeholders to create user experiences that would help in the regeneration of a historic site.

When Britain's industrial age went into decline in the early 20th century, many buildings and factories were demolished or, in a few cases, renovated to house new activities. Other industrial sites, however, were simply neglected and ignored. One notable site—the Hafod–Morfa Copperworks—was completely abandoned and left exposed to vandals and the elements for over 30 years.

The Hafod works is in the Lower Swansea Valley, located on a large site just to the north of the city of Swansea, UK. By 1890, the site was the largest copperworks in Europe, and it lay at the heart of a global network of supply. Since the 1830s, ores had been shipped in from not only Cornwall, but also faraway mines in Chile, Cuba, North America, South Australia, and elsewhere, giving rise to the world's first globally integrated heavy industry. The Lower Swansea Valley was one of the most heavily and intensively industrialized parts of the UK, and the sulfurous fumes given off by the smelting works poisoned the landscape and rivers.

Over the years of neglect, the site has drastically changed from its working appearance. Similar to other heritage sites that have missing buildings and artifacts that are in a state of disrepair, when visiting the Hafod Copperworks it is impossible to imagine the sheer scale of the industrious activity that went on at the site.

We saw a great opportunity for new, collaborative kinds of experiences, where visitors could explore together in groups and with different devices to reveal the dramatic past of the Copperworks. We imagined the site coming to life and people interacting with the environment to uncover its history.

So far we have designed and tested two mobile-based systems for future deployment at the Hafod site, the first using pico projection and the second using loudspeakers embedded in the environment.

## Pico projection

The Hafod Copperworks was once alive with molten metal, steam, rivers, and smoke, but it now lays bare, with no such visual activity or indicator of what it may have looked like in the past. The pico projection system that we developed was our attempt at visually enhancing a user's surroundings in a performative manner.

Rather than previous through-the-lens approaches, however, the augmentation in our design is projected directly onto the physical elements to which it refers. Our system uses a mobile device attached to a pico projector. The mobile is used to scan QR codes situated next to exhibits placed around the visitor space. After scanning, an image and sentence of context about the exhibit are shown on screen, along with a prompt to focus a projected target on the object of interest. The user presses a button when ready, and imagery or animation is then projected (see the image below).

As the Hafod Copperworks is currently under renovation prior to its opening as a heritage site, we partnered with the National Botanic Garden of Wales to test the system. We customized the prototype for use at this specific attraction, using imagery of insects, animals, or environmental factors that are related to the plants and other displays at the gardens.

The image below shows several such examples, where the projection appears next to or on top of the related artifact. Clockwise from top left, the projections show a witchetty grub; a sunbird flying to a plant; raindrops falling on a leaf; and a leaf miner's trail. Apart from the initial QR scan, the system does not implement any additional tracking of the object on which the projection is focused. This allows users of the system to project freely onto objects in an attempt to promote performative and playful behavior.

We carried out a study of the system with visitors working together in groups of on average three people. While there were many findings (as we compared the system to a conventional small-screen-only guide), let's focus on the behaviors and technology issues around the more public performances.

Three groups using the system reported that they demonstrated it to and engaged with nonparticipant visitors. One of these said that their performance involved 13 other visitors who became interested in what was happening.

As well as questioning visitors after their use of the system, we also observed interactions from a distance ourselves to see what was actually happening. Here we saw that there was evidence that projection encouraged participation beyond the device itself. Participants were not gathered around the device, but were seen to be focused on the projections instead. In one group, for example, an adult held the device and let the children direct his hand, pointing the projections at plants while other visitors stood by and watched.

## Audio

Turning now from group viewing to collective listening, the Hafod Copperworks was once filled with sounds. With the crackling of fired-up furnaces, the hammering of copper sheets, and the constant sound of boats delivering and exporting goods, it would have been a noisy place to be. When standing at the site now, apart from the neighboring roads, the site lays silent.

Outdoor audio guides are usually developed for use with headphones. These audio experiences attempt to immerse the user in their environment, providing them with useful and relevant audio information to interpret. Although these kinds of experiences are now fairly common, there are several limitations. The first issue is that audio guides of this kind can sometimes feel synthetic. Instead of augmenting the user's environment with sounds, a new environment is being created within the user's headphones. Secondly, in terms of a group experience, headphones can also be very isolating. While some researchers have tried synchronizing playback between multiple users' headphones, this solution still does not give people the ability to communicate with each other during the experience—when using headphones, you are on your own.

Our *Surround You* design attempts to look at spatial audio in a new way. The system is made up of a mobile client and a number of "sound points." Each sound point consists of a portable battery-powered speaker connected to a laptop (as shown in the image above). The mobile client is a controller app that is used to activate each sound point.

When designing Surround You, we focused on the performative aspect of users' interactions—we designed the system to amplify both the user's manipulations and the effects from these gestures. This way, in terms of the performance from a spectator's perspective, the interaction would be an expressive one (see the earlier *Different types of performance* box). By making an expressive interaction, we hoped that this would be the most engaging experience for bystanders, and would encourage them to become involved in the experience.

To activate a sound point, the user points their phone in its general direction. Each sound point is set up to appear to take up a much larger physical space than it actually does. For example, if one of these sound points were to be placed inside an old building at the Hafod heritage site, we would assign the dimensions of the building to the sound point. If the user then pointed at any point of that building, the sound point would activate and begin playing. We also used a tuning-in and tuning-out metaphor, so that the nearer the user is pointing to the center of the sound point, the louder the sound that is produced. We used this metaphor so that the audio would gradually fade in and not startle spectators or those standing close to the loudspeakers.

To get an insight into the impact of Surround You's expressive interaction on both the user and bystander experiences of a place, we also deployed three other systems that allowed us to consider the full spectrum of performances detailed in the earlier *Different types of performance* box:

- **Magical:** The user activated sound points by entering a code into their mobile. (Each loudspeaker had a number associated with it.) Bystanders would then hear the result of a hidden user interaction.

- **Suspenseful:** The user wore headphones with the audio only heard by them. They activated the playback by pointing at the location of interest. Bystanders only saw the gesture, and were left wondering what the point of the action was.

- **Secretive:** The user wore headphones and selected a sound source by entering the appropriate number into their mobile. Bystanders saw nothing unusual.

We asked people to use all of the systems in public. You can read up on the full results in the paper listed in the resources section, but some key highlights were:

- Performative interaction and being a performer is new to most, and people felt more comfortable using the hidden, conventional interactions.

- Some users were more comfortable with the notion of being a performer than others.

- Users saw how Surround You could be used sociably and playfully.

Looking at what our users say illustrates both the potential of more extravagant computing forms as well as challenges that will need to be overcome. Firstly, the vast majority of people decided that the number entry and headphones interactions offered the most solitary experience. When asked to comment on their views on a solitary experience in this context, the replies were universally positive, with one user saying, *"I was more comfortable, wasn't worried about others and could concentrate on the information."* When asked about number entry and headphones as individual factors, the view of most was encapsulated by a single participant who said, *"people didn't seem to take much notice, it's just normal behavior."*

At the other end of the spectrum, most users thought that the pointing and loudspeaker interaction offered the most sociable experience, with one explaining, *"they can see the interaction and listen."* Interestingly, around a third of the people who used the system chose to purposely try to get responses from spectators, whereas the rest aimed to be as inconspicuous as possible.

Opinion was divided between whether a system being performative in a public place was actually a good or a bad thing. One participant explained, *"I think it could be fun. I don't get embarrassed in public but some would."* Another user remarked, *"I don't want to be a performer. It wouldn't come naturally, but the system works well for a performance. Others always look and listen."*

## Writing your own script

While some of the illustrations we've used here are dependent on technological developments on mobiles and the infrastructure that supports them, think about what you could do in your next app to support more of the extravagant computing thinking. Here are some questions to prime your action:

■ In what ways could you use mobile loudspeaker output or activate the vibration motor in your mobile when it is placed on a table around which you and your friends are sitting?

- How could you get your mobile to listen to taps of that same table or objects on it (like the mugs you are drinking from) to control a service?

- How could you use highly visible shaking, spinning, or other gestures with your mobile?

- What could you connect to your mobile to enhance experiences? Think about the now cheap and easy ways to connect your phone to an external speaker or to a large-screen TV display.

# Resources

Going from mobiles as a support to a way of creating new performances all together, we began with a commercial example of how networking devices can change the listening experience. The video of the advert we mention is at [1].

Karl Willis and colleagues' impressive work on pico-projected interfaces and games is hugely inspiring [2]. As we saw, projectors and large-screen displays have the potential to expose what has previously been hidden under the glass of the user's device. More of Bert Bongers' videowalking work can be found in [3].

A range of other visual approaches including the *MobiSpray* and *Graffito* systems are detailed in [4] and you can watch a video of the *MobiSpray* mobile performance at [5]. As an aside we considered *injection* rather than projection as way of extending a user's experience of the world around them [6]—you can watch a video of the *Revel* system at [7].

With the move to outwardly visible, extravagant interactions, we took time to question whether this form of experience would be comfortable or embarrassing. We saw first that people do like to express themselves in certain, nondigital, contexts (e.g., [8]).

To help frame the exploration of how people feel when being more extrovert with their mobiles we used the helpful categorization in [9] and looked at two studies that shed light on the social acceptability of gesturing to operate mobile services in public [10,11].

We ended the chapter with a case study from our own work that illustrates alternative ways of being a performer in public to enhance UX. More details of those studies can be found in [12].

[1] Samsung Galaxy S4-Group Play (Commercial). 2013. Retrieved from https://www.youtube.com/watch?v=sDpwrd1mgMA.

[2] Willis KD, Poupyrev I, Hudson SE, Mahler M. Sidebyside: Ad-hoc multi-user interaction with handheld projectors. In: Proceedings of the 24th Annual ACM Symposium on User Interface Software and Technology; ACM; 2011. pp. 431–40. http://dx.doi.org/10.1145/2047196.2047254.

[3] Bongers B. The projector as instrument. Pers Ubiquitous Comput 2012;16(1): 65–75. http://dx.doi.org/10.1007/s00779-011-0378-0.

[4] Bedwell B, Caruana T. Encouraging spectacle to create self-sustaining interactions at public displays. In: Proceedings of the 2012 International Symposium on Pervasive Displays; ACM; 2012. pp. 15:1–6. http://dx.doi.org/10.1145/2307798.2307813.

[5] MobiSpray. 2010. Retrieved from http://mobispray.com/.

[6] Bau O, Poupyrev I, Le Goc M, Galliot L, Glisson M. Revel: Tactile feedback technology for augmented reality. In: ACM SIGGRAPH 2012 Emerging Technologies; ACM; 2012. pp. 17:1. http://dx.doi.org/10.1145/2343456.2343473.

[7] Revel: Programming the Sense of Touch. 2012. Retrieved from https://www.youtube.com/watch?v=L7DGq8SddEQ.

[8] Candy FJ. "Come on momma, let's see the drummer": Movement-based interaction and the performance of personal style. Pers Ubiquitous Comput 2007;11(8):647–55. http://dx.doi.org/10.1007/s00779-006-0136-x.

[9] Reeves S, Benford S, O'Malley C, Fraser M. Designing the spectator experience. In: Proceedings of the SIGCHI Conference on Human Factors in Computing Systems; ACM; 2005. pp. 741–50. http://dx.doi.org/10.1145/1054972.1055074.

[10] Montero CS, Alexander J, Marshall MT, Subramanian S. Would you do that?: Understanding social acceptance of gestural interfaces. In: Proceedings of the 12th International Conference on Human Computer Interaction with Mobile Devices and Services; ACM; 2010. pp. 275–8. http://dx.doi.org/10.1145/1851600.1851647.

[11] Wiliamson JR, Crossan A, Brewster S. Multimodal mobile interactions: Usability studies in real world settings. In: Proceedings of the 13th International Conference on Multimodal Interfaces; ACM; 2011. pp. 361–8. http://dx.doi.org/10.1145/2070481.2070551. ICMI '11. ACM.

[12] Betsworth L, Bowen H, Robinson S, Jones M. Performative technologies for heritage site regeneration. Pers Ubiquitous Comput 2014:1–20. http://dx.doi.org/10.1007/s00779-014-0766-3.

# CHAPTER 16

## Problem 5
## FROM DISTANCED TO MINDFUL INTERACTION

## WHAT'S THE PROBLEM?

Apps can distance people from each other.

As we have seen in previous chapters, this distancing can be direct, as a user disengages from others. But, apps also tempt us away from thinking about the real people we are connecting with. On our phones we have "contacts" and "friends"; perhaps these have just become another task to be done via an app.

Bringing a mindful perspective is about really helping your users think about who they are communicating with, in the moment. It is about moving from "me"- to "you"-focused interactions.

## WHY SHOULD YOU TACKLE IT?

Apps and frameworks that allow the user to be present and in the now—key parts of mindfulness—will help them have more meaningful experiences as they communicate and connect.

Encouraging your users to think less of the "me" (themselves, that is) and more of the "you" (the people they are communicating with) can also mean that more appropriate and efficient interactions are able to happen.

## KEY POINTS

- Telephones were originally about distance (*tele*) speaking (*phone*).
- Our apps and infrastructures are still orientated towards these sorts of distancing interactions.

- Apps are task-focused, and this also can lead to distancing from each other with people becoming "to-dos" or things we broadcast to.

- Mindful interaction, in contrast, is about thinking about who you are connecting with, and the value of the communication to them; it is about being very close to the person, in their "now," even when physically apart.

# Introduction

At the time of writing this chapter (late 2013), *The Lancet* published an article showing that, on average, people in the UK are having 20% less sex than they did in the year 2000. The authors speculate that one of the main causes is due to people taking electronic devices into the bedroom—they are checking emails and responding to posts until they fall asleep—leaving little or no time for one of the most intimate acts of human communication.

As we saw in the introduction to this book, much has been written in both academic venues and the popular press about how mobile communications disrupt face-to-face interactions. The rhetoric goes that we spend so much time broadcasting on Twitter, WhatsApp, and Facebook that we have lost the ability to narrowcast. We are no longer able to interact on a one-to-one basis, even with our most intimate partners.

But is the worry warranted?

Are we really losing the ability or desire to communicate mindfully to a person (local to us or elsewhere)? Or are the devices to blame—do they promote certain forms of communication over others?

In the last three chapters on performance, we looked at designing to enhance the togetherness of people by supporting their performances. To reinforce and extend the points made there, in these next three chapters we want to spend some time unpicking the experience of *being together*. We will see how the app model by default leads us to not be fully aware of others (who are nearby or, indeed, further away)—to a state of *distance* and lack of presence in the moment. By doing this, we will more clearly see the benefits of rebooting our design thinking so that we are mindful of others in our communications and interactions.

## Mindfulness

In using the term *mindful* throughout this chapter we are talking about raising the user's awareness of their surroundings, the people nearby or further afield *in and at the moment* they are interacting with their apps. There are lots of psychological techniques people can use to raise their level of mindfulness, but we are focusing on designing to support it rather than taking a strict cognitive or meditation perspective.

**Search for:**
*Mindfulness*

## Mindful interaction in physical forms

Kristina Niedderer's work on mindful interaction explores how the design of objects can force an awareness of other people's needs. For example, she created "social cups," which would tip over unless they were attached magnetically to at least two other cups (to form a tripod). She built them to explicitly force social interaction at parties, where if guests wanted to set down their cup on something they'd have to collaborate in a group, leading to chats.

# Distancing us

The reasons our apps and devices distance us from others are complex. We focus here on two problems:

- A legacy issue that comes from the original purpose and design of telephones; and.
- A more contemporary problem where "social" has become just another app.

## The legacy of the telephone

Sometimes it is possible to forget that the mobile devices we carry with us are derived from the telephone handset of Alexander Graham Bell—physically, the smooth glass of the smartphone looks a world away from its Bakelite and rotary-dialed ancestors. Yet, the philosophy of *"tele"* (distance) *"phone"* (speaking) still has a huge bearing on the apps we create for today's devices.

Due to the telephone, mobile communications and app services are hobbled by the idea that we wish to communicate with someone who is distant from us, with people in different locations. So, most apps assume that the other person you are communicating with is in a different place, and even a different time (with a person reading your post or adding your calendar suggestion, for instance, at a time different to the one when you posted or suggested it).

We connect with people through a medium of our convenience, arranged in a way that suits us: communication for our benefit. This perspective funnels our focus onto the device and away from anyone or anything around us that could distract us from the remote partner we are assumed to be communicating with. The default design basis is that if another person *is* in the room with us, then we would not need to use the mobile at all. So the telephone keeps us gazing in to the pool, like Narcissus.

Yet, this "distance" model of communication is clearly at odds with how we often use our handsets today. As we saw in the last chapters there are enjoyable, useful ways to use them when we are with our friends, not to detract from our conversation or performance, but to enhance it.

## Design Challenge

Have you ever passed your phone to a friend to share some piece of media that you both enjoy? Or, have you called up your mobile calendar to see when everyone in the physical group is free to meet again? What features of these apps helped you be mindful of the people around you, and what distanced you from them?

## Intimate interaction

In a paper published in 2007 by Microsoft Research, the researchers report the enjoyment people derived from swapping video clips at social gatherings. In particular, they noticed how people loved the clandestine intimacy of sharing a copyright-protected file over Bluetooth, subverting the DRM protection of the wider Internet by sharing media over a direct, person-to-person connection.

The astonishing thing is that, due to their heritage, these devices afford little extra functionality, or behave little differently, when you are communicating covertly with a friend in a pub or synchronizing calendars across time zones and geographic locations.

## Design Challenge

Why can't your handset automatically highlight the free dates in everyone's calendars when sitting around a table together? Or why, if we want to share media with someone beside us, must it go through a data center in Iowa? What redesigns are necessary to facilitate better local interactions?

We argue that it is time to rethink the design philosophies we have had since 1876 and start to build technology that keeps us *mindful* of the people around us and at a distance. Perhaps it is not that we have forgotten how to be mindful or intimate; it may be that our devices force us to communicate in ways that assume we are distant.

## The task fallacy

Computers—and now mobiles—are all about tasks, and this leads to a different form of distancing. It can make us think of people as things to be "done" rather than truly, mindfully connected with.

Let's explore this argument now by continuing our brief history lesson on how phones have developed from those early days. So, the telephone started as a way of enabling voice communication between people in different locations. Due to the nature of landlines and wired technology, telephones supported communication between one fixed location and another. When mobiles were introduced, their success came as they freed people from communicating at a location—communication was now between people and not places.

As the computational power of handsets increased, extra services were added to allow communication beyond voice (e.g., SMS and MMS), so communication could be asynchronous—at different times, that is—and in text or image, as well as voice. Rather than being a cheap alternative to voice calls, various studies (such as one by Alex Taylor of Microsoft Research and colleagues on teenage "gift" giving), show that these asynchronous systems allow communication that we value in different ways. For example, important texts or images can be stored on a handset and cherished as a gift, in a way that voice calls cannot.

Figure 16.1 Back to the future: Matt using a forerunner of the popular Personal Digital Assistants that become prevalent in the 1990s. Apps today mimic many of the functions of these past devices, as well as supporting so many more tasks.

At this point an interesting thing happened in the development of the handset, namely the Personal Digital Assistant (PDA—see Figure 16.1). Beginning with devices like the *PalmPilot*, PDAs were designed as a way of taking vital personal information, such as calendar and contacts, from your computer, and having it with you at all times. These devices were pocket-sized and became indispensable business tools, being carried around everywhere with the user. However, the chances were that same user would also be carrying around a cellular handset in their pocket at the same time. It seemed obvious, therefore, to merge the functionality of these devices.

The PDA evolution was being driven by a migration of tasks from the computer onto a portable device. Previously, handset development was being driven by the provision of new ways to communicate. But as Alan Cooper and colleagues' book *The Essentials of Interaction Design* teaches us, whenever you add computer functionality to any device, that device simply becomes a new form of the computer (Figure 16.2).

*The merging of phones with PDAs was a seemingly great idea, but we and other researchers believe that something was lost at this point in technological evolution, namely the focus on communication and people.*

Figure 16.2 The phone becomes a computer. Matt holding a Nokia mobile that appeared on the front cover of *The Economist* on November 21st, 2002 with the headline, "Computing's New Shape."

**Search for:**
*Economist computing's new shape*

Phones, and later smartphones, became about the functionality they could offer: how much you could do on your handset while mobile, without being shackled to a desktop computer. This thinking was most clearly articulated in the introduction of the iPhone, whose interface and ecosystem came to be based on the creation, installation, and management of what now became "apps"—small, task-based applications to simplify or enhance your life. "People," "contacts," and other social elements were relegated to one of many apps to be found in the pool.

So focused on tasks is the iPhone that its operating system (iOS) forbids users from having direct access to media through a mechanism like a file browser. The media we might wish to share and communicate to others is not available in a standalone way, rather it is locked into task-focused apps.

Interaction designers, such as us, have published many papers on how to improve these tasks and make people more efficient in the use of their mobile devices and apps. But in this striving for an improved user experience and fluidity in task completion, we may have taken our eyes off what the device is for in the first place—communicating with people. As Richard Buchanan says of interaction design:

> *"But you know, most interactions are not about computer interactions—it's a small part of our lives."*
>
> **Richard Buchanan**

Microsoft researcher Richard Harper also takes issue with the focus on communication-as-task, as we are apt to *"overlook the humans who are doing the communicating."*

It is a subtle thing, but the task-based nature of the app interface forces us into a particular way of thinking about communication. So, we "do" our email, relieved when we clear our inbox of all that bothersome communication. Following tweets or podcasts becomes akin to a "to-do list," where we tick off the feeds we need to read in order to get on with life.

# Becoming mindful

So, what's the solution to this distancing? In the next two chapters we propose two responses:

- **Mindful apps**: We want you to think more about what being mindful of others entails. To do this, we will consider ways of looking at communication that highlight the people involved rather than the task being done. We'll also see how thinking more deeply about the distance between people and their identities can challenge the forms of interaction we facilitate with our apps.

- **The end of apps**: More radically, we'll look at the arguments for moving away from app-based mobile design. Here we'll explore how alternative interaction infrastructures could lead to mobiles that help users to become more aware of the people, places, and possibilities that are meaningful to them in their here and now.

## What do you think?

Before we begin looking in detail at some solutions, here's a service to stimulate your own thinking. *Airwriting* is a beta service that allows messages to be written and shared in ways that focus on the receiver. The system is a generalized architecture for creating apps that allow people to post messages in a physical place for others to retrieve only when they too visit that place. So, messages can have a range of features that affect how they are communicated, as the following screenshot shows. It allows a user to be mindful of the people they are messaging in some simple but interesting ways. What do you think about it—does it support mindful interaction?

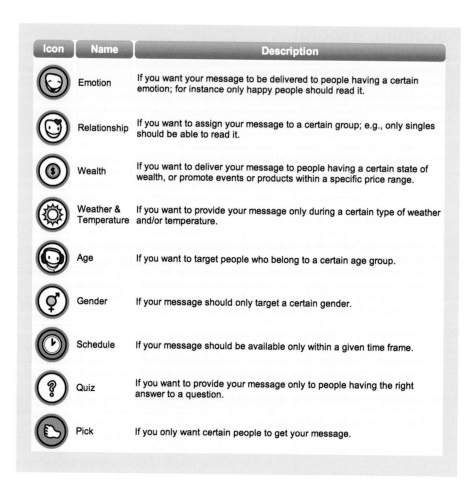

| Icon | Name | Description |
|---|---|---|
| | Emotion | If you want your message to be delivered to people having a certain emotion; for instance only happy people should read it. |
| | Relationship | If you want to assign your message to a certain group; e.g., only singles should be able to read it. |
| | Wealth | If you want to deliver your message to people having a certain state of wealth, or promote events or products within a specific price range. |
| | Weather & Temperature | If you want to provide your message only during a certain type of weather and/or temperature. |
| | Age | If you want to target people who belong to a certain age group. |
| | Gender | If your message should only target a certain gender. |
| | Schedule | If your message should be available only within a given time frame. |
| | Quiz | If you want to provide your message only to people having the right answer to a question. |
| | Pick | If you only want certain people to get your message. |

**Search for:**
*Airwriting*

## Resources

The study in *The Lancet* we mentioned can be found at [1], published over several detailed articles. Kristina Niedderer's work on mindful interaction by forced collaboration is explored in [2] The fun of swapping media at social gatherings is explored in [3], and the teenage "gift" giving in [4].

The different definitions of interaction design we mentioned can be found in [5,6,7], and Richard Harper's comments about communication-as-a-task in [8]. The *Airwriting* system is discussed in [9], and can be used at [10].

[1] The Third National Survey of Sexual Attitudes and Lifestyles. 2013. Retrieved from http://www.thelancet.com/themed/natsal.

[2] Niedderer K. Designing mindful interaction: The category of performative object. Des Issues 2006;23(1):3–17. http://dx.doi.org/10.1162/desi.2007.23.1.3.

[3] Harper R, Regan T, Izadi S, Mosawi KA, Rouncefield M, Rubens S. Trafficking: Design for the viral exchange of TV content on mobile phones. In: Proceedings of the 9th International Conference on Human Computer Interaction with Mobile Devices and Services; ACM; 2007. pp. 249–56. http://dx.doi.org/10.1145/1377999.1378015.

[4] Taylor AS, Harper R. The gift of the gab?: A design oriented sociology of young people's use of mobiles. Comput Supported Coop Work 2003;12(3):267–96. http://dx.doi.org/10.1023/A:1025091532662.

[5] Cooper A, Reimann R, Cronin D. About Face 3: The Essentials of Interaction Design. Indianapolis, IN: Wiley; 2007.

[6] Cooper A. The Inmates Are Running the Asylum. Indianapolis, IN: Macmillan Publishing Co., Inc; 1999.

[7] Buchanan R. Design research and the new learning. Des Issues 2001;17(4):3–23. http://dx.doi.org/10.1162/07479360152681056.

[8] Harper RHR. Texture: Human Expression in the Age of Communications Overload. Cambridge, MA: MIT Press; 2010.

[9] Mayrhofer R, Sommer A, Saral S. Air-Writing: A platform for scalable, privacy-preserving, spatial group messaging. In: Proceedings of the 12th International Conference on Information Integration and Web-based Applications & Services; ACM; 2010. pp. 183–91. http://dx.doi.org/10.1145/1967486.1967517.

[10] Airwriting. 2010. Retrieved from http://www.airwriting.com/.

# CHAPTER 17

## Opportunity 5.1
# DESIGNING MINDFUL COMMUNICATION APPS

## WHAT'S THE OPPORTUNITY?

Current communication and sharing apps are "me" centered: they're about "me" wanting to send or share something with "you."

The opportunity is to become more "you" focused. To think, that is, about apps that put other people at the center of a user's communication or sharing interaction. Let's look at designing to support users to think about the people on the other side of the interaction: how their friend, colleague, or acquaintance will receive the message, rather than simply seeing these communications as tasks to be done or transactions to be completed.

## WHY IS IT ATTRACTIVE?

As most apps today are still focused on the "me" element of the sharing and also major on sharing to a *remote* "you," there are lots of opportunities for new apps and services.

The "you" focus that is mindful of others can lead you to develop services that are creatively different in terms of how your users might craft, gift, and experience connections they make with others, both when they are together with others and when they are separated.

## KEY POINTS

- When we send a message to someone or share some content with them, it is useful to think about what our intention is and how the other person will make use of what we send.

- We present a design matrix that will help you think of these sorts of different communication scenarios with various sender intentions and receiver states.

- To build better apps for communication we can also fruitfully explore ideas about what being together is, and how we share and create identity when communicating.

## WHAT DO YOU THINK?

Many of us think our devices allow us to be more social, to empathize, to think about others. They keep us connected.

What's your experience? Does your mobile distance you or make you really mindful of others when you communicate?

The next time you post a status update or share a photo, pause and ask yourself what you are really saying and who you are saying it *for*: are you thinking about those who will receive your communication; thinking more about yourself; or not thinking about it all?

# Introduction

Guiding the creation of interactive systems for the past few years are the ideas of interaction design. One definition of interaction design is this, by Alan Cooper and colleagues: *"the practice of designing interactive digital products, environments, systems, and services."* But where are other people in that definition? Our friends are not products, systems, environments, or services, are they?

In contrast, Richard Buchanan sees interaction design as the communication and interaction between two people, mediated by a device such as a cellular handset:

> *"When you start to realize that we might design the way human beings interact in all sorts of situations; we might give thought to how people relate together. Not letting it happen by chance; serendipity or the whims of circumstance. We might be thoughtful about how we get together and do things together. When you start to form that idea you're in another world."*
>
> **Richard Buchanan**

But what does "another world" look like?

Let us first get inspired by an exploration of three elements that are important in inter-personal communication:

- The mode of communication;

- The space that the communication is taking place within; and,

- The way people construct and present their identities during the communication.

From this tour of how people communicate, we'll be then equipped to think about new app possibilities that make us mindful of others as we interact, rather than distancing us.

There's Not an App for That | Designing Mindful Communication Apps

# Modes of interaction

The discipline of HCI has a specialization known as Computer-Supported Cooperative Work (CSCW) looking at the general field of how people complete tasks together using computers (the inclusion of the term "work" in the title shows its task-based origins).

Search for:
CSCW

Despite the focus on work, it contains many ideas relevant to our discussion. Perhaps most critically, it provides a classification matrix of groupware systems, which allows people like us (developers and designers) to gain insight into the different types of systems we can develop to support human communication (see Figure 17.1).

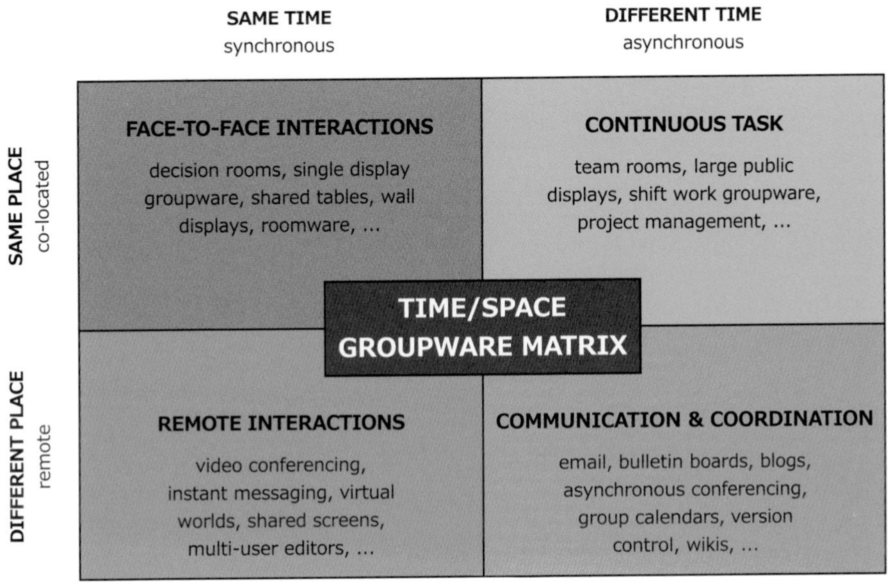

|  | **SAME TIME** synchronous | **DIFFERENT TIME** asynchronous |
|---|---|---|
| **SAME PLACE** co-located | **FACE-TO-FACE INTERACTIONS** decision rooms, single display groupware, shared tables, wall displays, roomware, … | **CONTINUOUS TASK** team rooms, large public displays, shift work groupware, project management, … |
| **DIFFERENT PLACE** remote | **REMOTE INTERACTIONS** video conferencing, instant messaging, virtual worlds, shared screens, multi-user editors, … | **COMMUNICATION & COORDINATION** email, bulletin boards, blogs, asynchronous conferencing, group calendars, version control, wikis, … |

**TIME/SPACE GROUPWARE MATRIX**

Figure 17.1 The Groupware matrix, adapted from Robert Johansen's original concept.

This matrix helps us classify forms of communication that do exist, but also gives us a framework in which to think about future ways of looking at communication. However, a *"me"* perspective drives this matrix—it is weighted towards the person who is doing the communication. We have categories for someone who wants to send a message to someone who is, or is not, in the same location at the current time, or at some other time.

*But what about the person receiving the communication? What about their needs? Communication is a two-way thing. Should we not start thinking of the person who is being communicated to?*

We have found the matrix in Figure 17.2, adapted from the one above to take into account the receiver, a better guide to help us create and understand applications that make us mindful of others. The horizontal dimension of the grid is the intent of the person wishing to communicate, while the vertical is the state of the listener.

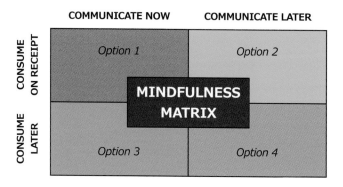

Figure 17.2 The mindfulness matrix—thinking about the state of the receiver ("consume") as well as the sender ("communicate").

Each cell in the grid represents a form of communication between two people. Some of these options are well served by apps currently, and others less so. Using the grid as our guide, we will explore each option in detail to see what forms of mindfulness they afford.

### Option 1: *Communicate now, consume on receipt*

This allows us to be mindful of someone who is absent from us but who we need to communicate with directly at this moment. This could be a voice call or instant messaging.

This is a very immediate form of communication in which both communicator and receiver are celebrating the "now" of their communication. We are mindful of someone and we want to communicate now and have their response now.

If we are physically with someone with whom we wish to share media, then mobile devices, due to their "tele" history, are very poor about supporting this form of interaction. In fact, they distract us from the people at hand.

## Option 2: *Communicate later, consume on receipt*

In this instance we want to communicate with someone, but the message we wish to send is not for immediate sending. Most likely the message needs explanation or makes sense only in a particular context.

For example, we see something we wish to discuss with a friend, so we take a photograph of it now to keep until we next see them. Or we may want them to receive information when we are not with them, perhaps in a particular location (geocaching) or at a particular time (e.g., sending them a gift voucher on their birthday).

This form of communication is really about the sender anticipating a communication. We are mindful of our recipient in the now, and anticipate their reaction to the receiving of the communication in the future.

## Option 3: *Communicate now, consume later*

Sometimes we wish to create some communication immediately, but know that the receiver will not be able to use our message until later. There are familiar technologies that allow us to do this at a distance, for example SMS and voicemail.

But let's extend the thinking. We may want to create something, an artifact that can be received and reviewed later, that is more about memorializing the past, whether that was a joint past in which sender and receiver did something together they wish to celebrate and treasure, or whether it is the sender sharing something from their *now* which the receiver will perceive as being from the past.

## Option 4: *Communicate later, consume later*

The easiest way to think of this category is mindfulness through gift giving. This form of communication is a communication that is of value independently of when it was created or received.

So, imagine you are thinking about a digital artifact (maybe something you've seen while online or something you've created), and you become mindful of someone that you then wish to give the gift to. When they receive the gift they may well use it or cherish it much later, and not immediately on receipt.

Much of our app communications are focused on the instant. What about apps that allow us to gather up and then give digital gifts that will provide persistent pleasure?

These artifacts may be passed through co-located means when we are together (for example, the video clip trafficking discussed earlier) or remotely (think again to the studies by Microsoft Research we mentioned in the previous chapter where teenagers saw their SMSes from friends as special gifts to be stored and revisited for a long time).

<table>
<tr><td>

## Design Challenge

Think about the following scenario. What app could you design in a "communicate later, consume later" way to provide the equivalent forms of communication digitally?

*You are going to a wedding of a friend. It's a month before the big day and you've purchased a lovely card in a shop and written a touching note wishing him well. On the big day, you tuck the sealed card into your tuxedo jacket pocket. There's a lot going on and you have to find the right moment to say "hi" to your friend. You get your card out and hand it over; the groom thanks you and places it on the gift table.*

*Several weeks later, after their honeymoon, the newlyweds go through their gifts and love what you've written. They place it on their mantelpiece where it stays for many years, its color fading in the sun over time but the message still valued and read occasionally by the pair.*

</td></tr>
</table>

A bit later on in this chapter we will examine each of these four categories to see how current apps can address each need and what opportunities there are for innovation. However, before we do so, it is worth considering a key assumption that helped shape this classification: physical space.

## Space

In the original CSCW matrix, great store was set by people being co-located or distant from each other. In other words "space" was one of the two key dimensions along which systems were classified. Yet, it is missing entirely from our alternative model, above. Rather than being laziness or oversimplification on our part, we find that space turns out to be a complex idea that has become blurred since the advent of mobile digital systems.

There's Not an App for That | Designing Mindful Communication Apps

A basic view of space is tied to the physical distance between two people—how far apart physically the atoms that make up the bodies of the two communicators are. While absolute physical space is vital for applications such as GPS location, it is less important when considering how humans interact, and their awareness of each other. For example, does communication change if people are 200 or 250 kilometers apart?

In his work on *proxemics*, Edward Hall allows us to think more deeply about space by considering people's perception of the space around them. He argues that people see space as being intimate, personal, social, or public—each in increasing concentric zones around the body (see Figure 17.3).

## Design Challenge

Hall was interested in physical closeness, but what can this mean for designs of digital services? How might digital communication forms differ between the public, social, personal, or intimate?

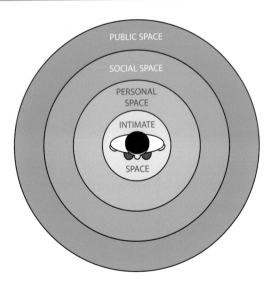

Figure 17.3 Edward Hall's classification of space: intimate for close contact, personal for friends and family members, social for acquaintances, and public for everyone else.

## Putting it into practice

Saul Greenberg and colleagues have used Hall's theories of proxemics to create the "Proximity Toolkit" to allow researchers to explore co-located interaction with an ecology of devices. This toolkit enables components to detect when they are close to each other and human users (using Hall's classifications as shown in Figure 17.3). This work is a very literal take on Hall's ideas—the toolkit divides physical space into interaction zones and sets distance limits such that between distance A and B, something is said to be intimate; between distance B and C, it should be considered personal; etc.

---

Another useful conceptualization of space is put forward by researchers such as Jason Farman, who advocate that physical and virtual space should be considered as a whole. Farman argues that space is a verb, performed between communicating humans, and that the space only exists when the communication is taking place. At first, this may seem like a strange, or perhaps irrelevant, perspective on space. But if we combine it with Hall's notions, we see that it is actually very powerful and a creative way to think about space.

Consider Hall's notion of an intimate space.

A literal interpretation would confine us to believing that that type of communication can only happen when face-to-face. However, many of us have experienced moments of intimate conversation when separated from family by thousands of miles; Gary, for example, has seen his daughter blow out her birthday candles over a Skype connection and had meaningful and touching conversations with her about her birthday and what it meant to her. In Farman's terms, we have performed in an intimate space, rather than being physically located in an intimate space.

Of course, many researchers are exploring the notion of a performed intimate space in many different ways. Some interesting work in this field comes from Adrian Cheok's

There's Not an App for That | Designing Mindful Communication Apps

research group in the form of systems like *Huggy Pajama*. This system is for parents who have to be away from their children for a period of time. The parent takes with them a teddy bear as a proxy for their child. The child wears pajamas with inflatable air bladders contained within. Both pajamas and bear are connected to the Internet such that, should the parent hug the bear, that hug is transmitted to the child through the inflation of the corresponding air bladders in the pajamas (see Figure 17.4). While this system may alarm some readers, it is primarily an attempt to explore these notions of performed space and see how to effectively create intimacy independently of location.

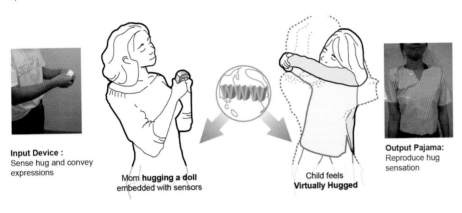

**Input Device :**
Sense hug and convey
expressions

Mom **hugging a doll**
embedded with sensors

Child feels
**Virtually Hugged**

**Output Pajama:**
Reproduce hug
sensation

Figure 17.4 *Huggy Pajama.*

By realizing that the communication space is a blended physical and digital activity, we can free ourselves to imagine systems that provide intimate communication over great distances. The demotion of physical space in our model is therefore a very deliberate one: we want you to think about how mindful, meaningful communications can occur regardless of where you and the person you want to connect to are physically located.

## Design Pointer

When you build your next social or communication app, think about the *space* that your users are performing in. Is it intimate, social, or public?

# Identity: Who we are

Following on from the idea that space is performed, it is also worth stopping to reflect on the subjects of our mindfulness: with whom are we communicating? Is a person a static entity (a recipient of a message) or is it more fruitful to consider them in some other way?

There has been a lot of research conducted on how we present ourselves in life, as well as online. As we write this (late 2013), no less an authority than the Oxford English Dictionary has declared "selfie" as word of the year. We are using social media to create carefully articulated versions of ourselves, always adding and managing our image online.

As early as 1959, Ervin Goffman was arguing that identity is performed; it is not a static thing. Using the metaphor of theatre, he argues that we need a *"backstage"* area (where we keep private the things that constitute us) and a *"frontstage"* area where we present a carefully created version of ourselves for a particular audience. While Goffman has his critics (see, for example, David Buckingham's critique in the book *Youth, Identity, and Digital Media*), he at least gives us a vocabulary to talk about the curation and presentation aspects of our personalities.

One problem with mobile devices from an identity point of view is that they reflect the act of constructing ourselves back to ourselves. We are caught up in taking photographs and producing tweets (or status updates) that we can then ourselves view in our news feeds, profile updates, and the like. We are drawn to reflect on our image without focusing on the readership and on their perception.

This lack of focus on the receiver can lead to narcissism, but can also have more severe outcomes. For example, Leigh Van Bryan tweeted *"Free this week, for quick gossip/prep before I go and destroy America"* and was deported when he arrived at the airport.

**Search for:**
*Leigh Van Bryan airport tweet*

There's Not an App for That | Designing Mindful Communication Apps

## Design Pointer

It is clear that more thought is needed in how to allow people to "do" identity in their communications with others via apps and services. We should design in ways that do not restrict us to present a single static image of our identity; they should allow us to create and present different aspects of our personality to different groups of people at different times. Apps should, for example, allow us to manage media privately in some backstage area before we reveal that construction of our identity on our frontstage. Friend groups and circles in social media sharing services are a start, but there's much more that can be done.

In the next section we will go on to look at the technologies needed to support these types of interactions, and how thinking in this way affects current apps.

# An app for that

Currently, many apps are created as a result of a technological imperative—because we can build something, we do. This is not necessarily a bad thing—with so many innovations, some really useful services emerge—but, if we are trying to be mindful of others, this approach can blinker us to more life-as-lived and human-centered opportunities. To redress this balance, in a small way, we'll use the matrix presented earlier to now classify existing applications and explore what other apps might be built.

## Option 1: *Communicate now, consume on receipt*

In this category we have message producers and consumers operating in real time; conversations and messages flow back and forward immediately whether the participants are co-located or not. Let's look now at issues and design solutions for enhancing the mindful sharing of content when our users are together with others.

### Connect users together through their devices and other resources

When used in a co-located way, current mobile devices now have much more to offer in terms of functionality than their text-based forbears. Devices can now be used to share and view media or access common data. With the advent of tablet devices, smartphones, laptops, and large displays, many researchers are investigating how ecologies of devices can be designed so that they interact with each other (and their users) in sensible and meaningful ways.

## MobiSurf: Communicating mindfully together through an ecology of devices

An exciting space for designers to begin to think about is using external large screens as part of the communication infrastructure when people are sitting together and want to share messages with each other. Getting people to lift up their heads from their own devices can offer more opportunities for them to be mindful of those around them. One useful example in this space is *MobiSurf*, which shows how working with a shared surface and personal mobile devices improves collaboration:

With the system, a group of users' own devices can be used in conjunction with a shared larger display. So, from left to right in the images above, when a user touches their phone to the surface, content is transferred from the small to the large display for easier group discussion.

There's Not an App for That | Designing Mindful Communication Apps

Typical examples of this would include the *Pass-Them-Around* platform and the co-present photo sharing system Gary and his colleagues produced in South Africa, which we encountered in Chapters 11 and 14.

Here, handsets are used in a co-located way to create an ad-hoc sharing group. Being somewhat older, our system was based on PDA technology and broadcast an image from one device to all other co-located devices. The system was designed to see how groups manage turn taking—who gets to show their photo at a given time. The *Pass-Them-Around* platform is much more advanced, whereby a device "knows" its location relative to other devices. In this way, users may flick an image from their screen to that of another user. While these systems are steps in the right direction, there is still much to change about the mobile interface to support co-located immediate sharing. By allowing devices to behave differently when people are co-located, we are facilitating a form of mindfulness between the participants.

Our own system was purposefully built to enhance a situation that a group had enjoyed together at some time. So, the devices would display photographs that a group had taken together. A user could take over the screens of other devices to display a photograph they wished to discuss. However, while they were talking, other people could doodle on the image to perhaps annotate an area of interest, but more often than not, modify the image in a humorous way (see Figure 17.5).

Figure 17.5 Co-located photo sharing via screen sharing.

So, the group could relive and retell an experience, but then enhance that experience through teasing and sharing in a new medium (that of shared image editing).

Even when the participants are not close by, "now" communications can create mindfulness. So, James Clawson created a system for remote but immediate communication of images. *Mobiphos* is a mobile imaging application that automatically sends every image taken to a group of subscribers. As this transmission of images is happening in real time, *pushed directly to the handset*, group members knew where people were and what they were taking images of. Capturers were mindful of recipients by taking images specifically for them. The real-time updates engendered playful usage, with people who were roaming round a shared location but not close to each other competing to take the "best" picture of a particular location.

## Allow people to manage their identities

Another consideration we can draw from the findings of Ervin Goffman with regard to frontstage and backstage is that people do not want to share everything when they are together. So while *Mobiphos* is powerful in how it can share images with users without any extra input, it does not allow us to perform our identities.

Even the gallery image application on every handset is fraught with peril when using a handset to physically show an image to another person. What if they should swipe to the next image and see a backstage shot? We need to start building this type of functionality into our apps, wherein images are tagged as private and only shown when explicitly frontstaged (Figure 17.6).

One exploration Thomas Reitmaier, our colleague, has made in this space is a system that allows a user to quickly tag images with one of three categories:

- For sharing;
- For keeping; or,
- For ignoring-for-now.

Figure 17.6 Grid view of some of Matt's photos. He'd be happy for someone to look at the images in the center, but there are pictures to the right and left that he'd feel uncomfortable with others viewing! Perhaps these photos should disappear when he's passing round his device in a group?

Given that most of us can't decide what to do with most of the images we take, his system defaults to a limbo state of photos hanging around on the device if they are not tagged explicitly. In the days of physical photographs, images in this state were referred to as "shoeboxed" as they never made it to albums, but were simply shoved in a shoebox.

However, if a user knows they want to share a picture some day, they flick the image in the camera review screen away from themselves (see Figure 17.7 where the cute dog photo is being made public by moving it up to the red zone).

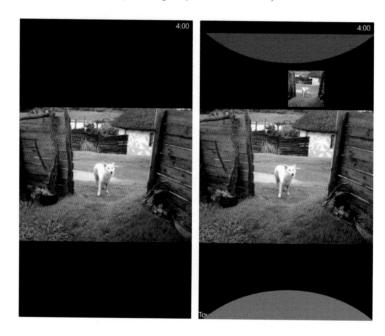

Figure 17.7 The dog is cute, but is it something you want to share publicly at some point? If "yes," move it up towards the red ellipse; if "no," tag it as private by flicking the image down to the green zone.

If they know that the image is private, then it can be drawn down to the bottom of the screen. In this way, quick private and public collections can be created, but most images drift in the backstage to be curated later or simply ignored.

In this age of mobile Internet, the models we have for files, permissions, and security are woefully out of date. As Richard Harper and colleagues at Microsoft Research bemoan, the abstraction of everything (in our case, a shared image) as a file with a set of permissions does not begin to address the needs of the app users in many forms of sharing.

For example, in systems that help people share content when they are sitting together, should the image disappear from the target handset when the receiver is "out of range"? Or should images be locked until the next time that group of people are together? Or, should images follow a *ShapChat* model and expire after a certain time? If we are to build apps for co-located situations, then these complex aspects of privacy and identity need to be taken seriously.

Finally, because handsets support various forms of communications, the "communicate now, consume on receipt" scenario can easily be interrupted and our identities exposed. Returning to Goffman's terminology for a moment, we might be engaged in some front-stage activity (perhaps photo sharing) when we receive a call. If we take that call, then the rest of that group become privy to some other aspect of our life—they might hear us discuss something to do with our children or physician. In a sense, we give our friends or colleagues a glimpse backstage.

## Design Challenge

For us as designers, the question then becomes about how we allow users to manage interruptions without disrupting the frontstage activity in which they have engaged. Clearly in the scenario above, automatic call barring when one is sharing images is too draconian. What else can you think of?

The challenge is not just around allowing people to perform their identity, but to move smoothly from one identity to the next.

## Awareness

Another way in which current apps can make us mindful of others in real time is by transmitting no message at all, but simply making us aware of other people. Crude ways of doing this exist already, such as *WhatsApp*'s "Last seen at" or *Skype*'s "Offline/Online/…" feedback. To some extent, this gives the sender some idea of the recipient's circumstances.

In co-located situations, apps like *Badoo* allow us to find out who is physically near to us, so that we can engage them in face-to-face conversation. *Facebook Mobile* has a more accountable version of finding nearby people in that it already knows who your friends are (and who the friends of those friends are).

The *Glancephone* project transcends this passive awareness of people and allows us to request an implicit status update from other people. So, if you wanted to find out how Simon was doing, Glancephone allows you to request that Simon's phone takes an image with its front-facing camera and sends it back to you. This is not as alarming as it might at first sound. Having used the Glancephone system, one soon gets into the habit of placing your handset in a position so that if someone does request an image, the shot taken is an appropriate one.

Although it needs to be thought through very carefully, the Glancephone system represents the beginning of the end of the "me"-focused view of the handset. Here, someone else may request *your* handset to perform an action on their behalf. Where does this end? Can they install or remove apps? Can they see what you are doing on your handset at that time? Until we break the model of an app-based, task-centric handset, we will be less inclined to look up from our device and be mindful of the people on the other side of our communication.

## Option 2: *Communicate later, consume on receipt*

This class of applications represents those that allow us to share with someone else, but not do the sharing immediately. So we are mindful of someone in the moment (for example, we take a picture of something we'd like to discuss with a friend), but we do not wish to send them the media in that instant; we want to savor discussing the image with them, or perhaps the image makes no sense without a lengthy verbal explanation.

At present, on most mobile handsets, the only way to share media is via the "Share" button in a contextual menu. You then select the application to do the sharing and off the item goes (see Figure 17.8).

There's Not an App for That | Designing Mindful Communication Apps

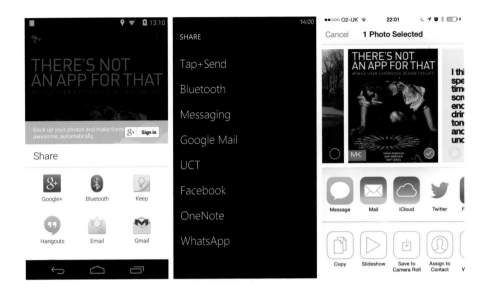

Figure 17.8 Sharing options on today's smartphones.

Again, this task-based way of doing communication robs us of a delayed, mindful form of communication, where the media is used to enhance a conversation. Instead, by being sent instantly, the sharing replaces the conversation.

(We are not saying that the instant sharing of media is a bad thing—far from it—rather, it should not be the only form of communication. Our argument is that we need to be aware that other forms of communication exist, and it is time we started exploring those.)

Furthermore, the share menu is orientated around apps, so the model is one of sharing with an app and not with a person. Even more problematic is that these apps do not embody any form of sharing that is familiar to humans. So sharing, for a human, can be broken down into actions such as "lending," "swapping," "trading," and so on. How can we be mindful of others when we abdicate our form of sharing to a choice between which transmission system we want to use to share our message?

One system that Thomas Reitmaier has been working on that does permit this delayed form of interaction is *Share Face2Face*, which adds a new option to the share button (as in Figure 17.9).

Figure 17.9 *Share Face2Face.*

Rather than becoming just another option in the selection of instant sharing apps, media that is shared in this way is kept on the handset until such time as the sender and recipient are in proximity. At that point, the sender is prompted to view the media and discuss it with the intended recipient.

This need for systems that support face-to-face discussion of media was highlighted in another mobile study by Thomas Olsson and colleagues, this time around the sharing of significant life events. Although the research was focused on the digital curation of such events, they found that participants wanted a system that would allow them to discuss, face-to-face, the digital artifact.

Participants did not want to send the artifact away to the recipient to examine on their own; rather, they wanted to remember together. You have most likely had the same sensation when buying a gift for someone—presents are often bought with the anticipation of the moment when you will see the recipient open the wrapping. Buying something online and sending it directly to a remote recipient is just not the same.

There's Not an App for That | Designing Mindful Communication Apps

Of course, the sender and recipient do not need to be located together. A message may be delayed until a certain time or delivered when the recipient is in a particular place. Mundane forms of this might be actions such as sending our children a message before they leave school reminding them not to forget to bring home their lunch box. A more whimsical version might be taking a photo of yourself in a particular place that is delivered to a friend when they too are standing in that place.

## Design Challenge
### Communicating later with strangers

After sitting in Euston station at rush hour one morning, and watching people stride from platform to platform with their headphones in and their eyes fixed on their target, Gary started to wonder if it would be possible for these people to lay down audio "trails." He found himself becoming fascinated by the idea of wandering through the trails left behind by commuters, and listening to the echoes of London heading to work.

What would this service look like? One possibility would be to implicitly tie media to a location; just as we see the paths through woodland where others have walked before us, we might hear the audio of the commuters who walk the same routes that we do. How would users subscribe to trails? What visualizations or audiolizations can you imagine to support this system?

One form of this type of delayed communication is geocaching—a popular hobby that involves leaving a hidden message for someone to find when then arrive at a certain location. When studying this phenomenon, researcher Kenton O'Hara saw the great joy that people have in not just finding these delayed messages, but also creating the locations for others to enjoy. So again, this notion of constructing a message in the present with anticipated joy of someone receiving it in the future is manifest in the people creating the cache.

The point is that, as app developers, we should not fall into the trap of only enabling immediate sharing. Certainly, as Hewlett-Packard researcher Tim Kindberg and colleagues found, the strongest urge to share media such as photos is when we think of people *"in the moment,"* but that does not imply that the act of sharing needs to be instantaneous. We can think of someone now and share with them later, *anticipating* a future communication which we will probably witness (as in *Share Face2Face*) or *imagining* a future communication that we will not witness (as in geocaching).

## Option 3: *Communicate now, consume later*

In essence, this category captures familiar asynchronous messaging. However, apart from the familiar technologies like email or SMS, it allows us to imagine new forms of app that are less familiar. One such group of applications is where we have multiple authors creating something together to share for the purposes of remembering a person or event.

A perfect example of this is the *Mobile Stories* project, wherein children used their mobile devices in a co-located situation to create stories together. Media on each child's handset could be used to co-author a joint story, which the children could then take away on their handset.

## Putting it into practice

We are familiar with sending messages to people who are not with us for later use. What sort of apps can you think of that allow people to create a shared memory of a situation they are in together for later enjoyment?

In Chapter 13, we saw one approach to capturing meetings for later review. Another of our responses is called *Com-Phone*—an Android app that can be used to capture an experience over time in photos, text, and audio in the style of a storyboard or comic strip. The following images show the app's interface—its simple main screen (left image) shows the stories, or narratives, that have been created. Any story can be added to at any point with photos, recorded audio, or text (center image), and stories can be played back on the phone (right image) or shared with others in either source (for editing) or video format.

We've used the app ourselves on vacations with others, creating a memory of a trip with the people we are journeying with and later sharing it with them and others as a souvenir of our travel. What other approaches can you think of for helping groups of people create a rich shared memory of their time together?

Rather than remembering a particular person, or explicitly creating a joint media artifact, there's also the intriguing possibility of implicitly capturing a co-located session. We are imagining that when a group of people gets together to use co-located applications (as described in the box on *MobiSurf*, earlier) that, after the event, the shared media and interaction are stored in the cloud, accessible to everyone who participated in the group.

These frozen collaborations could be anything from work meetings to family reminiscences. But they could be visited after the fact and allow people to remember the interaction in an undirected (browsing family photos) or a very purposeful way (*"I need to find the file that Brian shared when we met last week"*). By seeing the act of sharing merely as a file transfer, stripped of its embodied meaning, then, we close our eyes to these deep, rich, collaborations that are significant to us as human beings. And we miss the opportunity to build apps that support them.

## Option 4: *Communicate later, consume later*

The goal of this category is to support the thoughtful composition or collection of media and give it to a recipient for their consumption at some future date. Apps in this category are very scarce, yet there is evidence for the need to communicate in this way.

Some of our work with teenagers in resource-constrained parts of South Africa (who, amongst other things, cannot access desktop computers) shows that they spend a lot of time creating what they call "photo cards." Consisting, on average, of 12% of our subjects' collections, these were carefully constructed images, overlaid with messages and other graphics. They were created with a particular audience in mind, be it a single person or a group of friends.

These images were designed to engender a humorous response, act as a status update, or were heartfelt messages written specifically for the recipient. To create these photo cards, the participants had to use various pieces of editing software on the handset and then share the image via swapping memory cards or Bluetoothing the file directly to a handset (they could not afford Internet access or data connections).

Alex Taylor and Richard Harper of Microsoft Research write about similar behavior amongst teens in the UK, as mentioned earlier, where a text message is thoughtfully composed and sent as a "gift" to be treasured by the recipient. The recipient treasures such a gift and reads it (many times) when the giver is not present.

So valued are these gifts that the recipients in Taylor and Harper's study reported engaging in serious memory management on their handsets to delete other less-treasured messages in order to be able to preserve gift messages in the handset's memory (this study was conducted at a time when handsets had far more limited storage resources). Taylor and Harper argue against the viability of storing such important messages in the cloud somewhere, as the recipients attach meaning to the embodiment of the message on their handset. They also note that these gift-giving exchanges are highly ritualized, with an expected structure of communication containing well-understood forms of statements and responses.

While these forms of behavior have been observed from Cambridge to Cape Town, there are few applications that currently support these highly ritualized and meaningful forms of communication. Can a message be marked so that it is never deleted, for example? Or, why do handsets not have a "memorial area" where special media may be stored and mulled over at leisure?

Finally, what about support for the creation of these types of media? Messaging is often seen as ephemeral, but what if people wanted to create more meaningful media, such as the photo cards described above? Current handsets simply do not support this directly. At the time of writing, *Instagram*, with its fanciful photo editing, goes some way to creating modified images, but the modifications tend to be simple filters. And the mindfulness is not so much about the recipient, but to illustrate the prowess of the photographer.

We feel this is a rich area for exploration, both in the creation of apps that allow for the mindful construction of media on mobile platforms, and in apps that allow people to curate and to store shared media that has meaning beyond the mere content of the message.

## Solving the problem without apps

In this chapter, the focus has been on new app interactions that might help users think about the purpose and the person or people involved in their communications. Many of these ideas—and the ones they hopefully inspire you to come up with—can be relatively easily implemented with today's mobiles.

What if we started again, though, and imagined a world where apps disappear or operate quite differently from today?

In the next chapter we'll be looking at this more radical approach. As you read on, think about what the user experience would be like if the basic mobile design philosophy changed in these ways. We'd encourage you to also explore how you could enhance your current apps by recruiting some of the insights that underpin these unorthodox perspectives.

# Resources

Alan Cooper and colleagues' definition of interaction design can be found in [1], and Richard Buchanan's comments in [2]. The Groupware matrix is adapted from [3]. Proxemics and perception of space are discussed in [4], the proxemics toolkit in [5]. Jason Farman's arguments that physical and virtual space are a whole can be found in in [6].

The *Huggy Pajama* system is described and explored in [7]. Goffman's arguments for identity are in [8]; Buckingham's arguments against are in [9]. A news report about Leigh Van Bryan's controversial tweet can be found at [10].

*MobiSurf* [11] showed how working with a shared surface and mobile devices can improve collaboration. Andrés Lucero's *Pass-Them-Around* system can be found in [12]; our own co-located photo sharing system is in [13]. James Clawson's *Mobiphos* system for remote but immediate sharing is in [14], and Thomas Reitmaier and Pierre Benz's exploration of co-located interactions in [15].

Richard Harper and colleagues' analysis of how current permissions do not begin to address the needs of the app in collocated, delayed, immediate, group, and individual forms of sharing is in [16], and Harper's earlier work on the *Glancephone* is in [17].

The need for systems that support face-to-face discussion of media was highlighted by Thomas Olsson and colleagues [18]. Kenton O'Hara discusses the enjoyment from not just finding these messages, but also creating the locations for others to enjoy [19], and Tim Kindberg and colleagues discuss sharing "in the moment" [20].

The *Mobile Stories* project allowed media on individual handsets to be used to co-author a joint story [21], and our work with teenagers in resource-constrained parts of South Africa that showed that they spend a lot of time creating what they call "photo cards" in [22]. Finally, Taylor and Harper's gift giving through text messages can be found in [23].

[1] Cooper A, Reimann R, Cronin D. About Face 3: The Essentials of Interaction Design. Indianapolis, IN: Wiley; 2007.

[2] Buchanan R. Design research and the new learning. Des Issues 2001;17(4):3–23. http://dx.doi.org/10.1162/07479360152681056.

[3] Johansen R. GroupWare: Computer Support for Business Teams. New York: The Free Press; 1988.

[4] Hall E. The Hidden Dimension. New York: Doubleday; 1966.

[5] Greenberg S, Marquardt N, Ballendat T, Diaz-Marino R, Wang M. Proxemic interactions: the new ubicomp? Interactions 2011;18(1):42–50. http://dx.doi.org/10.1145/1897239.1897250.

[6] Farman J. Mobile Interface Theory: Embodied Space and Locative Media. Abingdon: Routledge; 2012.

[7] Teh JKS, Cheok AD, Peiris RL, Choi Y, Thuong V, Lai S. Huggy Pajama: A mobile parent and child hugging communication system. In: Proceedings of the 7th International Conference on Interaction Design and Children; ACM; 2008. pp. 250–7. http://dx.doi.org/10.1145/1463689.1463763.

[8] Goffman E. The Presentation of Self in Everyday Life. London: Penguin; 1999.

[9] Buckingham D. Youth, Identity, and Digital Media. (Chap. Introducing Identity). Cambridge, MA: MIT Press; 2008.

[10] Caution on Twitter urged as tourists barred from US. 2012. Retrieved from http://www.bbc.co.uk/news/technology-16810312.

[11] Seifert J, Simeone A, Schmidt D, Holleis P, Reinartz C, Wagner M, Gellersen H, Rukzio E. Mobisurf: Improving co-located collaboration through integrating mobile devices and interactive surfaces. In: Proceedingsof the 2012 ACM International Conference on Interactive Tabletops and Surfaces; ACM; 2012. pp. 51–60. http://dx.doi.org/10.1145/2396636.2396644.

[12] Lucero A, Holopainen J, Jokela T. Pass-them-around: Collaborative use of mobile phones for photo sharing. In: Proceedings of the SIGCHI Conference on Human Factors in Computing Systems; ACM; 2011. pp. 1787–96. http://dx.doi.org/10.1145/1978942.1979201.

[13] Ah Kun LM, Marsden G. Co-present photo sharing on mobile devices. In: Proceedings of the 9th International Conference on Human Computer Interaction with Mobile Devices and Services; ACM; 2007. pp. 277–84. http://dx.doi.org/10.1145/1377999.1378019.

[14] Clawson J, Voida A, Patel N, Lyons K. Mobiphos: A collocated-synchronous mobile photo sharing application. In: Proceedings of the 10th International Conference on Human Computer Interaction with Mobile Devices and Services; ACM; 2008. pp. 187–95. http://dx.doi.org/10.1145/1409240.1409261.

[15] Reitmaier T, Benz P, Marsden G. Designing and theorizing co-located interactions. In: Proceedings of the SIGCHI Conference on Human Factors in Computing Systems; ACM; 2013. pp. 381–90. http://dx.doi.org/10.1145/2470654.2470709.

[16] Harper R, Thereska E, Lindley S, Banks R, Gosset P, Odom W, Smyth G, Whitworth E. What Is a File? Microsoft Research; 2011.

[17] Harper R, Taylor S. Glancephone: An exploration of human expression. In: Proceedings of the 11th International Conference on Human-Computer Interaction with Mobile Devices and Services; ACM; 2009. pp. 24:1–0. http://dx.doi.org/10.1145/1613858.1613890.

[18] Olsson T, Soronen H, Väänänen-Vainio-Mattila K. User needs and design guidelines for mobile services for sharing digital life memories. In: Proceedings of the 10th International Conference on Human Computer Interaction with Mobile Devices and Services; ACM; 2008. pp. 273–82. http://dx.doi.org/10.1145/1409240.1409270.

[19] O'Hara K. Understanding geocaching practices and motivations. In: Proceedings of the SIGCHI Conference on Human Factors in Computing Systems; ACM; 2008. pp. 1177–86. http://dx.doi.org/10.1145/1357054.1357239.

[20] Kindberg T, Spasojevic M, Fleck R, Sellen A. The ubiquitous camera: An in-depth study of camera phone use. IEEE Pervasive Comput 2005;4(2):42–50. http://dx.doi.org/10.1109/MPRV.2005.42.

[21] Fails JA, Druin A, Guha ML. Mobile collaboration: Collaboratively reading and creating children's stories on mobile devices. In: Proceedings of the 9th International Conference on Interaction Design and Children; ACM; 2010. pp. 20–9. http://dx.doi.org/10.1145/1810543.1810547.

[22] Walton M, Marsden G, Haßreiter S, Allen S. Degrees of sharing: Proximate media sharing and messaging by young people in Khayelitsha. In: Proceedings of the 14th International Conference on Human-Computer Interaction with Mobile Devices and Services; ACM; 2012. pp. 403–12. http://dx.doi.org/10.1145/2371574.2371636.

[23] Taylor AS, Harper R. The gift of the gab?: A design oriented sociology of young people's use of mobiles. Comput Supported Coop Work 2003;12(3):267–96. http://dx.doi.org/10.1023/A:1025091532662.

# CHAPTER 18

## Opportunity 5.2
## MINDFULNESS WITHOUT APPS

## WHAT'S THE OPPORTUNITY?

This opportunity is thinking about a world without apps (or at least apps as we currently know them). What if the underlying mobile infrastructure was based on a mindful outlook? What if people and things around us triggered the services available on our phones? Or what if all our phone interactions were people based?

## WHY IS IT ATTRACTIVE?

Thinking about radical alternatives will further help you to see what's missing from today's established frameworks.

We don't expect apps to disappear, or for these solutions to address all of your users' needs (they *will* still want to play *Flappy Birds*, or whatever the next big app game is!). However, in terms of making people more mindful in their interactions, what you'll see here are two provocations that you could use to innovate in your own future services.

## KEY POINTS

- We argue that current app frameworks limit innovation for mindfulness.

- Two alternatives are proposed:

  - A just-in-time scheme, where apps and services appear and disappear from the handset to meet a user's present needs. People are encouraged to think about what's around them and what they should focus on, as opposed to being distanced and distracted by the screenfuls of apps at their fingertips.

- A people-centered interface that forces users to be mindful of who they are communicating with, and opens up new, flexible ways for people to interact, in contrast to the task-focused narrowness of current apps.

## WHAT DO YOU THINK?

Take a look at all of the apps on your own phone. Do you sometimes get lost when you are trying to find a particular one? Have you ever been frustrated when you realize that you have to download an app to do something you only want to do once or very infrequently? How many of the shops, airlines, museums, movie theaters, workplaces, clubs, churches, and so on that you interact with have tried to get you to install an app?

How does such app life differ from your digital surfing via a web browser?

# Introduction

The title of this book is *There's Not an App for That*. But, in this chapter, we would like to go a little further in exploring the limitations of apps. Actually, it is more the corrupting effect of apps, and how they limit current handset design that we want to explore. This is a logical consequence of the "task fallacy" discussed in Chapter 16, where our design efforts are focused on producing apps that complete tasks.

In order to achieve tasks, we need apps to support us. Therefore, the defining metaphor of handset design until this point has been focused on the installation, use, and arrangement of those apps. In breaking free from task centricity, we believe it is time to remove apps as the primary way of structuring our interaction with mobile devices.

In our move from old-style desktop operating systems to new mobile app-based systems we have gained much. Apps are easy to install and remove. The functioning of the operating system is hidden from the user—it just works. And everything is clearly organized around the app.

What we have lost, however, is access to the information and data we generate. So, unless we go in through an imaging app, we cannot access our images. Or if we want a music file, we need to find an MP3 player. On first glance this might seem sensible. However, it precludes many of the sharing possibilities and groups of app we have discussed earlier. If one cannot directly access a piece of media, then one cannot share it. So, unless a particular application has built-in sharing functionality, we cannot share the media it created. We limit the sharing as we cannot see the media independently of the application.

# Getting rid of apps 1: Building a just-in-time scheme

We are not alone in wanting to get rid of apps. Usability consultant Scott Jenson also lists many problems with an app-based interface in his article *Mobile Apps Must Die*. His argument is that we will be swamped by apps in the near future, and that the pain of installing and managing them will outweigh the value of using them. Instead, he proposes a *"just-in-time interaction"* model, whereby services make themselves available depending on location or activity (e.g., you might walk into a mall, and the application for navigating the mall installs on your device automatically, removing itself when you leave).

Jenson expands his thinking further in a subsequent discussion, *Of Bears, Bats, and Bees: Making Sense of the Internet of Things*, in which he imagines an ecology of devices including PCs, mobiles, small single-purpose devices, and embedded chips. In this *Internet of Things* world, interfaces on our mobiles not only have apps appear and disappear depending on context, but allow users to browse and search information from local devices (e.g., a bus stop transmitting arrival times).

This notion of a world of devices that our mobiles will interact with may seem far off, but the future is already with us. However, current forms of local or embedded devices tend to reinforce the digital narcissism in our lives. Whether these are fitness devices like the *Fitbit* or smart electricity consumption meters, they feed data into the pool to enhance our reflection about ourselves. The apps that come with these sensors encourage us to post our results (*"I used 5 kW today!"*) using social media, but this is a push model, to promote our achievements and ourselves. Jenson's agenda is to take us beyond these personal sensors and consider sensors and services in the wider environment, centered around the physical location or community and not on ourselves or just in our homes.

But how does that vision influence handset design? In the past two chapters we have explored an agenda of being mindful of other people and of favoring relationships over tasks. In Chapter 7, we also looked at being mindful of the physical location, freeing users from having to look at the screen.

Jenson's ideas lead us to a blending of these notions, allowing us to imagine mobile devices that communicate and interact with our (augmented) physical environments consisting of people and places around us. The device is still centered on apps, but, for many of those applications, their management (installation and deletion) is handled automatically.

**Search for:**
*Scott Jenson
blog*

We can also imagine an "environment" browser, which would allow us to see, store, and consume data from the device ecology around us. Although this browser may not seem all that different to location-based services, its conceptualization is radically different. Location-based services allow a particular app (e.g., a coffee chain's offering) to optimize its operation based on where the handset is located (e.g., by helping you locate the nearest branch)—app first, location second.

The new browser, in contrast, starts with being mindful of the location and then allows the user to further explore that location by drawing on lots of potential providers of data. It is essentially a generalized interface to ambient computer systems.

## Building browse and search into woodland

Many prototype research ambient systems have been built and their usage analyzed to understand what types of services people enjoy using. One of the more famous examples is Yvonne Rogers' *Ambient Wood*. Here, a research team augmented an area of woodland with various devices that delivered content or could be queried. They gave their child participants PDAs to interact with some of these data sources and also supplied them with other devices that could measure information about the environment (e.g., a moisture sensor). The Ambient Wood studies show how building devices to allow users to probe and ask questions of their environment enhances their awareness and enjoyment of their surroundings.

# Getting rid of apps 2: Back to people again

What if we centered mobile user interfaces on people instead of on apps? Seeing the electronic device as a mediator and not an end in itself, instead of app icons, our handsets could only show faces:

- We could arrange people into screens representing the different groups in our lives.

- Groups could be dynamically adjusted to reflect those in our physical location.

- We could drag media onto those groups or individuals to share.

- Only in the act of sharing would applications become active to facilitate the communication between people, thereby supporting relationships.

A big challenge for the next generation of mobile handsets is this: to orientate our communication around people, and make future apps that support that communication, rather than force it into the silos that each app creates. So, rather than start with media and how we wish to share it, we can start with people and add media to them.

Figure 18.1 Sharing centered around people.

In Figure 18.1, we tap Matt's image and then attach an item to him to be reviewed when we are co-located. When we eventually do meet, our device can notify us that there is media we may want to share with him.

But, if we take seriously this notion of person-to-person communication then the notion of a single media object that we might share no longer seems like an adequate abstraction. Imagine the scenario where you are with someone you have met and you are discussing music with them. You might want to know what music you have in common, or what music you have that your friend does not, or just grab all the music that your friend has that you do not.

Or, think about another scenario, where you meet a friend at college. You might want to plan your next meeting, and see when you both have a gap in your calendar. Or, you might want to find what classes you have in common, or what classes you take that they do not attend.

In other words, the model of using media jointly is not a simple share—it can mean so much more when viewed collectively to give form and meaning to a relationship. The notion of simply sharing a file seems very crude in this context.

The good news is that all of the scenarios listed above can be supported by the same set of canonical operators provided in every relational database, namely union, intersection, and difference.

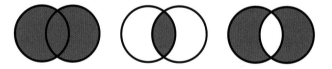

Figure 18.2 Sharing intersections: union, intersection, and difference.

- The **union** operator is the total of all the media on each device. Systems such as Apple's "Household" metaphor are instances of the union operator—they aggregate all the media for a group of people (see Figure 18.2, left).

- **Intersection** finds the overlap in two collections, as in Figure 18.2, center. Here, we can find when we will be in the same place together by the intersection of calendars, or what musical taste we have in common, or what movies we have both watched, and so on.

■ Finally, **difference** tells us what one has that the other does not, as in Figure 18.2, right.

These three operators are the core of a branch of mathematics called set theory, which is concerned with the relationships between collections of information. So useful are these operators that we believe they should be added to the core of every mobile operating system, so that users can explore their joint data sets together.

In our proposed metaphor, we could drag Matt's image onto ours and see what dates, songs, movies, books, etc. we have in common, or what we do not have. This would not be hard, as most mobile operating systems already store this type of data in relational databases that support set operations. However, we need to break the app metaphor in order to free the data so that users can perform these types of comparisons and use their collections of data to enhance their relationships.

## Resources

Scott Jenson's powerful critiques of mobile apps and device ecologies are available on his blog [1,2]. Yvonne Rogers' Ambient Wood system is detailed in [3].

[1] Jenson S. Mobile apps must die. 2011. Retrieved from http://designmind.frogdesign.com/blog/mobile-apps-must-die.html.

[2] Jenson S. Of bears, bats, and bees: Making sense of the Internet of things. 2012. Retrieved from http://designmind.frogdesign.com/blog/of-bears- bats-and-bees-making-sense-of-the-internet-of-things.html.

[3] Rogers Y, Price S, Fitzpatrick G, Fleck R, Harris E, Smith H, et al. Ambient wood: Designing new forms of digital augmentation for learning outdoors. In: Proceedings of the 2004 Conference on Interaction Design and Children: Building a Community; ACM; 2004. pp. 3–10. http://dx.doi.org/10.1145/1017833.1017834.

# CHAPTER 19

## Opportunity 6
## FROM SOME TO ALL

## WHAT'S THE OPPORTUNITY?

For most of this book we've been speaking about users who live relatively comfortable lives in what are called developed regions. They are educated, have reasonable salaries, and can access resources like the Internet and power grid.

To end our series of provocations, we want you to think about developing apps and services for the many hundreds of millions of users in developing regions who don't enjoy these luxuries.

We think there are huge opportunities to improve the quality of life in these regions through effective innovation. There are also big opportunities to do business in these areas, too.

We're not going to separate out our discussion into distinct chapters on the "problem" and the "opportunity" as we've done in other parts of the book. Instead, we want you to concentrate on the opportunities to make a difference.

## WHY IS IT ATTRACTIVE?

The size of the untapped market for effective apps and services that fit these contexts is vast. The impact new services can have on people's ability to collaborate, coordinate, and educate themselves is also exciting.

## KEY POINTS

- Resource constraints in these regions include lower literacy levels, low exposure to computing, and limited access to electricity and other infrastructures.

- We will look at interesting proposals and issues in tackling these constraints to build effective apps and services, including designs and infrastructures for sharing services, designs to accommodate literacy levels, and how platform thinking can empower people in these regions to take innovation into their own hands.

- Apps and services for these regions, perhaps more than anywhere else in the world, have the potential to make big differences in health, education, and business outcomes. If you are driven to change the world with your app skills, these are the regions to focus on!

## WHAT DO YOU THINK?

- Think about times when your battery level on your phone is low and you know that you can't recharge for several hours. How does your behavior change?

- What about when there is no cellular network, either due to where you are, or because the cost of using it would be prohibitively expensive (such as when you are roaming overseas). Again, how does your mobile use change?

- Now recall a time when you were in a foreign country and could not understand the signs, words, or norms when trying to find your way around. How did it feel? How did you cope?

# Introduction

Most estimates suggest that by the time of writing this book (2014), there are as many active SIM cards in the world as there are people: approximately seven billion. While this does not imply that every single person on Earth uses a mobile phone—many people have more than one SIM—there cannot be many people left who do not have some sort of access to a handset. This ubiquity has meant that for many people, all over the world, their first exposure to digital technology is in the form of a cellphone.

Much has been written about the rapid growth of the cellular market in developing regions. There are many reports of the effect mobiles are having, and the potential that exists for the technology to make a real impact on development goals. Within the academic community, there are several professional societies for the development of new forms of appropriate technology for the developing world. Research organizations have been expanding and setting up new centers in developing regions of India, Africa, and Asia for many years.

Commercially, this is an expanding market, so handset manufacturers and mobile software developers see the potential to increase their sales. However, they cannot simply cast off excess stock or old designs to the developing world and hope that people will buy them. For many in the developing world, a cellular handset represents the single biggest purchase of their lives. Buyers need to make sure that the phone will meet their needs, and those needs are unlikely to be the same as someone from the developed world. Consequently, companies spend a lot of time optimizing their handsets for these users and their needs.

But when we write about the developing world, what do we mean by this? How is it different from the traditional markets and population segments for which digital technologies are designed? In this chapter we will look at some of the existing technologies that have been created specifically for developing regions. We'll also look at some of the most common pitfalls and reasons for failure. More importantly, though, we'll look at why it is important to design for emerging markets, and the huge impact future mobiles will have in these areas.

# Inspired by the bigger picture

On a recent trip to Mumbai, India, we encountered many situations that made us reflect on some of the themes we've presented earlier in the book. We are lucky in our jobs to get the opportunity to travel and see many different ways of "doing" life.

We hope this book has inspired you to look around you, wherever you are based, or wherever you travel to, and see life's richness and diversity. Use these resources to challenge and direct your future UX designs.

## From heads down to face on

Here's a photo taken from the inside of a rickshaw. These three-wheeled public transports whizz through the city, nimbly avoiding collisions with cars and cows. You are not protected from the world outside as you might be in private car or taxi, but it's an exhilarating ride! Truly "face on" living.

## From clinical to clutter

As part of our fieldwork, we visited Dharavi, the slum featured in the film *Slumdog Millionaire*. It is a seemingly chaotic congregation of people and makeshift buildings, with a population of over a million people. There are few street signs, and many very narrow intersecting alleys—a maze that you can imagine being lost in forever. But, Dharavi houses thousands of entrepreneurial businesses and functioning families.

## From private and personal to public and performance

The image below is of a Rajasthani storyteller we interviewed to help our thinking around digital storytelling. His "mobile" is the box you can see: during the (long) story performance, the storyteller carefully opens up the physical elements of the box—doors, flaps, and trays—and points to illustrations with a peacock feather.

# Challenges

The key difference when designing digital technologies for developing markets is that of resource constraints. People have poor access to electricity, networks, devices, and education. As a consequence, their need for apps, their ability to use them, and the frequency with which they can access content are, literally, a world away from users in the developed world.

# Price sensitivity: Multi-SIM

When designing mobile interactions for the developing world, one cannot assume that there is a one-to-one mapping between a SIM and a person. Users are highly price sensitive. To many, it is worth the effort to swap one SIM for another so that they can take advantage of differences in network pricing structures (for example, it may be cheaper to receive calls on one network, but make calls on another).

This has led to behaviors ranging from disassembling handsets between calls in order to change the SIM through to purchasing several cheap phones, instead of a single smartphone, so that all networks are accessible simultaneously. Figure 19.1 shows the three handsets owned by one entrepreneur in Zambia, where there are three networks—rather than spend his money on a more advanced phone, he owns three cheap devices, each connected to a different network.

Figure 19.1 A trader's three handsets, each with a different SIM for each of the networks in Zambia.

For people who cannot afford multiple handsets, manufacturers are now offering devices that can support several SIMs simultaneously. Due to close ties between cellular service providers and handset manufacturers, these devices have not been common until now. However, Indian and Chinese handset manufacturers, who have no such ties to service providers, started making multi-SIM handsets specifically for developing markets (see Figure 19.2). When SIM swapping happens several times a day, the long boot times of some traditional single-SIM handsets move from inconvenient to infuriating, so multi-SIM handsets have proven very popular. Following suit, several mainstream device companies have started offering multi-SIM devices. These range from fully active dual-SIM handsets to others which have a main SIM and up to five alternatives that can be hot-swapped depending on the task at hand.

Figure 19.2 Indian manufacturer Maxx Mobile makes several Android phones that support hot-swapping of SIMs. Multi-SIM handsets are becoming increasingly popular in developing regions, as they allow phone users to mix and match networks to reduce costs.

## Price sensitivity: Sharing handsets

The popularity of Nokia handsets in the developing world led the company to create models with features or applications specifically for those markets. One such feature is the ability to store multiple address books on a single handset, based on the observation that many people in the developing world share handsets. Phones such as the Nokia 105, for example, allow individual users sharing the handset to keep their contacts completely separate.

But are distinct address books the biggest challenge of sharing a handset? This seems unlikely, as handsets are viewed as highly personal items with which people construct their identities. Digital media researcher Marion Walton and colleagues studied teenage phone users in townships around Cape Town, and identified a number of issues around the sharing of handsets that are more substantial than mixed contact lists.

- **Sharing things you do not wish to be shared**: Handsets are shared between all age groups and all genders. It is expected that if your handset has run out of charge or airtime, you are free to ask others to lend you their handset, and they cannot refuse. Added to this, many such communities expect everything to be open and public. So, if a phone user has content on their handset they wish to keep private, this is problematic, as anyone they know (friends, siblings, parents, grandparents) could reasonably ask to use the handset at any time. Holding private information, or even causing suspicion that the handset may have private information (such as by the creation of a folder marked as "private") is socially unacceptable.

- **Inability to share things you want to**: The flip side of living in a close, highly situated community is that there is information that people do want to share, yet they cannot afford the airtime to do so. This leads to behaviors such as swapping memory cards from handsets or using Bluetooth to broadcast media from phone to phone. At present, peer-to-peer sharing is poorly supported. There is no standard format for media cards (some handsets instantly format any card they do not recognize!). Some media items on handsets also cannot be shared over Bluetooth—text messages being chief among these. People simply cannot afford to forward messages through SMS. So, an owner can only share by lending their handset to other people.

## Price sensitivity: Exploiting free services

One of the few channels that GSM providers do not charge their users for is USSD. USSD is a simple command-response protocol that allows people to top up their airtime accounts, check balances, and request services. In terms of usability, USSD is a horrid protocol, with a typical interaction looking something like the one in Figure 19.3. Users who have access to alternative interfaces would be unlikely to use USSD for much beyond balance enquiries. But price-sensitive users with no alternative will put up with poor interaction if it provides a useful service. Because the channel is free, users in the developing world have also subverted it to their own ends.

Chief among these unexpected uses are the adoptions of the "call me" messages that many networks allow to be sent at no cost to the sender. These messages were originally intended to allow a caller with a low airtime balance to request that the other party call them instead. However, by prearranging meanings, a "call me" message might

Figure 19.3 A typical USSD menu interaction. Dialing an access code (e.g., *111#) activates the text-based USSD menu. Further content or services are requested by entering the number next to the item required.

There's Not an App for That | From Some to All

mean anything from *"come pick me up from school"* to *"I am missing you."* Many cellular service providers now limit customers to a fixed number of missed calls per day in order to limit this "abuse" of the system.

## Lack of infrastructure: Charging

Access to electricity for charging handsets is a large problem in the developing world. Again, manufacturers have tried to address this issue by releasing specially designed models, such as those that recharge using solar cells. These solar cells are built into the handset, so the device can be left in the sun to recharge when not in use.

Commtiva's Sola, for example (see Figure 19.4), can be charged through solar power alone. Samsung released the Crest Solar E1107, which used solar cells to top up battery power. While solar charging seems like a great feature, this handset has very limited functionality (no camera, for example) and is not designed to be charged on solar for extended periods—it needs to be charged periodically through an external source to keep the battery in good condition. None of the devices in this market have made a large impact, with most having only limited distribution before being withdrawn from sale.

Figure 19.4 Commtiva's Sola handset charged by solar panels on the reverse. While an admirable attempt at designing a handset specifically for developing regions, the handset was ultimately a commercial failure.

As an alternative to customized solar-powered handsets, device and accessory manufacturers are also constructing standalone solar devices to charge mobile phones. While many are of poor quality—both in terms of durability and charging rates—other innovative solutions to charging have been designed. Nokia created the DC-14, for example—a dynamo that connects to a bicycle wheel that is used to charge a handset. While this does seem like a good idea, evaluations by Susan Wyche and colleagues have shown that the device works least well in the markets where it is most needed. For example, most roads in the developing world are in such a poor state that it is impossible to ride a bicycle for a sustained period, meaning it can take up to six hours of cycling to charge a handset.

## Literacy: Speaking handsets

In Matt and Gary's previous book (*Mobile Interaction Design*), we argued that the question of literacy in mobile interface design spans beyond being able to read the written form of a language. We explained how many of the conventions (such as icon design) on handsets of the period had been influenced by desktop computer designs. Even concepts as core as the notion of hierarchical information (critical to navigating most menus) are not found in every culture. Since that book was written (in 2005), handset interface design has moved away from text-based menus to icon-based interfaces. Yet things have not really improved for the illiterate user. Interfaces now have even more conventions: tabs, press-and-hold, cloud-based or local data, multitouch gestures and, occasionally, the hierarchical menu (usually in the settings area).

**Search for:**
*Mobile*
*Interaction*
*Design*

In some cases, manufacturers have responded to the challenge of providing access to low literacy populations by supplying handsets with audio interfaces, which read out options to the user. The Motorola F3, sold primarily in Africa, would, when first turned on, ask the user to select between English, French, and Swahili (the most common languages on the continent) by pressing a corresponding key. So, assuming that the user can recognize the number symbols, they can select a language of their choice and have menu options read aloud to them.

Behavioral scientist Jan Chipchase's research documents the struggles illiterate users have with handsets, noting that often such users carry a paper notebook in which to record telephone numbers of regular contacts. Chipchase also explains that illiterate users are restricted in their ability to explore the device (one of the potential strategies they might use to learn how the system works), as selecting the wrong option could cost them money, in the form of airtime.

Some of the design solutions that Chipchase suggests in response to literacy issues can easily be implemented in existing handsets, and there is evidence that manufacturers have adopted these. Giving sensible default values for settings, for example, is a simple change to make. Some of the suggestions are more fanciful and are not yet possible in lower-end phones (such as using the handset's camera to interpret symbols or numbers from a written sheet).

One critical piece of advice Chipchase gives, in his closing reflections, is to state that handsets for illiterate users should be no different to those of reading users to avoid stigma. Most of the phones and other devices designed specifically for the needs of users in the developing world have been commercial failures. As we see in the following box, this particular element of Chipchase's advice is critical in the developing world.

## Two different approaches

Motorola and Nokia both introduced handsets designed specifically for the developing world market. Both designs had a rugged construction, were dust- and splash-proof, had long battery life, and were relatively cheap.

Motorola's F3 had an innovative e-Ink screen that could be read in full sunlight, a clever dual antenna that helped to improve signal strength for remote areas, and audio-menus for illiterate users. Nokia's 1100 was an evolution of the standard low-end handsets available at the time, but included a torch and a radio. Despite being launched globally, the F3 sold sporadically, and for only a few years. The model was soon discontinued. The 1100, on the other hand, went on to be the best-selling handset of all time, with some 250 million units sold. Variants of the handset are still on sale to this day (2014).

Of course, it is impossible to know the exact reasons why people prefer one design over another, but from interviews we conducted at the time, people preferred the Nokia as it looked like a "normal" phone. As Jan Chipchase reports, people did not wish to be stigmatized by using a handset optimized for users only in the developing world.

## Design Pointer

Don't emphasize the obvious "need" when designing for special user capabilities. Rather, think about how to support your users while accommodating their wider desires, aspirations, and values. Practice this thinking now—how would you design for elderly users? Take a look at Age UK's *OwnFone* to start your exploration. What's good (and bad) about it?

**Search for:**
*Age UK*
*OwnFone*

## Opportunities

Let's turn now from some of the challenges you'll face to look at examples of innovation that we hope will inspire you to develop successful apps, devices, or services for these regions. We'll consider:

- Designs for sharing

- Designs to accommodate literacy levels

- Designs to provide platforms to enable innovation locally

In the developing world, your apps and services have the potential to make a dramatic impact on not just "user experience" but quality (and even quantity) of life. So, afterwards, we will follow on from their discussion by thinking about designing to make such big differences.

# Designing for sharing

As everywhere, people in these regions want to share with others or with a wider community. They have privacy concerns, and also there are many times when their access to network infrastructures is limited. How do we design in this context?

## Person-to-person sharing

With the advent of cloud computing, sharing of data has become highly integrated into the mobile experience. Whether it is explicit data sharing through social media or services such as *Dropbox*, or implicitly through cloud-based editing suites such as *Office 365*, those of us with always-on Internet access might consider the problem of sharing to be solved.

In the developing world, things are more complex, and people have to improvise. For example, users in India have developed sophisticated ways of downloading multimedia content and sharing it out through peer-swapping of memory cards or from a central hard disk in a cellular repair and recharge center. Despite there being innumerable interface, network, and technology challenges, the desire for media sharing drives people to overcome these barriers.

Then there is the question of whom people want to share with. Orange Labs researchers Chantal de Gournay and Zbigniew Smoreda found, for example, that the majority of communication happens within a local community. Certainly networking initiatives such as *Village Telco*, which aims to create local mesh networks, were driven by the fact that up to 70% of GSM traffic in the developing world is intra-cell. This would imply that local sharing of information is viable. How, then, would you go about building a system to share media within a community?

As Thomas Reitmaier and colleagues have suggested, in some developing contexts you don't need a whole cloud, just a local cloudlet.

## Community sharing

One system we built to try to enable within-community sharing was based on the idea of a community noticeboard. The noticeboard in this case was a 42-inch LCD screen housing a media library computer. The system's display was simple, showing a grid of media packs that people might want to download onto their handset.

To initiate a download, the user takes a photo of the item on the screen in which they are interested. They then send that that image to the computer driving the screen, via Bluetooth. The computer runs image recognition algorithms on the photo and then sends all media relating to that topic, again via Bluetooth, to the handset that sent the initial image. There is no pairing required, no cost to the user, and no app to install—all you need is Bluetooth and a camera (see Figure 19.5).

We tested this *Snap 'n Grab* design in townships—disadvantaged communities with low social and economic profiles—around Cape Town in a library (see Figure 19.6) and in a training center. We had hoped that the system would be used for "development" purposes, and there was some evidence of that. However, one of the main uses was to share choir music: there were many different choirs in the area, and members of the choirs would record performances and share with others in the community.

Of course, given what we said earlier about the lack of electricity, keeping a 42-inch LCD screen running continuously would be a challenge in many areas. So, we ported our design to a mobile device, meaning that the phone can now be the media library. This new design was tailored to a common scenario within the developing world, namely, the

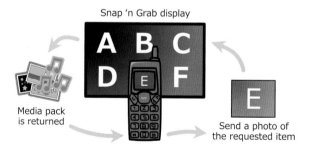

Snap 'n Grab display

Media pack is returned

Send a photo of the requested item

Figure 19.5 *Snap 'n Grab*: A user is interested in item "E" so takes a photo of it and sends the photo to the display. The display sends back a media pack over Bluetooth containing all the media objects related to "E."

There's Not an App for That | From Some to All

Figure 19.6 *Snap 'n Grab* installed in a library in Khayelitsha township.

Figure 19.7 The mobile *Snap 'n Grab* system in use on public transport. Taking a photo of any desired item and sending the photo via Bluetooth to a mobile media library phone causes the requested media to be sent back in response.

minibus taxi. Prevalent throughout Africa, the minibus taxi is probably the most common form of public transport on the continent.

Placing the media library phone in the taxi allows it to distribute media to a variety of communities. There is no visible screen, but users take photos of stickers placed inside the minibus. As before, the server handset processes the image and sends back the relevant information to the client handset. Furthermore, the taxis can act as part of a wider "mule" network, picking up and sharing information between geographically separated communities (see Figure 19.7).

Away from an extra piece of infrastructure, like a screen or a taxi with stickers, there has been little focus on thinking of handsets as information servers rather than consumers. With this idea of "cloudlet" computing, we believe there are opportunities to build cloud services that work across ad-hoc, highly localized networks. Building media servers into handsets, providing distributed backups, or allowing access to specialized information on demand are all, as yet, unexplored areas.

**Search for:**
*Cloudlet*

## Supporting privacy

One of the consequences of a lack of infrastructure is that media stored on a mobile device cannot easily be offloaded onto another device, such as a local PC or a cloud-based server. Coupling this with the culture of handset sharing leads to problems in how to separate out things that you want to keep private from those you don't mind sharing. This can be anything from teenagers receiving intimate texts to men trying to hide "blue" movies on their handsets. To date, the most prevalent form of hiding is to create innocuous sounding folder names, such as "presentations," or to hide files on a separate memory card.

So, while we are used to the idea of having family computers where different people have different accounts, we now need family, or community, mobile handsets, where there are separate user accounts or even a single guest account. Alternatively, one could provide handsets that store accounts on a memory card, or can quickly boot into an account from a card. Neither of these options is available for phones at the moment.

## A handset that's useful even when there's no "cloud"

As digital devices become more embedded into the cloud in developed regions, there is a danger that their utility is dramatically reduced for users who cannot afford to pay for access. One of the things Nokia got so right with the 1100 (see the *Two different approaches* box, earlier) was the realization that the device had to offer core functionality. So, in a household whose only consumer purchase was a handset, that handset should provide critical functionality like a radio and lighting. 250 million users all over the world can't be wrong.

The risk now is that more services will be offloaded from the device to the cloud, without clear consideration of the effects of this change for developing regions. This would be a huge mistake for users in the developing world. However, exploring some of the cloudlet ideas we have mentioned could offset its impact.

# Designing to accommodate literacy levels

Low literacy in many developing regions is complex and intricately linked to other social and education issues. The problems that literacy levels can cause with technology are widespread and well documented. However, many mobile research and development projects have helped to provide some support to those who are unable to use traditional text-primary devices. The most interesting of these often tend to be designs that use existing technologies in new and noteworthy ways.

## Voices not text

One particularly interesting mobile initiative to overcome low textual literacy is the *Spoken Web* project that we mentioned earlier in this book, developed by IBM Research India. The system is a modified Interactive Voice Response system, much like you might encounter when calling an automated customer service helpline. Dialing the service brings the user to a spoken menu, and the phone's buttons are used to navigate. Voice calls in India are very low cost, and the *Spoken Web* system allows users to create their own pages on a "voice site" by answering spoken prompts. For example, the system might ask users to give their name and contact details, and information about their business.

Each *Spoken Web* site has a unique number that can be dialed to access, and sites can be navigated using the keypad of any mobile or fixed-line handset. Whilst there is still some work to do in enhancing search and navigation functions, the *Spoken Web* is an intriguing solution to textual literacy issues that does not require the client to have any more functionality than that afforded by a standard touch-tone handset.

**Search for:**
*Spoken Web*

## Digital stories

Not only does poor literacy impede the use of mobile devices, but it also prevents users from creating content that they can share with others. One solution to this is the creation of videos, conveying the message by voice and moving image. However, the size and cost of video is prohibitive, especially over a mobile Internet connection.

A compromise that we have investigated is the creation of digital stories using mobile handsets. A digital story is essentially a series of still images linked with a voiceover. These can be used to convey a variety of information, ranging from training for health-care workers through to humorous stories. By working with low literacy users in our design sessions, we were able to create interfaces that were intelligible to the users by relying on icons with a minimum of text.

At present on the Internet, there is an underrepresentation of content from the developing world. Solutions like digital story creation apps are easy to create, and would allow users from the developing world to have a digital voice.

# Digital storytelling

 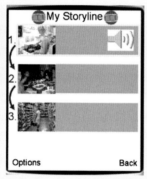 

A digital story is simply a collection of still images attached to a narrative. They can be created by recording a story by voice and then adding images later. Alternatively, they can be created by taking photos and adding voice to the images—as can be seen in the prototype above, which was designed for an early feature phone. In this instance, the user first takes a number of photos. On the second

There's Not an App for That | From Some to All

screen, the photos are arranged into the correct order. On the final screen, an audio narrative is added to each image. The story is then compiled into a single video file that can be shared with others.

## Direct manipulation

One of the benefits of touch-screen devices is that we have been freed from the physical constraints of button-based interfaces. However, if we look at the evolution of touch interfaces, we see that they are heavily informed by the physical interfaces and mouse-based interfaces that went before: there are buttons to click, objects to select, and dialogs to confirm.

More recently, multitouch and gestural interfaces have introduced entirely new ways of interacting with devices. However, rather than replace the old discrete interactions, most current interfaces blend the two techniques. But what if there was a group of users who were not familiar with discrete computer interfaces? What if they were not limited by having learned old ways of interacting? What type of interface should we create then?

This is the exciting prospect for anyone creating mobile software for many people in the developing world. In this case, their lack of interaction familiarity means that they can use entirely new forms of interface.

One project that we worked on allowed users from a rural South African community to record digital media and store them at a central communal tablet computer. The idea was that people could share media with others in the community, be this the community in general or individual members. Then, when those members visited the tablet, they could view the media that had been left for them. But how do you enable this kind of interaction (selecting people and sending them data) in an interface used by people who are not textually literate or familiar with widgets from computer interfaces?

The solution we developed centered on a panoramic image of the village that people could "swipe" around (see Figure 19.8). Donating media to another user then became a matter of finding the target person's house and choosing the correct resident.

Figure 19.8 The panorama-based Com-Tablet community media repository.

## Design Challenge

While our particular solution for community media sharing does not scale to very large communities, it is worth pointing out the kinds of opportunities that come about, as these first-generation users of digital technology have not been polluted by previous interface paradigms. The designer—you—is free to create entirely new forms of interaction.

What app designs would you create if you didn't have to conform to what your users expect given their years of exposure to computing concepts and norms?

## Proximate literacy

One final observation on literacy in the developing world is how communities work together to help overcome literacy issues. Often, illiterate users will engage the services of literate friends or family to help them solve a task. Tasks can range widely, from help in filling out forms to entrepreneurial activities, but the practice is rife in most of the communities that we have engaged with. In order for the literate party to help the user, they will have to take over usage of the handset. This, once again, leads to privacy issues, as what the designers assumed to be a private device is used in a shared context. This is another clear motivation to provide handsets and applications that have a more fine-grained control over information than current mobile operating systems permit.

> ## Design Pointer
>
> The message, then, is that we need to take our focus off literate individuals using apps on cloud-connected personal handsets and instead look at low-literate communities using shared handsets to interact with local and global information platforms in resource-constrained environments.

## Designing platforms that empower

If you are an app developer reading this book, you will most likely be living in the developed world. It is understandably hard for you to understand the needs and constraints of handset users in remote African villages. You could go and conduct studies there, but to generate the kind of insights that would lead to useful products would simply take too long. Of course, the best solution would be for people from those regions to create their own solutions. However, most people living in these regions are not skilled in coding or interface design.

What platforms do is allow local people to solve their own problems. As we will see later, *M-Pesa*, the "platform" of allowing people to move airtime from one account to another, started an e-commerce revolution. People were then able to adapt it to address a need that was apparent to them. As the following box illustrates, the question now is not *"What app should I create?"* but *"What platform should I create?"*

*Platforms are important; they allow people to innovate for themselves.*

# The "open source" bicycle

The following image shows a bicycle similar to a "Unix" bike Gary saw in Zambia (photos inset). Being an "open" bicycle, the owner adapted it with a pannier with which he runs an egg delivery business. Bicycles have been adapted in other ways to run other businesses, such as taking paying passengers or providing cellphone charging. The goal, then, is to provide platforms that, like the bicycle, can facilitate creativity and innovative usage of cellular handsets.

# Designing to make a big difference

Besides the broad themes of sharing, literacy, and infrastructure, there is an active community of researchers trying to address development needs through the use of technology. Termed ICT4D (or HCI4D—4D meaning "for development"), this community of researchers, NGOs, practitioners, and government agencies seeks to create technology that is not driven by a commercial imperative but, instead, aids human development.

Clustered broadly around the topics of health, education, and poverty eradication, many new technologies and apps have been created that directly address these concerns.

With too many to report in detail, we shall focus on poverty eradication to give some examples of systems that have been successful in this area, and draw conclusions about mobile technology design from the common themes. We will see, in particular, how important the platform thinking we've just encountered is when you are trying to do important things at scale.

## Poverty eradication

There are a number of ways in which mobile technology is being used to address poverty eradication in developing countries. One of the most highly publicized is the *M-Pesa* system from Safaricom in Kenya.

Around the mid-2000s, researchers, ourselves included, noticed that in many rural areas, airtime had become a de facto local currency. By moving airtime from the account of a buyer to the account of a vendor, goods or services could be purchased. This system immediately overcame the limitations of cash, such as limited availability in remote regions and potential for theft, without incurring the overheads of formal banking, such as lack of access to branches and needing a formal address to open an account.

But airtime is not a stable currency. So, Safaricom in Kenya introduced "e-float"—effectively an electronic analog to the Kenyan shilling. Users could pay money to a Safaricom vendor and be credited with an equivalent amount of e-float. Using menus (e.g., USSD) on the handset, clients could transfer money, pay bills, and conduct general banking services. To avoid regulatory issues, *M-Pesa* clearly states it is not a bank—it does not offer loans or pay interest—but provides the other services one would expect of online banking.

M-Pesa now exists in other countries, and similar services have also started to appear (*Airtel Money* and *Wizzit*, for example), all providing "cash" services from a handset without the need for full banking services.

Now that this backbone of low-impact financial services exists, the opportunities to create businesses on top of it greatly increase. One key piece of the digital marketplace has been put into place—people can pay for services securely, provided they have even a basic cellular handset; we now need to create digital services around this capability.

One such service is *Kuza*. Essentially, Kuza allows small informal traders to create websites and mobile sites. One of the founders, Andrew Maunder, was inspired to build the service after trying to contact various township businesses by calling the cell numbers they used in their advertising (see Figure 19.9). None of the numbers he called was active; most of those SIM cards had been lost or stolen.

Figure 19.9 The cell number painted on the shop no longer works.

Kuza allows small business owners to create a permanent website for their business, as shown in Figure 19.10. Not only does the service give current contact and location details, but it can advertise deals or offers to potential customers. The websites can be created interactively using nothing more than a feature phone, but can also be browsed on the desktop or mobile Internet.

Creating systems such as Kuza lowers the barrier for micro enterprises to leverage digital technologies. So, rather than creating an app, which none of these businesses are able to do, Kuza affords them a mobile digital marketing solution.

Besides local business platforms, there are other solutions using crowdsourcing on mobiles to provide occasional employment to people with skills and access to a mobile handset. One such system is *mClerk*, where local people with basic handsets earn money for translating and digitizing documents. Other variants of this include the *Umati*

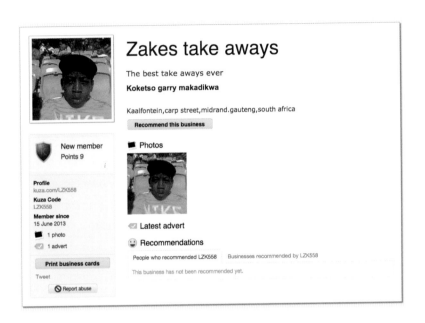

Figure 19.10 A permanent website created through the *Kuza* system.

system—a novel approach to vending machines, which dispenses food when users complete a task.

For the non-entrepreneurially inclined, Shikoh Gitau created *Ummeli* to find people employment in existing businesses. The system is based on the observation that companies were offering jobs on websites, but potential employees had no access to desktop computers to see these advertisements or create a CV. Ummeli allows feature phone users to create an online CV by asking them a series of simple questions. Once the CV is created, the system matches their skills to web-based advertisements and informs them of employment options automatically.

What we hope is clear from all of these systems is that it is not a sole app that is likely to have an impact. Taking the Ummeli example, the team could have created an app for one of the local job websites. While this makes it possible for phone users to read the advertisements on mobiles, it excludes small companies from advertising their

> "Ummeli connects poor people to opportunities, opening up a world they never knew existed"
>
> Shikoh Gitau

vacancies (those who do not have the funds to post on larger sites or to run their own website) and applicants from submitting a CV (those who cannot afford the resources to create the document in the first place).

These systems are much more than an app: they are platforms that empower local users to have a mobile presence. Few organizations in developing regions possess the skills or financial resources to create their own app, but new platforms are being created that could allow them to exploit mobile digital technology. The platforms must therefore lower the barrier of entry for those wishing to provide a service and for those wishing to consume it. Those barriers may be technical (where the target is a simple feature phone), human (where lower literacy levels must be accommodated), or commercial (where cost must be at an absolute minimum).

Moving beyond poverty eradication to further explore this idea of a platform, we see it repeating in fields as diverse as governance and entertainment.

The *Ushahidi* mapping platform grew as a response to the violence that broke out during the 2008 Kenyan elections. Incidences of violence were being reported using SMS, Twitter, email, and other services, but an overall picture was difficult to see. Ushahidi was created to try to coordinate and merge information from a variety of sources on an interactive map. So, users with any technology could cheaply make reports and see that information represented in a visual form that was familiar to them. While creating this specialist system, the team realized that they had actually created a platform that could be used to solve a wide variety of problems. At present Ushahidi is still primarily used for governance issues and keeping track of protests, but the service is also used for diverse applications such as tracking the favorite restaurants in Johannesburg.

## The importance of partnering

In all our own efforts in these areas, we have worked closely with what have been called Human Access Points. Typically, this would be a person or organization in the developing world that is trying to address the challenges in their region. This can be a large organization such as the UN, or a highly localized nongovernmental organization (NGO); it could even be an individual community member.

In the case of the *Ummeli* job system discussed earlier, a skills training agency in a township near the University of Cape Town were able to explain the problems that graduates had in finding jobs. Note that the developers did not talk to the graduates directly, but relied on the NGO as an access point to mediate their concerns in a form that could be understood.

The benefits of Human Access Points are many, and this approach is able to help both developers and designers, and the eventual users of a product. Just as it is unlikely that we could ever fully understand the resource constraints and information needs of a jobseeker living in a township, they would have had a hard time understanding what the technology could provide and how it might meet their needs.

Working closely with the NGO, then, the Ummeli team built a series of prototypes and technology probes to explore the problem space fully. Throughout this development, jobseekers were giving feedback mediated through NGO employees. The team was able to continue refining the design to the point where a philanthropic organization adopted and refined the code to release quality, and made the system freely available across South Africa.

## Design Pointers

Of course, building links with local organizations and creating a platform infrastructure takes a large amount of time. Before this, though, there are other, quicker opportunities for improvement. So, if you've become excited about the possibilities of developing in these regions, either as an individual or as a company, here are some suggestions about how to improve the relevance of your systems for the developing world in the medium term.

## Relocate

Design consultant Jens Fendler stresses the importance of basing developers in the field along with the people they are developing for. So, if you are developing an app for users in India, and your company has an office there, move the developers into that context. Not only will they have greater connection with those who live there, but iteration cycle times are cut greatly, as developers can get feedback on prototypes directly.

If you cannot afford to relocate a team, then you might want to try a tool such as Batya Friedman and David Hendry's *Envisioning Cards* (see the images below). These are simple cards that a designer can use to remain mindful of users from differing cultures or environments, helping to place the designer in the context of the user. Each card holds a summary of an important aspect of a new technology, and encourages designers to think carefully, via practical tasks, about the effects of these concerns.

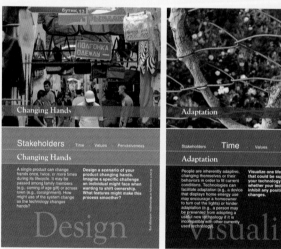

## Build apps that promote sharing

As a minimum, you should support peer-to-peer sharing in your applications. But do not rely purely on the default option of cloud-based or Internet sharing—users in developing regions will have limited, if any, access. Instead, use Bluetooth.

Allowing ad-hoc Wi-Fi connections between handsets can help further, as can thinking seriously about the handset as a server as well as a client.

It is important to remember that handsets are often not personal devices. If your design contains media that you think a person may wish to keep private, allow them to hide it away in a covert fashion: while it may seem counterintuitive, do not use padlock symbols or name folders "private." Let the user choose their own name and location for private media.

## Focus on lowering cost

Price sensitivity is more important than you can possibly imagine. For someone living on $2 per day, spending airtime on something that could be avoided is not an option. As a possible solution, cache as much as you can on the device, or in community cloudlets. Most importantly, let people choose whether they want your app to go online or not, and offer alternatives if they choose to remain offline.

# The road ahead

It may seem that creating devices and software for the developing world is a niche undertaking. However, that would be to misunderstand the nature of design. As we hope to have shown you in this chapter, the goal of design in the developing world is really no different than for anywhere else—people want useful technology that fulfills a need in their lives. The difference comes in the specific constraints that apply. In designing for those constraints, one explores different classes of solution that may, in turn, be relevant to the developed world.

Take, for instance, Nokia's profile manager feature, which was created for the developing world to support multiple users on a single device. Move forward to the advent of tablet computing, where many households share a single tablet amongst several different people. Google introduced a near-identical "profile" feature in Android 4.2, which allows multiple people to maintain separate profiles on a single tablet device.

Many designers, however, will look at the discussion above and conclude that, if we wait long enough, the issues around pricing will go away—costs will come down, as they have for us with so many other technology aspects. Unfortunately, this is simply not the case. Maintaining infrastructure in the developing world is more costly than doing so in the rest of the world, and many factors prevent beneficial refinements from being applied. There is often no reliable power grid, so base stations must provide their own power; many roads are poor, meaning access costs to install and repair base stations are higher; and components cannot be manufactured locally, which means incurring shipping and import costs.

You might, instead, assume that someday everyone will be able to read, so decide not to worry about illiterate users. Again, there are different forms of literacy, and while we hope that some day everyone will be able to read and write in their language of choice, the visual and information formalisms that are used in designing handsets for one market will not necessarily translate to another context.

Ultimately, the "solution" in all of this is for developing countries to become developed, so that people can live fulfilled lives where costs are relatively low. Although this is a problem far beyond the scope of this book—there are plenty of governments, NGOs, and billionaires pondering how to achieve that end—it is worth noting that technology alone is not sufficient to bring about transformation. The term "digital divide" is unfortunate, as it gives the expectation that purely by inserting the "digital" we can close the divide. This is patently not true. However, given the relative cost of technology to individuals in the developing world, we as designers and technologists should be doing all that we can to ensure that the technology we deliver is as appropriately designed and empowering as we can make it. Just because "digital" alone cannot close the "divide" does not mean it is not a large part of the solution.

## Resources

The incredibly rapid growth of the cellular market in recent years has been documented by the International Telecommunications Union [1], and the impact of this technology in the developing world is discussed in [2]. The professional societies we mentioned can be found at, for example, [3] and [4].

The personal status of phone handsets is discussed in [5]. Marion Walton's research into teenage phone use in and around Cape Town can be found in [6]. The kinds of meanings built up around missed calls all over the developing world are discussed by Jonathan Donner in [7]. Susan Wyche and Laura Murphy's work on evaluating solar chargers' appropriateness can be found in [8], and Matt and Gary's previous book is at [9].

Jan Chipchase's studies on the struggles illiterate users have with handsets are given in [10], and research into mobile media sharing via SD cards and hard disks can be found in [11]. Chantal de Gournay and Zbigniew Smoreda's findings around community communication are in [12]. Thomas Reitmaier and colleagues discuss the concept of local cloudlets in [13]. Our *Snap 'n Grab* system can be found in [14], and the mobile version in [15].

The *Spoken Web* can be found in many publications; the original description of the system can be found in [16]. Our *Community Media Toolkit* work, including the *ComTablet* media browser, can be found at [17]. The relationship between illiteracy and entrepreneurial activities is discussed by Nithya Sambasivan and colleagues in [18]. The various web platforms we have discussed can be found at [19,20,21]. Some of the example systems mentioned have also been written about in academic papers—see, for example, *mClerk* [22] and *Umati* [23].

The concept of Human Access Points is proposed and debated in [24], and arguments for basing developers in the field, rather than in the lab, can be found in [25]. The *Envisioning Cards* technique is documented in [26].

[1]  The World in 2013: ICT Facts and Figures. 2013. Retrieved from http://www.itu.int/en/ITU-D/Statistics/Pages/facts/default.aspx.

[2]  Bagchi K, Kirs P, López F. The impact of price decreases on telephone and cell phone diffusion. Inf Manage 2008;45(3):183–93. http://dx.doi.org/10.1016/j.im.2007.12.005.

[3]  ACM DEV. 2014. Retrieved from http://acmdev.org/.

[4] ACM SIGCHI HCI4D Community. 2014. Retrieved from http://www.sigchi.org/comm unities/hci4d.

[5] Cukier KN. Handsets are highly personal items: Let the good times roll. In: Intelligent Life. 2005 (Summer, pp. 24–25).

[6] Walton M, Marsden G, Haßreiter S, Allen S. Degrees of sharing: Proximate media sharing and messaging by young people in Khayelitsha. In: Proceedings of the 14th International Conference on Human-Computer Interaction with Mobile Devices and Services; ACM; 2012. pp. 403–12. http://dx.doi.org/10.1145/2371574.2371636.

[7] Donner J. The rules of beeping: Exchanging messages via intentional "missed calls" on mobile phones. Journal of Computer-Mediated Communication 2007. 13(1):1–22. http://dx.doi.org/10.1111/j.1083-6101.2007.00383.x.

[8] Wyche SP, Murphy LL. Powering the cellphone revolution: Findings from mobile phone charging trials in off-grid Kenya. In: Proceedings of the SIGCHI Conference on Human Factors in Computing Systems; ACM; 2013. pp. 1959–68. http://dx.doi.org/10.1145/2470654.2466260.

[9] Jones M, Marsden G. Mobile Interaction Design. Chichester: John Wiley & Sons; 2006.

[10] Chipchase J. Handbook of Mobile Communication Studies (Chap. Reducing Illiteracy as a Barrier to Mobile Communication). Cambridge, MA: The MIT Press; 2008. http://dx.doi.org/10.7551/mitpress/9780262113120.003.0007.

[11] Smyth TN, Kumar S, Medhi I, Toyama K. Where there's a will there's a way: Mobile media sharing in urban India. In: Proceedings of the SIGCHI Conference on Human Factors in Computing Systems; ACM; 2010. pp. 753–62. http://dx.doi.org/10.1145/1753326.1753436.

[12] Gournay C, de, Smoreda Z. Space bind: the social shaping of communication in five urban areas. In: Nyiri K, editor. A Sense of Place: The Global and the Local in Mobile Communications. Passagen Verlag; 2005. pp. 71–82.

[13] Reitmaier T, Benz P, Marsden G. Designing and theorizing co-located interactions. In: Proceedings of the SIGCHI Conference on Human Factors in Computing Systems; ACM; 2013. pp. 381–90. http://dx.doi.org/10.1145/2470654.2470709.

[14] Maunder A, Marsden G, Harper R. Creating and sharing multimedia packages using large situated public displays and mobile phones. In: Proceedings of the 9th International Conference on Human Computer Interaction with Mobile Devices and Services; ACM; 2007. pp. 222–5. http://dx.doi.org/10.1145/1377999.1378010.

[15] Smith G, Marsden G. Providing media download services in African taxis. In: Proceedings of the South African Institute of Computer Scientists and Information Technologists Conference on Knowledge, Innovation and Leadership in a Diverse, Multidisciplinary Environment; ACM; 2011. pp. 215–23. http://dx.doi.org/10.1145/2072221.2072246.

[16] Kumar A, Rajput N, Chakraborty D, Agarwal S, Nanavati A. WWTW: The world wide telecom web. In: Proceedings of the 2007 Workshop on Networked Systems for Developing Regions (Article No. 7); ACM; 2007.

[17] Community Media Toolkit. 2012. Retrieved from. http://www.digitaleconomytoolkit.org/.

[18] Sambasivan N, Cutrell E, Toyama K, Nardi B. Intermediated technology use in developing communities. In: Proceedings of the SIGCHI Conference on Human Factors in Computing Systems; ACM; 2010. pp. 2583–92. http://dx.doi.org/10.1145/1753326.1753718.

[19] Kuza. 2012. Retrieved from http://kuza.com/.

[20] Ummeli. 2014. Retrieved from http://ummeli.com/.

[21] Ushahidi. 2008. Retrieved from http://ushahidi.com/.

[22] Gupta A, Thies W, Cutrell E, Balakrishnan R. mClerk: Enabling mobile crowdsourcing in developing regions. In: Proceedings of the SIGCHI Conference on Human Factors in Computing Systems; ACM; 2012. pp. 1843–52. http://dx.doi.org/10.1145/2207676.2208320.

[23] Heimerl K, Gawalt B, Chen K, Parikh T, Hartmann B. CommunitySourcing: Engaging local crowds to perform expert work via physical kiosks. In: Proceedings of the SIGCHI Conference on Human Factors in Computing Systems; ACM; 2012. pp. 1539–48. http://dx.doi.org/10.1145/2207676.2208619.

[24] Marsden G, Maunder A, Parker M. People are people, but technology is not technology. Philos Trans Royal Soc A Math Phys Eng Sci 2008;366(1881):3795–804. http://dx.doi.org/10.1098/rsta.2008.0119.

[25] Fendler J, Winschiers-Theophilus H. Towards contextualised software engineering education: an African perspective. In: Proceedings of the 32nd ACM/IEEE International Conference on Software Engineering - Volume 1; ACM; 2010. pp. 599–607. http://dx.doi.org/10.1145/1806799.1806888.

[26] Friedman B, Hendry D. The envisioning cards: A toolkit for catalyzing humanistic and technical imaginations. In: Proceedings of the SIGCHI Conference on Human Factors in Computing Systems; ACM; 2012. pp. 1145–8. http://dx.doi.org/10.1145/2207676.2208562.

# CHAPTER 20

# Bringing Things Together

## The way forward

At the very start of this book we claimed that apps are changing the world. And they clearly are: as users, we pick up an app for everything we do on our mobiles, and we often find them effective, satisfying, and enjoyable. As developers we build apps to connect more personally with our customers and improve their experiences—we hear how engaged they are from Twitter and Facebook feedback and in-app analytics, and they are clearly enjoying themselves. Finally, as device manufacturers we create app store platforms and rely on the treats that get submitted to invigorate and push our new device designs—as a result, app stores are massively successful.

Over the previous chapters, we've shown many demonstrations of what can be good about apps. No doubt you will have many more examples of good design of your own in mind. But, as we've argued, it's time for some new thinking.

The mobile market seems focused and driven to develop more apps, better screens, longer battery life, and faster networks to keep us satisfied with our mobiles, drawing us more and more into the digital. In contrast, we hope that in this book we've been able to offer a few alternative perspectives on the future of the mobile, starting now.

We've designed this chapter to summarize and integrate the rest of the material in the book, so if you're the kind of person who jumps to the end of a book first, reading it now will give you many of the main messages.

If you've just read the book cover to cover—great! The best thing you can do now is to skip to the *Pathways to the future* section at the end of this chapter, and then return to read the rest later when you've let all the material sink in through practical application.

# What have we learned so far?

We've looked at six UX areas where there are clear opportunities—we'd argue *needs*—for new approaches.

1. Initially, then, we saw how interacting with a mobile could move from being about stroking a hard, glassy, and emotionless screen to feeling truly alive as any or all of our devices are used to interact. The *food*, *fashion*, *fitness*, and *material* design opportunities helped us to see particular example areas, but these are by no means exclusive: the future devices we will own will use these techniques to embrace real feeling in any appropriate situation.

2. Moving outside the device itself, we explored the benefits of "face on" computing. Current apps and services tend to expect—or even force—us to use them with heads bent down in deference to a screen. Face on designs may be difficult to get right, but we've demonstrated that the effort is worth the reward. The *in your face* and *in the world* technology opportunities showed two ways of achieving this goal with glances or wand-based interactions. Future designs that really embrace this face on thinking will lead the way in getting the right balance between our devices and our lives outside our technology.

3. Next, expanding to look at the space around us, we turned to think about the clutter—or, the lack of clutter—in our interactions with technology. Human lives are so often messy and disorganized, but at the moment our apps do not appreciate this, and we are pushed towards order and clinical effectiveness. We argued that the current approach—striving to organize the humanness out of our lives—is not the right answer. Instead, the *mess* and *uncertainty* opportunities demonstrated how mobiles need not take this approach. Clinical, never-lost, always-ordered designs leave a lot to be desired, and your future designs can quite easily make big contributions in this area.

4. The performative aspects of our mobile interaction are far less explored in both research and commercial mobile designs than perhaps any other

problem area in this book. The opportunities in this section showed how mobiles can be both *props* and *extravagant* performative objects themselves. We looked at performative interaction ranging from group games to heritage sites, and saw how shared emotions and characters can enrich interactions. We also saw how performances are moving and influential not through small bursts of content, but because of their deep narratives and the way they connect us to each other.

5. From this point, we took a leap to more outward-looking, mindful interaction. Our current devices and apps are set up to favor impersonal, task-focused interactions that assume we are distant from the people we are communicating with. Four categories of looking at communication and consumption of digital content, either now or later, demonstrated less-prescriptive ways of handling sharing. Most current research and commercial sharing work focuses on real-time communication and consumption, but the opportunities in this section helped us to imagine new fundamentally *mindful communication app* forms. Redesigning our apps to support all four scenarios would greatly improve our sharing experiences. We also turned drastically to think about a world of *mindfulness without apps*, arguing that thinking about such an unusual alternative can help refocus our design, spurring radical innovation.

6. Finally, we looked at how everybody in the world might benefit from these new forms of interaction. The so-called "developing" world is an expanding market—mobiles are the main and perhaps only computer that many people in these regions will ever own. But, it is not enough to simply cast off old versions onto those who are unable to afford the latest, most expensive designs. Instead, as we've shown, the different viewpoints of ICT4D approaches can not only profoundly influence the Western-oriented app and service models that we rely on today, but can provide entirely new ways of thinking about the technologies that are being developed, moving our narrow design focus from *some to all*.

# What can we do right now?

This book is not packed full of tips about how to fit your apps to the interaction guidelines of your chosen mobile operating system, or new GUI themes for mobiles; far from it. We've also stayed away from looking at basic, well-known interaction and usability principles of smartphones and touch-screen devices—there are many other books that will help here (see the *Resources* section at the end of this chapter for a few tips on where to start).

Instead, we've laid out a collection of new design spaces, and shown how some of the thinking that has been bubbling away in research labs for some time could truly change the way we use our devices. We chose to call these areas "problems" because we truly believe that they are the foremost areas in which to unpick and reshape the current app hegemony. Indeed, adopting the new ways of interacting that we've shown in any of the chapters in this book may help you to change the core of what we think of as a mobile device:

- If you're a researcher or student you might be wondering about how you can use the starting points throughout this book to define and guide your own research areas. One way to begin would be to take a closer look at some of the research papers detailed in the *Resources* section for each chapter. Each of the references for the examples we've given is listed here, and you'll be able to find out about the designs in far more detail than we've been able to give in the relatively short space available.

- On the other hand, particularly if you're a mobile app developer, or want to make a start in this area, you may be reading this book and thinking more practically about what you can do in your current work. How can you use these new ideas and ways of thinking to give fresh interaction perspectives to your existing designs? And, perhaps more importantly, what can you do in future, with the next generation of mobiles that are on the horizon?

From this point, then, we'll look at what you can do right now. We'll give a synopsis of techniques that you can adopt to take on the themes from the disruptive problems that we've been exploring. Then, we'll turn to think more generally about what might be possible if some of the research prototypes we've seen turn into commercial reality.

# No time like the present

If you were to start to apply the themes from this book to your designs right now, what approach should you adopt?

In each chapter of this book we've given a raft of examples of existing ways of operating that can be changed—apps, services, and tools that illustrate how things might be done differently. Each of the sections below outlines the departure points that we've identified for new mobile perspectives.

## Lessening the impact

One of the main overarching themes throughout this book has been to lessen the impact of current digital designs on our full experience of everyday living. We want to help you to help your users to avoid the same fate as Narcissus, drawn into the dark pool, captivated by the beauty they see there:

- One issue raised as a priority in Chapter 7 is the problem of giving in to the temptation to look at a screen. And, once that temptation has been succumbed to, it's far easier to justify carrying on using the mobile, heads down. Part of the cause of this issue is the decidedly "stop-to-interact" ethos in current mobile designs (see Chapter 5; Joe Marshall and Paul Tennant). Often this is due to the sheer complexity of the tasks we now perform on mobiles; but there are also other constraints, such as the thinking required to use an app, the physical environment we're in, other tasks we're trying to perform simultaneously (e.g., walking, cycling, driving), or the impact on other people. So, as designers, we need to think about the pressure we're putting on our users to stop and interact. One way of doing this is to design for more "face on" interactions.

- Visual displays are clearly more attractive than audio or tactile interfaces in many ways (turn back to the illustration of the effectiveness of screens in the

*Screens are effective* box in Chapter 7 for an example). So, it can be challenging to think about alternative approaches without dampening the user experience. The face on approach, though, is about trying to lessen the impact of the device, restoring the link between the user and people and places physically present. Face on thinking need not involve entirely removing screen interactions.

- Many of the face on techniques we saw in Chapter 7 and the two accompanying *Opportunity* chapters could be implemented right now, on the sensor-laden devices that many of us own. The around-body interaction demonstrated in the *BodySpace* prototype, for example, aims to supplement visual interfaces with quick gestures that are far easier to design and implement now than they were when this prototype was originally created. Another example we saw—the *Laid-back search* tool—which tries to prompt slower, more reflective searching by waiting to conduct queries in bulk, would be very easy to replicate on a smartphone.

- Speech recognition, such as *Siri*, Apple's speech-controlled agent for the iPhone, or Google's *"Ok Google"* always-on assistant, is one other option for lessening the impact of our devices. But, as we saw in Chapter 8, simply using conversational audio is no guarantee that situational awareness is being enhanced or even sustained. However, audio need not mean speech— take *TapBack*, the casing tap and scratch system we saw in the *More than prod or pinch* box in Chapter 4. Its goal was to enhance a remote interactive telephone service, but these sorts of methods could easily be used on-device. Simple applications of this technique could let users define their own interactive areas of the phone casing: anywhere can be a button. A more nuanced approach could be to support quick scratches or swipes around the edges of the device to check for updates without risking being drawn into the screen.

There's Not an App for That | Bringing Things Together

- Design for face on interaction where possible. Giving your users a chance to step away from the device will ultimately benefit them more than a full-time focus on the screen.

- Think about the effect your designs might have on the user's current behavior—would they need to stop to interact? What would they need to do if your alert caught them while they were cycling, or walking—could they carry on uninterrupted?

- Audio interfaces can be part of face on designs, but speech recognition is unlikely to be a panacea, at least in the near term. Other uses of sound, though, such as ambient detection of audio gestures, could help lessen the impact of interacting with the device.

## Glancing

Glance-based techniques are a clear part of lessening the impact of our digital interactions, and in this area there is a great deal of development going on. Google's *Glass* may be a tempting fit for the future of technology, for example, but its approach might only increase the screen time at the expense of the physical. Google's other ambient update approach—*Now*—is a more positive development here. Its bite-sized chunks of information are timely and often helpful, and, more importantly, are mini nuggets of content that need not distract us from the world outside for too long.

- A better approach than *Glass* apps right now, then, could be to design your apps using *glance* app strategies for screens. You could approach this technique by thinking carefully about when it is really necessary to alert the user. Pop-ups monopolize people's attention: they steal focus and shout for someone to take notice of them. When the user absolutely must know about the information you're giving them, this is a good idea. At other times they are little more than an annoyance.

■ Alerts that are more background level can get caught up in a queue of notifications that are easy to ignore and might just be cleared en masse at the end of the day. So, in this case less can be more: a few important glanceable notifications that can be assessed and dealt with quickly are more likely to be noticed than a deluge of irrelevant content. See, for example, how *Gmail*'s inbox is now grouped into tabbed categories based on importance or source. Or, if it makes sense for your design task, a more practical alternative might be to link with the many wearable device accompaniments that are now available. A smart watch's small notification-based display is probably a better place to glance at a meeting reminder than a phone's screen, anyway. Just be careful that the glance doesn't prompt or require a further interaction to look at the phone's screen—this would be worse, not better!

■ This same design principle applies just as much to the design of your app itself. Right from the start of the app design process, it is crucial to think about what the user's primary goal is. The more confusing and complex the first impression is, the more time they must spend building familiarity. Better, then, to design from the starting point of what needs to be done immediately, as soon as the user gets to the app. This applies to both first visits and repeat interactions, too—the more information you have about the user, the more specific your app can be to meet their needs at a glance.

## Design Pointers

■ Think about whether your app might work better with different ways of giving information to its users. Accessories such as smart watches are one option, but a more general way to approach small bursts of interaction is to think about what would be helpful to have at a glance as soon as you select the app; and, conversely, what would get in the way and make you spend longer interacting than you need to.

- Design user notifications to be accessible at a glance if they need no action. Better still, consider whether a notification is necessary at all. Could you get away without it?

## Pointing

In Chapter 9, we saw how location can combine with mobiles in far better ways than just showing a map with a cluster of icons overlaid. The first geopointing designs for mobiles came along around 1999; since then this field has seen much research work, but rarely commercial interest.

The one style that has seen the most attention is that of augmenting a camera preview with digital overlays: the phone becomes a lens to view the world through. While the benefits of this method may seem obvious—the user can see what they are doing—the interface in reality picks up the worst of both map overlay clumsiness and sensor inaccuracy.

- There are more options for pointing-based interaction, however. Far more interactive, but rarely adopted, is the use of the mobile as a direct pointer to objects around you—as a magic wand. Think of how easy it is to touch the icons on your phone screen, or hold your phone up to a poster to transfer NFC content. The same interaction methods can work for the places in the physical environment around us, too. The real benefit here, then, is that the phone is used only as a tool to indicate a direction; the real experience of discovering things in the wild is preserved.

- One way to get the best of both worlds here is to offer the wand technique as an alternative. Obviously, sometimes it really is best to see the big picture on a map. So, your users could point to something, then view detail on a map on the screen. Or, perhaps they could gather up a collection of interesting places with a sweeping gesture. Issues with pointing accuracy can be dealt with by snapping toward popular items (or, perhaps more interestingly, *away* from popular items, showing you less discovered things, promoting new insights rather than making you follow the crowd) and filtering sensor data.

## Design Pointers

- Interaction with geolocated content is most often achieved with map overlays. While these are very effective for overviews and broad indications of where items are located, for more personal, nuanced selection, gesturing and pointing can be an option.

- There's a lack of interest in these direct manipulation techniques in current mobile apps. If you're developing apps that rely on geotagged content, consider using these techniques as a way to interact when screens aren't necessary.

## Feeling truly alive

We are physical beings, built to manipulate and sense physical materials in a multitude of different ways. The touch screens we use so often have truly transformed mobile user experiences. But as we have seen, they rarely offer "real" touch. Instead, we have grown accustomed to interacting through a glass barrier, blunted by the screen instead of enhanced by the experience. For the time being, however, this glass barrier is the main method we have for touch interaction; so, what could we do differently? Here are some of the ideas we considered:

- As we suggested right at the beginning of the book, a good way to start is by imagining a world where certain characteristics commonly taken for granted are removed. A severe way of looking at this would be to design an app that doesn't need to use the screen at all; instead, think about how you could rely on the other ways of touching the phone and still provide a great user experience.

■ Another way of approaching this is to design to enhance the outside world, rather than try to dampen its impact. So, a fast-moving journey might occasionally show the thrill of moving at such speed: imagine the true sensory overload of being outside an airplane rather than cocooned in the interior. Or, strong sunlight shining on to the screen might simply prompt the mobile to turn off or dim the visuals, encouraging the user to see the world around them, instead.

■ The *Stane* device we saw in Chapter 4 is an example of an attempt to simulate physical touches digitally. Its textured outer shell provides a range of surfaces to scratch, tap, or poke. But there's no need to add an extra casing to use these sorts of interactions on modern mobiles: their processing power is well capable of recognizing taps and scratches around the edges of the casing. How could you move touches from the screen to the case, and would this enhance the user experience?

■ Modern technology profoundly changes our perspective on life. We've become accustomed to smart devices, making sure we're never lost, never without social contact, rarely too hot or cold. The everyday acts that used to require practice, patience, or substantial effort are pushed to the background—few of our mobile interactions require learning new skills. Imagine instead a design that brought a sense of effort into the engagements with your apps. Positive interactions could involve gentle gestures, cradling the device, and calmly releasing content to the cloud. Negative ones would be more forceful—throwing gestures and tight squeezes could show the strength of your feeling, transferring the effort into a digital form for others to see.

- A good way to design for real feeling is to think about what you could design your app to cope without. So how would your app design respond if the screen size got progressively smaller as the battery time drained away? Or, what if you couldn't use text entry? The point, here, then, is not to design future apps without key attributes, but to use their absence as a prompt to think differently about how you could achieve the same interaction in other ways.

- Consider exploring designs that express the effort and care that certain interactions might involve. Sending a tenderly written note to a loved one is not the same as replying with a quick meeting acknowledgement to a work colleague. How could you reflect these types of contexts better in your designs?

## Embracing physical expressiveness

- Small-scale expressive gestures can work on-device to help interact more naturally with, for example, files and folders. Take a look back to *BumpTop*, explored in Chapter 11, which allows circling a group of documents to cluster them together, or quick flicks to browse through a pile. Gestures can be hard to learn, so many developers stick to the basics. This is best for the user initially, but is also quite shortsighted. If your app is going to be used regularly then your users should have access to the best interface possible. For example, direct manipulations might be better, in many cases, than complex menu structures. Initial training (with new features learned over time) can help far more in the long run than the simpler approach of sticking to the now-standard pinch-zoom and other similar gestures with no real basis in physicality.

- More ambitiously, using the small phone in big ways can enliven physical activities. So, large-scale gestures can be both useful—such as with the pointing gestures we've looked at in the *Pointing* section earlier in this chapter—and intriguing: how could your app react to someone walking in a circle around a building, for example, or repeatedly visiting the same place?

- Going beyond your own device, the tangibility of other objects can give a far wider aspect to everyday interactions. In Chapter 11, we saw how the *BookMark* navigation system recruited books on shelves around the user, rather than relying solely on a digital map. The *Marble Answering Machine*, *Dirti*, and *Tokens of Search* examples we have seen in various chapters show other ways to incorporate physical, tangible objects into the interaction experience. Are there interesting and fulfilling ways in which you could recruit other physical items around the user into the interaction they have with your app?

- A useful crossover point between fully physical interactive objects and the screen-focused interactions we are now used to is supported by near field communication (NFC). Research prototypes have shown how the "touch for information" boards in large cities could be enhanced by being grids of tags, rather than a single item; other near field approaches such as Bluetooth or Apple's *iBeacon* help to move interactions from under the glass to the tangible objects around us.

## Design Pointers

- Consider using expressive gestures (both large and small scale) to enhance the ways your users can interact with your apps.

- Don't be afraid to go beyond the basic pinch-zoom and swipe that have become the norm. New gestures can be overwhelming if presented right at the start of a user's journey with your app; but, learning new features over time could enrich the experience far more in the long run.

- Think about how you could recruit some of the other physical objects that surround your users into the interaction experience. In the short term this could involve short-range tags (e.g., NFC/RFID) and geofences, but future mobiles will be far more able to recognize objects that aren't explicitly tagged.

# Messing things up

In Chapter 10 and the two associated *Opportunities* we looked at how "messy" designs can often be more appropriate than clinical, neatly ordered systems.

- Think back, then, to the photo collage layout of the *StoryBank* system. This approach showed one possible way to view a collection of photos that is less prescriptive than the grid layout commonly used on smartphones. The *Flutter* example in Chapter 5 showed a similar way of interacting, but with added gestures, both on-screen and with the whole device.

- Both of these designs embraced messiness, and also flexibility. In our interactions with physical objects we're used to messiness—folding down a book corner or tearing off a sheet of notepaper. Mobiles are usually more rigid—look at the home screen of your phone and try moving an app to a place that isn't in the defined grid, for example. There are good reasons for this—the small screen size being one of these. But flexibility can be beneficial—accessing things on a work surface becomes an act of muscle memory (e.g., pointing to the right place reflexively), rather than a visual search for the right name in a sea of icons that are visually very similar.

- The same approach applies from browsing to working. Synchronization of all our files wherever we are is something we've become used to, whether it's provided by apps such as *Dropbox*, or handled manually by emailing a file to yourself. There can be benefits in taking a break from the always-on synchronization, though. Often a fresh start helps to clear and reinvigorate people (the "inbox zero" movement, for example). Can you stimulate less-clinical ways of keeping your users up to date with their digital possessions?

- One barrier to this approach is the lack of flexibility in searching through your digital content. You can see this for yourself by trying a query on any modern search engine, but intentionally spelling your term slightly incorrectly. Notice how your query is automatically modified (but with the option to switch back if desired), and the correct results are still found. Try the same thing with the built-in search tool on your mobile, searching through your own content, and the results are very different: nothing is found. There's an urgent need for this type of interaction on mobiles, then.

## Design Pointers

- Think carefully about whether a neatly ordered collection is the best display for the content your users access with your app. Could you help them become more at home by relaxing the standard layout and ordering restrictions, and letting them take things into their own hands?

- Let your users make a fresh start, without having to worry about where they were before.

- Provide search that allows for flexibility: search engines have had this functionality for many years; apps are sorely lacking here.

## Experimentation and uncertainty

Experimentation is a key part of how we learn and shape ourselves as we grow from child to adult. We learn to hide our "childish" behaviors as we grow older—we assume that others will think us immature.

- Allowing experimentation and playfulness in apps can be exciting for your users, however. One way of doing this is to allow them to customize the app, letting personal expression fill their mobile. There is a fine line between customization and overload, but the rigidity that has become the norm can often be relaxed.

- We've also looked at how being lost can be both exhilarating and nerve-wracking. Outdoor navigation is often seen as a solved area, but it is actually one that could benefit a great deal from a significant helping of uncertainty. Leading users directly to their destination via the quickest or shortest route is the obvious choice from an implementation point of view, but this is not always optimal from a user experience perspective. Think, also, of the frustration when GPS gets it wrong: by that stage we're so reliant on the instructions that all we can do is sit back and accept our fate.

■ Instead, with a more uncertainty-laden design, we might feel empowered to make our own choices. For walking in particular, uncertainty in navigation can be very appropriate. So, could your apps be more aware of the user's surroundings? What would happen if the navigating system gave us a list of routes based on the interestingness of the places they pass through (rather than time or distance), letting us pick the one we thought looked most fun? Our own designs in this area have looked at using vibration feedback rather than path directions, trying to reduce the screen focus at the same time as increasing flexibility. But there's no reason why a mobile navigation system couldn't just point you vaguely in the right direction (an arrow on the screen), then leave you to your own explorations.

## Design Pointers

■ Experiment with relaxing the restrictions on the look and feel of your app: customization and playfulness can be part of a good user experience just as much as familiarity.

■ If you're designing apps that make use of navigation, think about how you could include other perspectives beyond fastest time or shortest path. Routes that take in points of interest are a good start here, but would it be better if your users could forge their own paths and truly explore, relying only on the most basic forms of guidance from the device?

## Mindful communication

Due to the legacy of the telephone, mobile communications and app services that want to let us share content are constrained by the idea that we always wish to communicate synchronously with people in different locations. The assumption is that if another person is in the room with us, then we will not need to use the mobile at all. But this ignores a large segment of mobile interaction—passing a phone around to share a photo, for example, or huddling around a screen together to check a movie's availability.

- Our current mobiles make no distinction between communication that involves someone right next to you, compared to talking to someone on the other side of the world. When you're all in the same room, there's actually no real reason for something you're sharing to go through a data center halfway across the world. There's also no reason why some tasks—such as calendar comparing, or updating music collections—can't be handled automatically. At the moment, our devices force us to communicate in ways that assume we are far apart from each other.

- The four types of mindful communication and sharing we explored in Chapter 17 each lend themselves to new ways of interacting. For a start, we could bring the focus back to people, rather than apps. The current focus on apps pushes the people into the background, but it is actually the people that are the most important parts of our mobile interactions.

- This way of thinking, as a starting point, opens up a whole new way of interacting with our devices. For example, once a phone is all about the people, we can group people to see common themes, or drag two people together to share media items. Another very different way of thinking could be to let other people request temporary control of your handset to perform actions on their behalf.

## Design Pointers

- Make people the focus, rather than the app itself: they are the most important parts of our mobile interactions, and deserve to be at the forefront.

- Rethink the way you treat tasks that involve people who are close, compared to those who are distant.

# Designing for everyone

For some people in the developing world, a mobile phone is the largest purchase they will ever make. As a result, existing mobiles sold in these regions have been designed with as many context-appropriate features as possible. They are robust, often multi-SIM, and include extras such as a radio or a torch. They are also often shared between multiple people. This sharing reveals a number of user experience design areas that can be addressed right now.

- Many of the same sharing issues related to mindful communication are relevant in this context: sharing with people in a tight-knit rural community is difficult with current devices, and the difficulty is even more obvious (and untenable) than our own experiences of the slight inconvenience of not being able to share easily. A crucial factor here is the lack of reliable or fast data connections, due to either cost or coverage. So, designing quick and—most importantly—straightforward to set up local clouds (or, *cloudlets*) should be a priority for anyone working in this area. New designs should not rely on Internet access without clear consideration of the effects of this choice. Systems like the *Snap 'n Grab* photo-based community sharing design in Chapter 19 show one way local cloud sharing could work. The prototype uses Bluetooth for transferring media, but works around the usual hassle of setting up pairing and access codes. How could your own apps work together to provide simple, feature-rich local sharing?

- A related issue is the lack of privacy when devices are shared. Think about how you would feel if your friends or family regularly used your phone as their own. If you are anything like us, you would feel the need to change your current behavior, hiding some meaningful private items and deleting others, constantly aware of the lack of personal space. This sharing of devices directly affects app designs, then, and can be limiting to your users if not handled sensitively. One straightforward way to lessen your users' worries would be to provide a way of storing accounts and private data on a memory card that could be removed, rather than on the phone itself.

There's Not an App for That | Bringing Things Together

- While sharing and privacy challenges are partially caused by the huge growth in apps and services (each requiring their own content to be considered), other issues—such as literacy—have been around since early text-based handsets. Modern devices do now use less text, preferring icons instead, but there are far more conventions that the user must learn in order to effectively use the device. Imagine trying to learn to use a new smartphone without any prior experience, and being unable to read the manual or follow a tutorial. How would you find out about all the swipes, pinches, and long-presses?

- Issues such as these lead to coping strategies that use only the bare minimum of the phone's features. So, a sensible set of default settings, and simple built-in apps that have been carefully designed with illiterate and non-tech-savvy users in mind will bring benefits.

- It would be nice to think that in the future everyone in the world will have an always-on, reliable electrical connection, so power considerations would not be too much of an issue. Unfortunately, this is unlikely to be the case. So, particularly if you are designing with developing regions in mind (which you should), battery life is a key concern. Other limitations in these areas, such as data connectivity, are likely to persist into the future, too. One solution to network costs is the voice-based telephone services that are popular in developing regions where voice calls are cheaper. While it might seem lacking to have to design a feature-rich modern app without Internet access, these voice sites can provide similar features if integrated well.

- More than just apps, what is needed in these areas is new *platforms* that exploit digital technology to provide new services. Platforms can lower the barrier of entry for those wishing to consume content from them, integrating a large set of different app-like services into one coherent core. What people can do next, then, is innovate for themselves on the platforms that you have created.

When this book was in a draft stage, some readers took issue with our final *Opportunity* chapter that explores designing for everyone, rather than a wealthy, Western perspective. The main comment was that designers and developers would not want to make apps for emerging markets if there isn't lots of money to be made. They argued that we should use this book only as a means to identify issues in richer countries.

To put it bluntly, this is missing the point. Firstly, there clearly is money to be made in developing regions (see, for example, the sheer number of low-end handsets Nokia sold in these markets). Secondly, as we have seen throughout the rest of this book, mobile app designers are currently stuck in an insular, inward-looking mindset. The apps we have on mobiles now are ultimately evolved from early PCs and work-focused personal organizers. Many people in developing regions have no such pre-conceived notions of how a phone must look or operate, having not been through the PC, landline, or laptop stage. Instead, their entire experience of computing is from their mobile. Designing for everyone, therefore, can lead to far more groundbreaking designs because there is not the same underlying expectation of what the design must be. Entirely new forms of interface can be created, without needing to rely on the physical interface paradigms and discrete computer interfaces that came before.

## Design Pointers

- Think about supporting ways of sharing that can use local clouds. Could your app detect that others nearby are using it too? Sharing apps such as *Bump* are one way to approach this, but here the shared content still goes via a remote data center. Could you use more local ways to communicate content, and break the reliance on a constant Internet connection?

- Incorporate ways of importing or exporting private content in your apps, preferably automatically. Imagine using your app on a phone that is shared with other people as a main device—how would that change the interactions you provide?

There's Not an App for That | Bringing Things Together

- Designing for low literacy or low technology familiarity can enhance the user experience, and unlock previously off-limits areas of functionality for large numbers of potential users. The best approach here is to work with users themselves to shape the design from an early stage.

- In many developing regions there are opportunities to create interconnected platforms, rather than standalone apps, as innovation hotspots. One way of starting is by looking at the way that apps can also transform into platforms—see *Ushahidi*, for example, in Chapter 19.

- Sticking to the Western-oriented rich-country mindset is an insular way of thinking. Looking wider to the hundreds of millions of people who don't fit the standard cloud-connected personal handset model can break new ground and help expand your user experience horizons.

## Backgrounding the digital

We've tried to make it clear throughout this book that we're not simply arguing for people to put away their phones all of the time. However, a running theme has been of ways to move the digital interaction to the background, rather than letting it draw us in. Here are some of the starting points we looked at:

- One way to approach this is to wean us off our device dependence. So, in Chapter 3, for example, we saw how nudge techniques can be used to draw users towards healthy lifestyles or fitness goals. The examples here were not designed as a set of screens of objectives and targets. Instead, simple messages and an ambient display helped prompt behavior changes. There's no reason why nudge techniques could not be used to encourage your users to take a break and engage with the world, too.

- Another way of hiding the digital is to make your designs more convenient, so less effort is required to get to the bottom of the task at hand. Human-computer interaction practitioners have been designing toward this goal for many years. Meanwhile, search and shopping providers have quickly seen the benefit of designing for convenience in interaction. Holding a transaction state that is shared between all the devices a user might adopt to access the service is now common. So, for example, your online shopping list and previous search queries are available whether you use a laptop or simply sign in to a newly downloaded app. This strategy has been gradually adopted in messaging apps, too—while "drafts" used to be a way of storing temporary messages, now you can just close the app and know that your partially written message will be where you left it when you come back. How could your apps adopt this approach, making usage more convenient for your users?

■ Building apps that are clearly useful for people is an obvious strategy for attracting app store shoppers. But, as we have seen throughout this book, it can often be worth stepping back and designing to satisfy the feelings, or the emotions of your users instead. Physical experiences can drastically shape the activities we are involved in; the same could be applied to the digital experiences we create. For example, this might involve cutting off the cloud for a while, immersing the user in the physical world around them instead; or, perhaps just designing for primary interactions—apps that don't require us to use our dominant hand, or our entire vision. This might seem like an odd strategy for app developers looking to create the next bestseller, or those keen to increase in-app advert revenue. But, in the long term, you might find that users appreciate the thought and consideration that you have put in to their well-being, too.

## Design Pointers

■ If you are designing for behavioral change, nudge techniques can be just as effective as screens of detailed advice. Aim to give simpler, meaningful visualizations and messages, rather than overwhelming your users. The full detail can be given in a separate page, accessed only when specifically requested.

- Design ways to quickly resume actions started at other times and places—the less time the user needs to spend getting back to where they were, the less impact the digital interaction will have on their everyday life.

- Interactions that are considerate about your users' feelings and emotions are more likely to create meaningful user experiences than those that strive only for quick fixes.

# Beyond phones and apps

So far in this chapter we've looked at pointers to how some of the ideas and concepts we've explored in this book might be achieved right now, with current technology. However, in the book we've also surveyed a wide range of entirely new interaction designs and future concepts that aim to prepare you for the future interaction possibilities in the coming years. Some of these have shown how your existing designs might be enriched; others take a step away from the interaction design norms and give new perspectives on exactly what interaction design and user experience really mean. Some highlights are revisited and integrated in the following sections.

## Malleable mobiles

Imagine that someday in the near future you've ordered a new mobile phone. The parcel arrives and you eagerly open the box. Inside, rather than a single part, there's a collection of separate components: one you slip on to your wrist; another is shaped like a pill for you to swallow; the third is placed in your pocket; and the final part is left on your desk. Each part is carefully designed to fit the interactions it will be used for. Later, using the touch screen on your wrist, your interaction is supported by a display that pops up buttons where they are needed, giving you a real sense of what you're feeling on the screen. Rather than *"pictures under glass,"* then, the glass (or, rather, a layer above it) shapes itself to fit your needs.

This future is not as far off as it might seem—the smart watch is the device of the moment, smoothly displaying notifications from paired smartphones, and deformable touch screens are often demonstrated at technology fairs. Before that future, though, it's far more likely that we'll be designing interactions for a plethora of devices that must all work smoothly together. Current mobiles are already well capable of synchronizing our information between mobile and laptop; future versions will need to deal with yet more interactions at once.

Next, think further ahead to how devices might work if the screens themselves could reshape into intricate patterns—highlighting the contours of the shapes they are displaying, and demonstrating, rather than simply illustrating, depth. Or, what if your device could gently shape itself to your hand, or to your pocket when appropriate? As MIT researcher Hiroshi Ishii showed in Chapter 2, deformable devices could lead the future of interaction to support far more tangibility.

This malleability also hints at the ubiquity of devices that will need to be coped with by our future designs. What does it mean for interaction when each and every device we use is merely temporal? Unlike the computer mainframes of old, this temporality is personal—we aren't leasing computer time from a large corporation; we own all the devices, but we choose to use them on our own terms.

## Design Pointers

- Now is the time to start thinking about how your user experiences might work when scattered over several devices that a person carries at the same time. Think not just of a few devices, but tens or hundreds, where each gets merely a fraction of our interaction time and attention.

- A future packed with the sorts of radically deformable devices we've seen as research prototypes is, realistically, probably some way off. But physical flexibility is almost here today, and devices that are reshapable based on context will come soon. How could your designs take advantage of these new forms?

# Future touchables

Try interacting with your phone by waving your hand in front of it, and think about how difficult it would be to accurately manipulate your body to provide the right motions for more than just simple actions. Of course, this is a not-so-futuristic interaction style—camera-based games and face recognition login screens are already using this technique; the *Leap Motion* accessory provides similar capabilities for desktops. But, none of these techniques give any tactile feedback about the motions you're performing, so can be difficult to use and react to accordingly.

Now, imagine that you felt what was happening when you waved your hand—an invisible in-air pulse of vibration that gave you feedback just like real buttons or keys. Think how this new dexterity of feedback could let you feel the shape of a model you were designing, or shape the intensity of a sound wave. This type of in-air feedback, as demonstrated in the *UltraHaptics* prototype in Chapter 6, could hugely expand the interactive area around your device, then, and in a far more accessible way than current gestures, where tactile feedback is limited to that given on the device itself. So, this type of interaction would open up many more possibilities for great user experiences that don't require much of a device at all.

Turn now to the undeniable tangibility of food. Think back to the *Noisy Jelly* kit that we saw in Chapter 3—the physical form of the jelly makes for a fun, playful interaction device. Other ways of interacting with more physical objects are likely to arise in the coming years. Designing solely for touch screens seems a little weak, then, when we could be using all the objects around us instead.

Food also highlights how we could use a plethora of tools to interact. At the moment a dull swipe gesture is used for so many interactions. In the near term we might be able to simulate the materials the user is touching by, say, giving slowed-down, jerky scrolling for rough surfaces, or fast scrolling for smooth ones. In future devices, though, we're likely to be able to simulate much more than this. A starting point here, then, is to think about what sort of material you are asking the user to manipulate, and use the answer to help select the interface to use.

While food enhances our inside, clothing protects our outside. Clothing is also a way of personalizing our bodies temporarily. The richness of the fabrics we wear is rarely reflected in the ways we choose them on our digital devices, though. Simulations are used at the moment to try to enhance this richness. What if in the future you could stretch out your mobile to feel the fabrics? Or, what if the fabrics themselves became the interaction focus? A touch might light up or expand a section of clothing, playfully illustrating how the material has been used.

A more intimate system might communicate with a similar garment worn by a partner, or respond differently to more intimate actions—a whisper from a loved one being gently blown on to your face, or a gentle stroking motion reassuring you of their far-away touch. Much more emotionally connective than a "like" or SMS, perhaps your phone might eventually transfer the loved one's kiss via more refined versions of the methods we saw in the *Futuristic to feasible emotional communication* box in Chapter 6.

## Design Pointers

- Future ways of feeling touches from our mobiles will drastically change the way we can interact. Mobiles are not destined to be interacted with solely by poking and stroking a glass panel. In fact, future devices will likely be anything but what we currently call mobiles.

- Explore the different materials that you could use in your designs. One way to start here is to think about what sorts of items the user is manipulating, then choose the most appropriate interface to enrich the user experience.

- Think about how the gentle interactions of devices designed for intimacy could support remote touch. How does this make you feel about the real touch and emotional connection with others?

# Pathways to the future

Think back to the way we opened this book, with Narcissus at the pool, staring lovingly into his own reflection, the wood nymphs watching him slowly dying, captured by the beauty of his own reflection. At the moment, many of us as users are falling into the same trap as Narcissus.

The problem, we've argued, is that people find apps effective, satisfying, and enjoyable. They meet our needs, solve our problems, and fill our spare time. But they are not perfect—they can be much better. And, in the process of looking for alternatives, we've argued, our users' experiences will become better, too.

In this final chapter of the book, we've highlighted what we think you could do right now to improve your users' experiences. We've also looked at how to change your interactions to focus away from screens and onto the people who use them.

If you're an app developer, the first thing to do right now is to look through the apps you've made, thinking about the specific focal points of each chapter as summarized here. Can you make your apps more about real touch and less about glassy stroking? Or, could you make your apps less clinical and more about the clutter of human life? There are plenty of examples in this book to get you thinking about new user experiences that you could create.

If you're a researcher or student then we hope that we've been able to spur you on to think about areas outside the norm. The examples we have reviewed give you a shortcut into some of the hot research topics in user experience. Reading further into these areas will help you get a footing into the leading current research themes.

If you began this book simply as an intrigued onlooker we hope that we've piqued your interests, too. We've tried to reassess the certainty of current design thinking, bringing other possibilities into the fray and connecting all of these together into general problem areas that could greatly impact mobile user experience. Some of the far-out thinking that we've explored may be a long way off; yet more will no doubt never happen. What we've tried to do, however, is connect these ideas with today's design concerns. In the process, we hope that we've been able to spur you on to change the way you think about mobiles and apps.

Now it's over to you: be provoked by what you've read in the book; be motivated by it; or, in disagreeing with us, see your own other ways forward. Whatever you do, though, go out and change the world for your users. Help them to benefit from the richness of the digital services they carry around with them, but empower them to be in the world and not apart from it. Let them experience life face on, not heads down, using their natural abilities to physically and tangibly express and sense. Equip them to revel in complexity and uncertainty and to keep their eyes on others and not just narcissistically on themselves. Above all, remember that this technology is for *everyone*.

*Now it's over to you.*

## Resources

The main resource for this chapter is the rest of the book: turn back to each referenced section to see in more detail the design pointers and the research or concepts that prompted them. For even more detail, follow through from each chapter's *Resources* section and *search for* hints to find the paper, article, or other resource that is referenced for each example we've given.

If you'd like to start developing some of the new ideas we've explored in this book, and you don't have a background in interaction design, we'd recommend that you have a look a some of the key existing user experience materials before you start. There are, of course, far too many to comprehensively list here. However, here are a few ways in which you might like to start:

- Read key books in the HCI and user experience communities. Two great places to start are the comprehensive *Interaction Design: Beyond Human-Computer Interaction* (Yvonne Rogers, Helen Sharp, and Jenny Preece), and *Designing the User Interface: Strategies for Effective Human-Computer Interaction* (Ben Shneiderman and Catherine Plaisant). Another resource, from a consumer electronics perspective, is the inspiring *The Simplicity Shift* by leading designer Scott Jenson. Or, of course, there's the classic book on usability, *The Design of Everyday*

*Things*, by Donald Norman. There are many, many books in this area—we'd suggest that the best way to start is just to get stuck in and follow your interests.

- Research the state-of-the-art and look through previous findings in the area you're working in. Good places to start are the *ACM Digital Library* (requires an annual fee, but often free in libraries and universities) or, for a wider range, *Google Scholar*, which often manages to find direct (free) PDF links to the articles in question. Most researchers have personal websites, where you can download all their research articles or get in touch with them for more details.

- Read interaction designers' and usability gurus' websites. For a general view, look for websites such as Jacob Nielsen and Donald Norman's user experience consultancy *NN/g*—their regular free articles on design issues can be a great resource when designing apps and encountering common usability problems. In addition, many researchers and developers have blogs or social media feeds on which they post articles, tips, or examples that can be a useful resource.

- Read through design guidelines, such as those for Android and iOS, which are freely available online—these will help you fit the platform norms if necessary. However, don't forget that the aim of this book is to break away from the predicted future—don't be afraid to go it alone!

# Index

*Note:* Page numbers with "*f*" and "*b*" denote figures and boxes, respectively.

## A

Aestheticodes, 211, 211f
*Airwriting* system, 307b–308b, 308
Android, 114
Angst, 6–7
Apple, 2–3
Apps that bite back, 167
App selection, 247b–248b
*Audio Gift* system, 248b–250b
*AudioCanvas* system, 208, 209f

## B

Barcodes, 211, 213b
Ben's origami model, 34f
Bits-*out* interaction, 42–43
Board games, 264b
Body awareness, 93
*BodySpace* prototype, 137, 138b, 139
*BookMark* system, 210, 212f, 213
Breaking glass, 39–43
*BumpTop* system, 196f

## C

Careful information design, 163–166
Centaurs, 103–104
Charging handsets, 357–358
*Chewing Jockey* system, 52
*Chop Chop* prototype, 53
Clutter
   chaos, 182

digital clutter, 186–189
physical clutter, 182–184
cyborgs, 179b–181b
Collaborative interaction, 271
Collective interaction, 271
*Com-Phone* story maker, 332b–333b
*Com-Tablet* community media repository, 368f
Commitment, 173
Computer-Supported Cooperative Work (CSCW), 313
   groupware matrix, 313f
   space, 316–319, 317f
Context data, 162
CSCW. *See* Computer-Supported Cooperative Work
Cyborgs, 103–104, 179b–181b

## D

Deformables, 123–125
Developing regions, 350, 365. *See also* Literacy levels, designing to
Difference operator, 347
Digital backgrounding, 403–404
Digital clutter, 186–189. *See also* Physical clutter

*"Digital is natural"* video, 38b
Digital purveyors, 92
Digital scrapbooks, 204b
Digital stories, 365–366, 366b–367b
Direct manipulation, 169–171, 367–368
Direct token, 262b–263b

## E

*EATProbe* prototype, 241b–242b
End of apps, 307
Enlivening interactions, 140b
Environment browser, 344, 344b
Ephemeral interfaces, 60–61
Ergonomics, 94
Experimentation, 397–398
Expressive performance, 284b–285b
Extravagant computing boombox, 276b–277b
   brick-style mobiles, 276
   embarrassment, 283–294
   Hafod world heritage site, 288–294
   large screen, 278–282
   performance types, 284b–285b
   principles for new performances, 280b–281b

Extravagant computing
(*Continued*)
projected performance,
278b–279b
self-expression, 283–294
small screen, 278–282

**F**
Face on, 136–140. *See
also* "Heads down"
computing, 384
on-screen menu
frustration, 137f
voice services,
155b–156b
*Ubi displays* project, 149f
speech recognition,
150–151
Facebook, 241b–242b,
300, 327b–328b
Fashion, 72
intimate interfaces,
84–85
*iShoogle* system, 78f
phone as an accessory,
73b–74b
traces of past
interactions, 83f
wearables to wear,
81–84
*Fat Thumb* technique,
76b–78b
Feeling, 30
barriers, 33, 33f
breaking glass, 39–43
uncomfortable
interactions,
36b–37b
Fitness, 92
body movement, 95–99
cyborgs, 103–104
effortful design, 99–101
feelings, 93
Flexibility, 184

Fluid dexterity, 55–56
*Flutter* prototype, 103–104
Food
fluid dexterity, 55–56
material properties, 59
consumed material,
60–61
function follows form,
59–60
instant gratification, 61
learning from feelings,
61–63
multisensory interaction,
51–56
*FoodieFab* system, 60
Friction-free future, 178
Future touchables, 407–408

**G**
*GeoPointing* design, 169,
170f
Glanceable displays,
160–166
travel apps, 166b
*Glancephone* project,
327b–328b
Glancing, 389–390
Google *Now*, 161, 161f, 178
Google *Glass*, 147, 389
Google+, 241b–242b
Graphical user interface
(GUI), 35
Gustatory, 51

**H**
Hafod world heritage site,
288
audio, 291–294
Pico projection, 289–291
Hands-*in* interaction, 40–41
*Haptic Lotus* prototype,
18b–19b
HCI. *See* Human-computer
interaction

Heads down, 132–133
effectiveness of screens,
135b–136b
thinking, 20–21
Heads-up displays
(HUDs), 146
Hidden performance, 293
HUDs. *See* Heads-up
displays
*Huggy Pajama* system,
318–319, 319f
Human Access Points,
374b–375b
Human-computer
interaction (HCI),
5b–6b, 220

**I**
Illusions, 39–40
Inter-personal
communication, 312
Internet of Things, 344b
Intersection operator,
346–347
Intimate interaction, 302b
iOS. *See* iPhone operating
system
iPad art installation, 3f
iPhone operating system
(iOS), 306

**J**
*Jenga* game, 234
Just-in-time scheme,
342–344

**K**
Knowledge Navigator,
23–24
*Kuza* system, 372, 373f

**L**
*Lambent* design, 62
*Lean-in* design, 246–247

Literacy levels, designing to
    *Com-Tablet* community
        media repository,
        368f
    digital stories, 365–366,
        366b–367b
    direct manipulation,
        367–368
    mobile research and
        development, 365
    proximate literacy, 369
    voices not text, 365

## M

*M-Pesa* platform, 369,
    371
Magical performance, 293,
    284b–285b
Malleable mobiles,
    405–406
Many-to-many
        performance, 237
Material properties, 59
    consumed material,
        60–61
    function follows form,
        59–60
    instant gratification, 61
    learning from feelings,
        61–63
Materials, 114
    emotional
        communication,
        126b–127b
    modalities, 114–116
    multimodality, 114–116
    tangibles, 117–120
    touch, 119f
Maxx mobile, 354f
Mess
    using clutter, 207–213
    customization,
        197b–198b
    barcodes, 213b

mess and creativity,
    206–207
mess media, 203–205
messiness, 189
messy interaction,
    198–202
messy organization,
    194–197
Microsoft Research, 205f
mobile user interface
    components, 194
physical clutter, 214b
signaling experience, 204f
voicemail access, 214b
*MetaCookie+ prototype*, 51
*MimicTile* system, 123,
    124f
Mindful apps, 307
Mindful communication
    apps, 398–399
    awareness, 327b–328b
    identification, 320
    inter-personal
        communication, 312
    interaction design, 312
    *MobiSurf* system, 322b
    modes of interaction,
        313–316
    solving without apps, 335
    space, 316–319, 317f
Mindfulness, 25, 93,
    300b–301b
    end of apps, 307
    interaction in physical
        forms, 301b
    telephones, 301–303
    mindful apps, 307
    task fallacy, 303–306
Mobile
    angst, 6–7
    austerity conditions, 1
    clinical helpfulness,
        21–23
    ecstasy, 1–4

future, 26–27
heads-down thinking,
    20–21
iPad art installation, 3f
life under a lid, 16–26
physical container,
    43b–44b
projectors, 289–291,
    198–202
as props
    app for conferring,
        258b
    board games, 264b
    capturing moments,
        256, 256b–257b
    designing to
        encouraging
        people, 261
    digital traces, 267b
    interaction types, 271
    inviting interaction,
        260b
    *Pass-Them-Around*
        prototype, 261,
        262b–263b
    personal devices,
        267b–270b
    prop principles, 260b
    public devices,
        264–266
service, 1
    clouds, 25
    touch screen
        dominance, 18
Mobile apps
    browser, 344, 344b
    Internet of Things,
        344b
    just-in-time scheme,
        342–344
    limitations of apps, 342
    sharing centered around
        people, 345f
    sharing intersections, 346f

Mobile designing
    constraints
  designing digital
    technologies, 352
  differences in designing,
    370–374
  exploiting free services,
    355–357
  goal of design, 377
  importance of
    partnering,
    374b–375b
  lack of infrastructure,
    357–358
  literacy, 358–359,
    365–369
  mobile software
    developers, 350
  Motorola and Nokia,
    359b–360b
  multi-SIM, 353–354
    Maxx mobile, 354f
  opportunities, 360–361
  platform designing,
    369
  for sharing, 361–365
  SIM cards, 350
  solar handset charging,
    357f
  UX designs, 351b–352b
Mobile interaction
    designers, ancient,
    7b–9b
*Mobile Stories* project,
    332
Mobile technology
  adopting new ways,
    386–387
  approaches to adopt,
    387–404
  designing for everyone,
    400–402
  digital backgrounding,
    403–404

  embracing physical
    expressiveness,
    394–395
  experimentation,
    397–398
  feeling truly alive,
    392–393
  future touchables,
    407–408
  lessening impact,
    387–388
  malleable mobiles,
    405–406
  messy designs, 396–397
  mindful communication,
    398–399
  beyond phones and
    apps, 405
  problem areas, 384–385
  uncertainty, 397–398
*Mobiphos* application,
    324
*MobiSpray* prototype, 281,
    282f
*MobiSurf* system, 322b
Modalities, 114–116
Motorola, 359b–360b
  F3, 358
Multi-SIM, 353–354
  Maxx mobile, 354f
Multimodality, 114–116
  guidelines for, 117b
Multisensory interaction,
    51–56

**N**

Narcissus, 6–7
  losing ourselves, 9–12
Natural user interfaces
    (NUI), 18
Near field communication
    (NFC), 119, 395
Negotiated interaction
    approach, 104

NFC. *See* Near field
    communication
NGO. *See* Nongovern-
    mental organization
*Noisy Jelly* prototype, 59
Nokia, 359b–360b
  DC-14 dynamo, 358
  mobile, 305f
  popularity, 354
  profile manager feature,
    377
Nongovernmental
    organization (NGO),
    374b–375b
Nostalgic design,
    185b–186b
NUI. *See* Natural user
    interface

**O**

One-to-many performance,
    237–238
Open source bicycle, 370b
Ordered chaos, 182
  digital clutter, 186–189
  digital fridge design,
    187f
  physical clutter,
    182–184
  physical kitchen clutter,
    187f
Orthodoxy, 225b

**P**

*PalmPilot*, 7b–9b
*Panavi* system, 56
*Pass-Them-Around* system,
    200, 200f, 261,
    262b–263b,
    264–265, 323
PDA. *See* Personal Digital
    Assistant
*Pebble* smart watch, 163
*Perfect Red* digital clay, 43

Performance
  design opportunities,
    252
  *EATProbe* prototype,
    241b–242b
  *lean-in* design, 246–247,
    248b–250b
  many-to-many, 237
  one-to-many, 237–238
  performance at
    periphery, 243–245
  pub quiz, 234
  quiet performance,
    238–239
  small group games, 234
  strategies for app
    selection,
    247b–248b
  technology gathering,
    240b–241b
Performance aspects,
  236b
Persistence, 172
Personal Digital Assistant
  (PDA), 262b–263b,
  304–305
Photo browsing
  application,
  105b–107b
Physical clutter, 182–184,
  214b
Physical risk, 220b–222b
Pico projectors. *See* Mobile
  projectors
*PicoTales* design, 201–202
Platforms, 369
*Point-to-GeoBlog* system,
  170
Pointing, 391–392
Poverty eradication,
  371–374
Price sensitivity
  exploiting free services,
    355–357

multi-SIM, 353–354
sharing handsets,
  354–355
Progression, 172
Projected performance,
  278b–279b
Props, 237–238
  principles, 260b
Proximate literacy, 369
Proximity Toolkit, 318b
Psychological risk,
  220b–222b
Pub quiz, 234

**Q**

*Questions not Answers*
  prototype, 222–223
Quiet performance,
  238–239

**R**

Radical atoms, 42
Realistic paper interactions,
  79b–81b
Rebellion, 13–15

**S**

Samsung, 276b–277b
Scrap computing, 265
Secretive performance,
  284b–285b
Self-expression, 283–294
Set theory, 347
Sharing, designing for, 361
  community sharing,
    361–364
  handset usage, 364–365
  person-to-person
    sharing, 361
  *Snap 'n Grab* design,
    362, 362f–363f
  supporting privacy, 364
*Siftables* research,
  267b–270b

*Snap 'n Grab* design, 362,
  362f–363f
"Sofalising" performance,
  243, 246–247
*Soft(n)* system, 75,
  75b–76b
Space, 316–319, 317f
Speaking handsets,
  358–359
Speech approaches,
  150–151
  bigger problems,
    152–154
  technical and
    performance issues,
    151–152
Speech recognition, 388
*Spoken Web* sites, 365
*Stane* device, 393
Stop-to-interact ethos, 387
*StoryBank* system, 198,
  198f, 396
Suspenseful performance,
  293, 284b–285b

**T**

Tactile displays, 123,
  123f
Tangible user interfaces
  (TUI), 117
Tangibles, 117–120
*TapBack* system,
  76b–78b
*Tearaway* game, 40b
*3in3out* prototype, 179
Three-second rule,
  262b–263b
*TicQR* prototype, 210
*Tilt Display* prototype, 125,
  125f
*Tokens of Search*
  prototype, 120, 121f
Touch screen dominance,
  18

TUI. *See* Tangible user
    interfaces
Twitter, 25, 241b–242b,
    243, 300

## U

*Ubi displays* project, 149f
*Ultrahaptics* prototype, 122
*Umati* system, 372–373
Uncertainty, 189, 397–398
    experiences, 220b–222b
    orthodoxy, 225b
    *Questions not Answers*
        prototype, 222–223
    seven stages of action,
        220

value of, 224–227
Union operator, 346
User experience (UX),
    5b–6b
    alternative trajectories,
        26b
    design features, 17
USSD protocol, 355–356,
    356f

## V

Videowalking, 280
Visual clutter, 211–213
Visual displays, 387–388
Voicemail access, 214b
Voices not text, 365

## W

Wand metaphor, 160
    direct manipulation,
        169–171
    glanceable displays,
        160–166
    heads down, 172–173
    beyond instant, 168–169
    power of, 169–171
WhatsApp, 126b–127b,
    263b
*Whereabouts Clock* design,
    188, 188f
Wireless Application
    Protocol (WAP),
    7b–9b